Praise the Lord!
I pray Heavenly Father &
Our Lord Jesus Christ that
the Holy Spirit will teach me
guide me thru this Book.
Occupy till He cometh the
"Day of the Coming of our Lord!
Hes Coming Back
I want to hear that Mother
busy with His when He comes
My Big Big Love
the King of Kings + Lord of Lord
Our Lord Master
Jesus Christ

Alma Harris
630 Pickus Ct.
Waukegan, IL 60085

THANK YOU

Thank You Lord using the Holy Spirit
for the Living Snapshot Here I Love
in the Lord. Thank you for being His
Both in the Lord!

My Dearest :)
Cuz Mimi
Mickey

I leaving you this Book
Because I feel that you
Would Be Spiritual Friend
to Help the Family & Friend
in Communion or on what
to Say when you know
Minister and Biblical Way
According to the word of God.
But that Birth & Life so
when the Problem is there
I will Pray that you Dress
up the Good & that may come
the God & that may come true.
Don't to walk with me through
in my Life & my Life & fine
Except the Cross & five
Except the walk the
Loving Spears

May I the
Become Heavenly Father
Praise the

J.B.

Brother Swaggart, How Do I Live A Victorious Life?

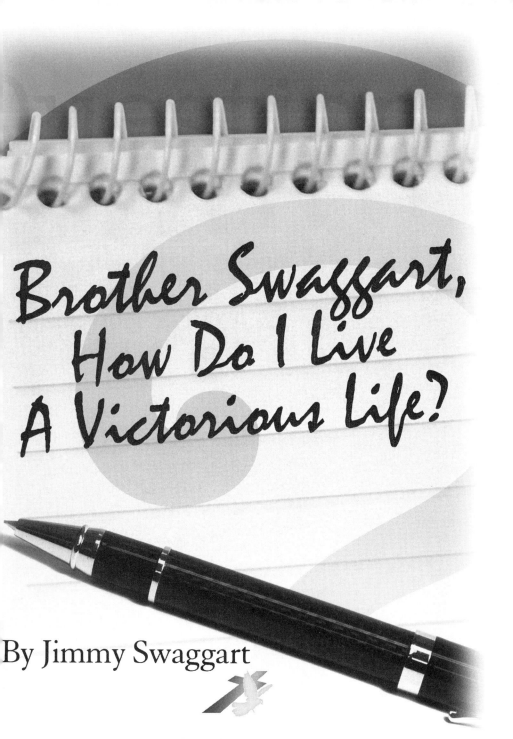

Brother Swaggart, How Do I Live A Victorious Life?

By Jimmy Swaggart

Jimmy Swaggart Ministries
P.O. Box 262550 • Baton Rouge, Louisiana 70826-2550
Website: www.jsm.org • Email: info@jsm.org
(225) 768-7000

TABLE OF CONTENTS

INTRODUCTION

The material that we will give you in this book, as it regards life and living, in other words, living a victorious, overcoming, Christian life, victorious over the world, the flesh, and the Devil, is by far the most important material that you will ever read. I'm saying this because it's not something I have originated, not at all, but rather, that which was given to the Apostle Paul nearly two thousand years ago. He gave it to us in his fourteen Epistles. Unfortunately, most of these great Truths have been lost to the modern church. As a result, those who truly love the Lord, and who truly want to live the kind of life they ought to live, simply are unable to do so.

SHOCKED!

The Christian world is always shocked at the revelation of failure regarding Preachers of the Gospel, and actually any Believer, for that matter, and rightly so.

Whatever the problem is, those who fail are culpable, as all who fail are culpable. Yet, those who fail, and virtually all do in one way or the other, do not want to commit the sins they are committing. In fact, they are struggling with all of their might, strength, and power not to commit them, whatever they may be. But, the evidence proves that no matter how hard we struggle, no matter how hard we fight these ungodly impulses, not knowing God's Prescribed Order of Victory, we are doomed to failure. The truth is:

A STARTLING STATEMENT

Whatever the problem, most of the modern church is struggling with sin in some fashion, and they are losing the battle. Once again, I state that this is the case because the modern church simply doesn't know the Scriptural way to Victory. Not knowing God's Way, the sin nature is ruling most Believers and, even though they are Saved, their life and living is anything but that which Jesus said it ought to be. He said:

> "The thief comes not, but for to steal, and to kill, and to destroy *(speaks of Satan and his emissaries who peddle a false way of Salvation)*: I am come that they might have life, and that they might have *it* more abundantly *(the Source of this 'Life' is Christ; all true Believers have such; however, all true Believers enjoy such only by constant Faith in Christ and the Cross)*" **(Jn. 10:10).**

When I made mention that most Christians presently, and I speak of those who truly love the Lord, are struggling with sin in some fashion, that is exactly right; however, that particular struggle is because of the real struggle, which is with the Lord.

THE CHRISTIAN'S TRUE TRIUMPHS ARE GOD'S TRIUMPHS OVER HIM

Let me give the entire statement:
"The Christian's true triumphs are God's triumphs over him, and God's triumphs over His People are our only Victories."
That's where the real struggle is. It is the same as Jacob of old. Please notice carefully the Biblical account. Incidentally, all quotes in this book will come from THE EXPOSITOR'S STUDY BIBLE. The Scripture says:

> "And Jacob was left alone; and there wrestled a Man with him until the breaking of the day. *(In this Chapter and in Hosea [Chpt. 12], this Man is called God, the Angel, Elohim Sabaoth, and Jehovah. In this scenario, we find that it was not with Esau, his brother, with whom he had to contend, but with Jehovah Himself. This is always the case with every Believer.)*
> "And when He saw *(the Lord saw)* that He prevailed not against him *(against Jacob)*, He touched the hollow

of his thigh *(Jacob's thigh)***; and the hollow of Jacob's thigh was out of joint, as He wrestled with him.** *(The great principle that God cannot give victory to 'the flesh' appears in this night scene. It is the broken heart that begins to experience what Divine Power means. Better for the sun to rise upon a limping Israel than to set upon a lying Jacob. Jacob, for his misconduct, was exiled from the Promised Land, having nothing but his staff. He returns a wealthy prince, but lamed. So, Israel, cast out of Jehovah's Land because of her sin, will return with abundance, but broken and contrite in spirit.)*"

BLESS ME

"**And He said** *(the Lord said)***, Let Me go, for the day breaks. And he said** *(Jacob said)***, I will not let You go, except You bless me.** *(Williams says, 'When sore broken by that mighty Hand, he ceased to wrestle and clung with weeping and supplication to the very God Who wounded him, then it was that he got the Victory and the glorious name of Israel.')*

"**And He** *(the Lord)* **said unto him, What is your name? And he said, Jacob.** *(Of course, the Lord already knew Jacob's name. So, why did He insist on Jacob pronouncing his name? He wanted Jacob to admit who and what he actually was, which the name Jacob adequately portrayed. True Faith requires that we admit what we are, before we can receive what He is!)*"

A PRINCE OF GOD

"**And He** *(the Lord)* **said, Your name shall be called no more Jacob** *(meaning deceiver or supplanter)***, but Israel** *(a Prince of God)***: for as a Prince have you power with God and with men, and have prevailed** *(as we shall see, Jacob's change was instant, but yet gradual)***.**

"And Jacob asked Him, and said, Tell me, I pray You, Your Name. And He said, Wherefore is it that you do ask after My Name? *(The Lord's answer is revealing. He responds with another question: the idea is, Jacob, by now, ought to know Who the One is with Whom he has been struggling. And the next statements prove that he did.)* and He *(the Lord)* blessed him *(Jacob)* there *(He gave him power with God and with men).*"

A CRIPPLED JACOB

"And Jacob called the name of the place Peniel *(means 'the Face of God')*: for I have seen God face to face, and my life is preserved *(Jacob will never be the same again).*

"And as he passed over Penuel the sun rose upon him, and he halted upon his thigh. *(The sun is now rising, but upon a crippled Jacob. If the Lord is to reveal Himself to an individual, the flesh must be crippled. That is an absolute necessity!)*

"Therefore the children of Israel eat not of the sinew which shrank, which is upon the hollow of the thigh, unto this day: because He *(the Lord)* touched the hollow of Jacob's thigh in the sinew that shrank. *(This particular sinew is the proper name for the large tendon which takes its origin from the spinal cord and extends down the thigh unto the ankle. It was called by the Greeks the 'tendo Achillis,' because it reaches the heel. So, the 'heel-catcher' became a 'Prince with God')*" **(Gen. 32:24-32).**

A PERSONAL EXPERIENCE

If I remember correctly, it was the first part of April. The sun would rise that morning on a beautiful day, but it was anything but beautiful to me. The world's largest Evangelistic effort, touching nearly half the world for Christ, with hundreds of thousands being brought to a saving knowledge of the Lord Jesus Christ, and I exaggerate not, had crashed. The world, which I knew had crashed, and the fault was mine, but at that time I did not even remotely understand how that it was my fault. In fact, that's what this book is all about. Untold millions of Christians are failing the Lord each day, despite struggling with all of their strength not to do so. They are being ruled in some way by the sin nature, and they don't understand what is happening. The Apostle Paul had much to say about this, which we will deal with in this book. The great Apostle said:

"For that which I do *(the failure)* I allow not *(should have been translated, 'I understand not'; these are not the words of an unsaved man, as some claim, but rather a Believer who is trying and failing)*: for what I would, that do I not *(refers to the obedience he wants to render to Christ, but rather fails; why? as Paul explained, the Believer is married to Christ, but is being unfaithful to Christ by spiritually cohabiting with the Law, which frustrates the Grace of God; that means the Holy Spirit will not help such a person, which guarantees failure [Gal. 2:21])*; but what I hate, that do I *(refers to sin in his life, which he doesn't want to do and, in fact, hates, but finds himself unable to stop; unfortunately, due to the fact of not understanding the Cross as it refers to Sanctification, this is the plight of most modern Christians)*" (Rom. 7:15).

If, in this book, I can relate to you that which the Lord gave to me by Revelation in 1997, it will be, as we've already stated, the greatest Truth that you as a Believer will have ever heard. The Lord has a pattern for Victory. While the Bible doesn't teach sinless perfection, it most definitely does teach that sin is not to have dominion over us, not in any way (Rom. 6:14). What I will attempt to do in this effort is to proclaim to you, in no uncertain terms, that Prescribed Order which the Lord has given us in His Word. In fact, He gave it to us in untold Types and Shadows in the Old Testament, but plainly and clearly through the Apostle Paul in the New Testament. So, what I am giving, as also stated, will not be new but that which has already been established.

A BROKEN HEART

I had slept very little that night and had actually gone downstairs and was lying on the couch. It must have been somewhere near five o'clock that morning. I lay there with the tears rolling down my face, and then I said to the Lord, *"Why did it have to be this way? Why did it have to be so humiliating?"* I went on to say, *"Lord, You are able to do all things. Whatever needed to be done with me, You could have done it in any number of ways, without making it so humiliating and so public over the entirety of the world."*

I lay there for a few moments locked in my own thoughts, when the Lord very quietly and very tenderly spoke to my heart. *"I had to cripple you as I crippled Jacob of old,"* the Lord kindly spoke to me.

AGAIN, THE LORD SPOKE

Some time later while sitting on the platform in Family Worship Center, looking out over the congregation, all of a sudden the Spirit of God once again greatly moved upon my heart relative to my own particular problem and situation. Softly He spoke to me saying, *"This sickness is not unto death, but for the Glory of God, that the Son of God might be glorified thereby"* (Jn. 11:4).

The Greek Text actually says, *"He shall not fall prey to death."*

In essence, the Lord was saying to me that He was the only One Who could take our terrible wrongs, put them into His total Right, and make everything come out right. Years have now passed, and I am watching the Lord do exactly what He said He would do. While the Lord most definitely does not get any glory out of sin or failure of any nature, He most definitely does get glory out of Victory over sin. Sometimes the Lord has to push us against the wall until we have no place else to turn, in effect, until all hope of the flesh has died, and then He can do with us and for us what needs to be done. That's the reason I stated some paragraphs back that *"The Christian's true triumphs are God's triumphs over us, and God's triumphs over His People are our only Victories."*

When I said, as well, some paragraphs back, that virtually the entirety of the modern church is being controlled in some way by the sin nature, which makes life miserable, to say the least, that was not at all meant to be sarcastic and certainly not meant to be said with a holier-than-thou attitude. I've been there! I know the heartbreak, the pain, and the suffering, so, anything I say in the capacity of correction is meant only to pull the Believer to a place of Victory, where the Lord desires that he be. And, if the Lord can use this unworthy vessel to bring that about, then the broken heart of past experiences will not have been in vain.

THE CROSS OF CHRIST

Please note the following very carefully. Due to its great significance, it will probably be repeated in other Chapters.

• Jesus Christ is the Source of all things that are given to us from God (Jn. 14:6).

• The Cross of Christ is the Means by which we receive all things (Rom. 6:1-14; I Cor. 1:17-18, 23; 2:2).

• The Cross of Christ must be the Object of the Believer's Faith (Gal. 6:14; Col. 2:14-15).

• The Holy Spirit, Who works totally within the parameters of the Finished Work of Christ, and will not work outside of those parameters, is the One Who does the doing once our Faith is properly placed (Rom. 8:1-2, 11).

FAULT!

As we've already stated, failure on the part of any Believer is always the fault of the Believer; however, the fault is not exactly where most people think it might be. No true Believer wants to sin. In fact, every true Believer hates sin (Rom. 7:15). As we will deal with in this Volume, even though most Believers do not understand what I am about to say, the truth is, if the Believer doesn't understand God's Prescribed Order of Victory, in other words, of life and living, then Satan can override that Believer's will and force the Believer into a course of action that he doesn't want to engage, but will find that he has no choice. In other words, Satan will override the will of the individual.

Now, many would argue, if that is the case, then the person isn't responsible. Oh, yes, the person is responsible, but the responsibility doesn't come about over whether the individual says *"yes"* or *"no"* to sin, but rather, *"yes"* or *"no"* regarding God's Way.

IGNORANCE

The sad fact is that most of the modern church is ignorant of God's Way of life and living, His Way of Victory over the world, the flesh, and the Devil. While most Believers have a modicum of understanding respecting the Cross regarding Salvation, they have no understanding at all respecting the Cross as it pertains to Sanctification, in other words, how we live for God on a day-to-day basis. Then, there is the problem of *"unbelief."* Sadly and regrettably, much of the modern church simply doesn't believe that what Jesus did at the Cross is the answer for every sin, every perversion, and every aberration that may plague the human race. In fact, there is no other answer, no other panacea. There remains but one sacrifice for sin. Not five, not two, only one, and that is the Cross of Christ (Heb. 7:27; 9:28; 10:12). Now, the truth is, while there most definitely is gross ignorance regarding what the Bible teaches about this

all-important subject, still, and sadder yet, it is a willful ignorance on the part of many, if not most. They have adopted the
ways of the world, which is humanistic psychology, and they do
not desire to hear anything else. But, there are many who do love
the Lord supremely and want to know and to have all for which
He has paid such a price. To be sure, even though it's not easy,
we most definitely can have everything for which Jesus died.
Admittedly, we only have the Firstfruits now (Rom. 8:23), the
balance awaiting the First Resurrection of Life, but still, there
is enough in the *"Firstfruits"* that we may walk in total Victory
before the Lord. Don't you think, considering the price paid
by our Lord, that He desires that we have all that He intends,
considering all that He has done to bring it to us. Every single
Believer in the world has *"more abundant life;"* however, most
Believers aren't realizing or enjoying that more abundant life.
That is not the intention of our Lord.

"He Who spared not His Own Son *(concerns the Great
Gift of God, i.e., the Lord Jesus Christ)*, but delivered Him
up for us all *(the Cross)*, how shall He not with Him also
freely give us all things? *(We can have all things that
pertain to Life and Godliness, which Jesus paid for at the
Cross, providing our Faith is ever in Christ and the Cross
[II Pet. 1:3-7])*" (Rom. 8:32).

"Oh, when shall my soul find her rest,
"My struggling and wrestlings be o'er,
"My heart by my Saviour possessed,
"Be fearing and sinning no more?"

"Now search me and try me, O Lord;
"Now Jesus, give ear to my cry:
"See, helpless I rest on Your Word;
"My soul to my Saviour draws nigh."

"My idols I cast at Your Feet;

"My all I return You, Who gave;
"This moment the Work is complete,
"For You are almighty to save."

"O Saviour, Your Word I believe,
"Your Blood for my cleansing I see;
"And, asking in Faith, I receive,
"Salvation — full, present, and free."

"O Lord, I shall now comprehend,
"Your Mercy so high and so deep;
"And long shall my praises ascend,
"For You are almighty to keep."

CHAPTER ONE

The Revelation Of The Cross

THE REVELATION OF THE CROSS

It is impossible for the Believer to live a victorious life unless the Believer understands God's Prescribed Order of Victory. That Prescribed Order, that Way, is in short, *"Jesus Christ and Him Crucified"* (I Cor. 1:23). In other words, if the Believer doesn't understand the Cross of Christ as it regards Sanctification, such a Believer, no matter how hard he tries, no matter how much he struggles, will not be able to live a victorious life. He can be Saved without understanding this great Truth, but he can never be what he ought to be in Christ without understanding this great Truth.

Most Believers have had a modicum of teaching regarding the Cross of Christ respecting Salvation, but almost none as it respects the Cross of Christ and our Sanctification, i.e., how we conduct ourselves, how we live, how we order our behavior. That's strange when one considers that virtually the entirety of the Bible is given over to telling us how to live for God. There is a small portion which tells sinners how to be Saved, but that small portion would make up far less than even one percent. And to be frank, for the most part, that small portion that's given is meant to be directed to those who are Believers, so that we may tell the unbelievers how to come to Christ. Paul plainly stated as it regards understanding the Word of God:

"But the natural man receives not the things of the Spirit of God *(speaks of the individual who is not Born-Again)*: for they are foolishness unto him *(a lack of understanding)*: neither can he know *them (fallen man cannot understand Spiritual Truths)*, because they are spiritually discerned *(only the Regenerated spirit of man can understand the things of the Spirit)*" (I Cor. 2:14).

THE NEW COVENANT

As it regards the New Covenant, the meaning of which was

given to the Apostle Paul, and he then gave to us in his fourteen Epistles, almost all of his writings are given over to telling us how to live for God. This refers to the Cross of Christ as it regards our Sanctification (Rom. 6:1-14; 8:1-2, 11; I Cor. 1:17-18, 23; 2:2).

But sadly, virtually the entirety of the modern church is completely lacking in knowledge as it regards this all-important Truth. It staggers from one fad to the other, all to no avail, because there is only one solution, and that is the Cross.

A short time ago, a Brother e-mailed me stating, *"Why do you keep talking about the Cross? We already understand everything about the Cross."* The truth is that our dear friend did not know anything about the Cross of Christ; however, sadder yet, that is basically the attitude of most of the modern church.

The Truths I will give you in this Volume can completely change your life, and in totality. As one dear Preacher friend told me, *"When I first gave my heart to Christ and set out to live for Him, everybody told me what I had to do, but no one told me how to do it."* That Preacher, after several years of struggling, finally just gave up and quit. He went into deep sin, but the Lord still had His Hand over him. One fine day, the Lord put him in contact with this great Message of the Cross, and it totally and completely revolutionized his life and living. He is now back in the Ministry, pastoring a great Church, and seeing great things done for the Lord. His story is just one among many. In fact, every Victory that's ever been won in this world, every Victory over the world, the flesh, and the Devil, has come by and through the Lord Jesus Christ and what He did for us on His Cross. As we have stated, He is the Source, while the Cross is the Means.

THAT WHICH THE BELIEVER IS FACING

The first thing I want to deal with is that which each and ever Believer is facing. I am speaking of the powers of darkness.

Paul said:

"**Finally, my Brethren, be strong in the Lord** *(be continually strengthened, which one does by constant Faith in the Cross),* **and in the power of His Might.** *(This power is at our disposal. The Source is the Holy Spirit, but the Means is the Cross [I Cor. 1:18].)*

"**Put on the whole Armour of God** *(not just some, but all)*, **that you may be able to stand against the wiles of the Devil.** *(This refers to the 'stratagems' of Satan.)*"

THE POWERS OF DARKNESS

"**For we wrestle not against flesh and blood** *(our foes are not human; however, Satan constantly uses human beings to carry out his dirty work)*, **but against principalities** *(rulers or beings of the highest rank and order in Satan's kingdom)*, **against powers** *(the rank immediately below the 'Principalities')*, **against the rulers of the darkness of this world** *(those who carry out the instructions of the 'Powers')*, **against spiritual wickedness in high** *places. (This refers to demon spirits.)*"

RESOURCES

"**Wherefore take unto you the whole Armour of God** *(because of what we face)*, **that you may be able to withstand in the evil day** *(refers to resisting and opposing the powers of darkness)*, **and having done all, to stand.** *(This refers to the Believer not giving ground, not a single inch.)*

"**Stand therefore, having your loins gird about with Truth** *(the Truth of the Cross of Christ)*, **and having on the Breastplate of Righteousness** *(the Righteousness of Christ, which comes strictly by and through the Cross)*;

"And your feet shod with the preparation of the **Gospel of Peace** *(peace comes through the Cross as well)*;"

THE SHIELD OF FAITH

"**Above all, taking the Shield of Faith** *(ever making the Cross the Object of your Faith, which is the only Faith God will recognize, and the only Faith Satan will recognize)*, **wherewith you shall be able to quench all the fiery darts of the wicked.** *(This represents temptations with which Satan assails the Saints.)*

"**And take the Helmet of Salvation** *(has to do with the renewing of the mind, which is done by understanding that everything we receive from the Lord, comes to us through the Cross)*, **and the Sword of the Spirit, which is the Word of God** *(the Word of God is the Story of Christ and the Cross)*" **(Eph. 6:10-17).**

JOHN THE BELOVED

John gave us another glimpse into the spirit world in his great Book of Revelation. Once again, we need to study this very carefully, inasmuch as this is an example of what we as Believers are facing. I'm giving these things simply because I want the reader to understand that what is arrayed against us is greater than we within ourselves can overcome. Yet, the Lord has a way that we can have Victory and that we need not fear. As I have stated, and will repeatedly state, that Way is the Cross of Christ and the Cross of Christ alone. Read carefully what John gives us here and, as well, please note that I am using exclusively THE EXPOSITOR'S STUDY BIBLE.

"**And he** *(Satan)* **opened the bottomless pit; and there arose a smoke out of the pit, as the smoke of a great furnace; and the sun and the air were darkened by reason of the smoke of the pit.** *(This will probably be concentrated* *in the old Roman Empire territory.)*

"**And there came out of the smoke locusts upon the earth** *(these are demon locusts, even as the following Verses prove)***: and unto them was given power, as the scorpions of the earth have power** *(refers to the sting in their tails, and the pain this will cause).*

"**And it was commanded them that they should not hurt the grass of the earth, neither any green thing, neither any tree** *(normal locusts destroy plant life; but these are not allowed to do so)***; but only those men which have not the Seal of God in their foreheads** *(refers to the one hundred and forty-four thousand Jews who have accepted Christ as their Saviour [Rev. 7:2-8]).*"

TORMENT

"**And to them it was given that they should not kill them, but that they should be tormented five months** *(this will be literal, yet these creatures will be invisible)***; and their torment** *was* **as the torment of a scorpion, when he strikes a man** *(pain and swelling).*

"**And in those days shall men seek death, and shall not find it; and shall desire to die, and death shall flee from them.** *(For pain to be so bad that people want to die is bad indeed! Evidently painkilling drugs will not work. It will be interesting how medical doctors diagnose all of this, to say the least.)*

"**And the shapes of the locusts** *were* **like unto horses prepared unto battle; and on their heads** *were* **as it were crowns like gold, and their faces** *were* **as the faces of men.** *(These are demon spirits, but will be invisible. If they could be seen, this is what they would look like. We aren't told their origin in the Bible. We know they were not originally created in this manner, but evidently became this way in the revolution instigated by Lucifer against God [Isa. 14:12-20; Ezek. 28:11-19].)*"

THEIR POWER

"**And they had hair as the hair of women, and their teeth were as *the teeth* of lions.** *(They were, no doubt, originally created by God to perform a particular function of praise and worship, even as the 'living creatures,' but they have suffered this fate due to rebellion against God.)*

"**And they had breastplates, as it were breastplates of iron; and the sound of their wings *was* as the sound of chariots of many horses running to battle.** *(We are given a glimpse here into the spirit world. This is the reason such foolish efforts as humanistic psychology are helpless against such foes. The only answer is Christ and the Cross.)*

"**And they had tails like unto scorpions, and there were stings in their tails: and their power *was* to hurt men five months.** *(This Judgment is limited to five months, which tells us Satan can only do what God allows him to do.)*"

THE ANGEL OF THE BOTTOMLESS PIT

"**And they had a king over them, *which is* the Angel of the bottomless pit** *(gives us further insight into the spirit world of darkness)*, **whose name in the Hebrew tongue *is* Abaddon, but in the Greek tongue has *his* name Apollyon.** *(This is a powerful fallen Angel, who evidently threw in his lot with Lucifer in the great rebellion against God. Only four Angels are named in Scripture, 'Gabriel, Michael, Lucifer, and Apollyon,' the first two being Righteous)*" **(Rev. 9:2-11).**

John the Beloved now gives us another glimpse into the spirit world in which we are shown another type of these spirits of darkness. As we have briefly alluded in the notes, these creatures were not originally created in this manner. They evidently became this way because they threw in their lot with Lucifer and his rebellion against God. Demon spirits fall into the same category. Demon spirits aren't fallen Angels, as some claim, because Angels have spirit bodies. Demon spirits have no spirit body or any type of body, therefore, they seek to inhabit a human being or even an animal.

Some Bible scholars believe that demon spirits are the spirits of the creation that were on Earth when it was ruled by Lucifer, which he ruled under the Lord in Righteousness and Holiness, which was before Adam and Eve. And when Lucifer fell, that creation of beings, whatever they were, threw in their lot with Lucifer, and these are the demon spirits referred to in the Word of God.

John further says:

"And thus I saw the horses in the vision *(demon horses)*, and them that sat on them, having breastplates of fire, and of jacinth, and brimstone: and the heads of the horses *were* as the heads of lions; and out of their mouths issued fire and smoke and brimstone. *(All of this presents demon spirits riding demon horses.)*

"By these three was the third part of men killed, by the fire, and by the smoke, and by the brimstone, which issued out of their mouths. *(Quite possibly, over three hundred million people will die as a result of this particular plague. Whatever they think to be the cause, the actual cause will be what is described here.)*

"For their power is in their mouth, and in their tails: for their tails *were* like unto serpents, and they had heads, and with them they do hurt. *(Once again, we are here given a glimpse into the spirit world. That's the reason Paul said we 'wrestle not against flesh and blood, but against principalities, against powers, against the rulers of the darkness of this world, against spiritual wickedness in high places' [Eph. 6:12]. As well, that is why all efforts to oppose such are fruitless, other than Christ and the Cross)*" **(Rev. 9:17-19).**

A DREAM GIVEN TO ME BY THE LORD

If I remember correctly, the time of this dream was in late 1953 or early 1954. Frances and I were married in 1952, and Donnie was born in 1954. Frances was pregnant with Donnie at the time.

We lived then in a little tiny thirty-two foot long house trailer that was eight feet wide. The particular night in question, Frances retired for bed, and I remained up to study the Word for awhile. At a given point in time, there was a terrible oppressive spirit that came over me. I was trying to read the Bible, but I finally just laid it down, unable to continue. I stepped outside so as not to disturb Frances and started walking on the little road beside our trailer, which offered a modicum of privacy, trying to pray. I couldn't pray, either. It was like the heavens were brass, and the words choked in my throat.

DEMON OPPRESSION

Demon spirits function in two ways, either by demon possession or demon oppression. It is not possible for a Believer to be demon possessed. Paul said:

"Know you not that you are the Temple of God *(where the Holy Spirit abides)*, and *that* the Spirit of God dwells in you? *(That makes the Born-Again Believer His permanent Home)*" **(I Cor. 3:16).**

Paul also said:

"You cannot drink the Cup of the Lord, and the cup of devils *(if we are going to associate with demons, the Lord will not remain)*: **you cannot be partakers of the Lord's Table** *(the Lord's Supper)*, **and of the table of devils** *(that which the world offers)*" **(I Cor. 10:21).**

Demon possessed, no! Demon oppressed, yes! In fact, every single Christian who has ever lived has been oppressed by demon spirits at one time or the other. The Scripture also says concerning this:

"**How God anointed Jesus of Nazareth with the Holy Spirit and with Power** *(as a Man, Christ needed the Holy Spirit, as we certainly do as well! in fact, everything He did was by the Power of the Spirit)*: **Who went about doing good** *(everything He did was good)*, **and healing all who were oppressed of the Devil** *(only Christ could do this, and Believers can do such only as Christ empowers them by the Spirit)*; **for God was with Him** *(God is with us only as we are 'with Him')*" **(Acts 10:38).**

Demon oppression can cause certain types of physical illnesses, emotional disturbances, nervous disorders, etc. When one is oppressed by demon spirits, it feels like there is a hundred pounds of weight on his shoulders. It is the major cause of depression. There's only one cure for this, and that is, once again, the Cross of Christ.

THE REVELATION OF THE CROSS

One Sunday morning at Family Worship Center, I was ministering on this very subject. Right in the midst of me explaining this subject, it suddenly dawned on me, even while I was preaching, that I had not experienced even one moment of demonic oppression since the Lord gave me the Revelation of the Cross in 1997. As well, that holds true unto this very hour (October, 2009). All Victory is found in the Cross, and no victory is found outside of the Cross.

THAT WHICH THE LORD SHOWED ME

It was fairly late when I retired for bed. It must have been pretty close to daylight when the Lord gave me the dream in question.

I dreamed that I was in a large house, actually in the front room, which was all of the house that I saw. There were no windows in the room, only a door which led outside, with not even any furniture in the room. I looked around in the dream, not knowing where I was and wondering why I was in this particular place. I started toward the door to leave when, all of a sudden, there appeared in the door the most hideous man/ beast that one could ever behold. He stood in the doorway, seemingly seven or eight feet tall with a bulk of several hundreds of pounds. This thing had the face of a man and the body of a bear.

As I looked on his face, I've never seen such evil in all of my life. The two eyes seemed to be pools of evil, and they were looking straight at me.

FEAR

I stood there looking at this thing and it slowly started to lumber toward me. It seemed to say, *"I have you now."* I slumped to the floor; I was so weak I could not stand.

This type of fear, as would be obvious, is an awful thing and it completely immobilized me. Paul also said concerning this:

> "**For God has not given us the spirit of fear** *(refers to a disposition of the mind; the Apostle is telling the young Evangelist not to fear)*; **but of Power** *(could be said, 'the spirit of Power,' for such comes from the Holy Spirit)*, **and of love** *(again, given by the Holy Spirit)*, **and of a sound mind** *(a 'spirit of self-control,' all made possible by the Holy Spirit, Who demands that we ever keep our Faith in the Cross [Rom. 8:1-2, 11, 13])*" **(II Tim. 1:7).**

THE WEAPONS OF OUR WARFARE

I was lying on the floor so weak that I could not get up. This beast was slowly lumbering toward me with his huge paw-like arms outstretched, and again, with the attitude, *"I have you now."* I began to feel around over the floor, trying to find something with which I could defend myself with, but all to no avail. There was nothing there. Of course, looking back, I know that the Lord was telling me the following:

> **"For though we walk in the flesh** *(refers to the fact that we do not yet have Glorified Bodies)*, **we do not war after the flesh** *(after our own ability, but rather by the Power of the Spirit)*:
> **"(For the weapons of our warfare** *are* **not carnal** *(carnal weapons consist of those which are man-devised)*, **but mighty through God** *(the Cross of Christ [I Cor. 1:18])* **to the pulling down of strongholds;)**
> **"Casting down imaginations** *(philosophic strongholds; every effort man makes outside of the Cross of Christ)*, **and every high thing that exalts itself against the Knowledge of God** *(all the pride of the human heart)*, **and bringing into captivity every thought to the obedience of Christ** *(can be done only by the Believer looking exclusively to the Cross, where all Victory is found; the Holy Spirit will then perform the task)*" **(II Cor. 10:3-5).**

As well, even if there had been something on which I could have laid my hands, what good would it have done me? I was so weak that I could not stand, but still, that's the natural reaction of the flesh. We try to defend ourselves by our own machinations, etc.

THE NAME OF JESUS

Without premeditation, without forethought, I shouted as

loud as I could, even though my voice was only a whisper, *"In the Name of Jesus."* The moment I uttered that Name, that thing clutched its head and screamed like someone had hit it in the head with a baseball bat. Actually, it began to stagger around across the floor, continuing to hold its head, and continuing to scream.

I learned from that dream that the Power of that Name was not predicated on my personal power or strength. In reality, I had none. Nevertheless, when that Name was uttered, as weak as I was, this man/beast was defeated, for all practical purposes, from that moment.

I said it the second time, *"In the Name of Jesus."* Now my voice had much greater strength and power. And when it was said the second time, *"In the Name of Jesus,"* this thing fell to the floor, writhing like a snake that had just received a death blow. And now, instead of it towering over me, I was towering over it.

I said it the third time, *"In the Name of Jesus."* This time, it was like my voice was attached to a powerful public address system. It literally reverberated off the wall.

THE SOUND OF THE MIGHTY RUSHING WIND

As I said it the third time, I heard a noise that was coming toward the room, sounding something like a freight train. I didn't see anything, but I distinctly heard it. It was the *"noise of the mighty rushing Wind,"* i.e., *"the Holy Spirit."* It came into the room, hit that man/beast on the floor, and despite its bulk of hundreds of pounds, blew it out the front door like it was a piece of tissue paper. Actually, I ran to the door and saw it wafting away on the wind like a leaf.

AWAKE AND SPEAKING WITH OTHER TONGUES

The dream then ended, and I awakened myself by praising the Lord in other Tongues.

I knew the Lord had given me the dream. At the time I

thought I knew what it meant; however, I was to learn years later as to exactly what the Lord had shown me that night so long ago.

He was showing me that I would face the powers of darkness, and it would seem as though I would be totally defeated, but the end result was the opposite. Because of the mighty Name of Jesus, Whose Name, incidentally, means *"Saviour,"* and which refers to the Cross of Christ, I found a total and complete Victory.

The point being, what we are facing in the spirit world of darkness is so much greater and more powerful than we are personally. So, if we use any other method, such as humanistic psychology, or whatever it might be, other than our Faith in Christ and what He has done for us at the Cross, we will surely be defeated.

Jesus said:

> **"And these signs shall follow them who believe** *(not these 'sins' shall follow them who believe)*; **In My Name shall they cast out devils** *(demons — Jesus defeated Satan, fallen Angels, and all demon spirits at the Cross [Col. 2:14-15])*; **they shall speak with new Tongues** *(Baptism with the Holy Spirit with the evidence of speaking with other Tongues [Acts 2:4])*;
>
> **"They shall take up serpents** *(put away demon spirits [Lk. 10:19] has nothing to do with reptiles)*; **and if they drink any deadly thing, it shall not hurt them** *(speaks of protection; in no way does it speak of purposely drinking poison, etc., in order to prove one's faith; the word, 'if,' speaks of accidental ingestion)*; **they shall lay hands on the sick, and they shall recover** *(means to do so 'in the Name of Jesus' [Acts 5:12; 13:3; 14:3; 19:11; 28:8; I Tim. 4:14; II Tim. 1:6; Heb. 6:2; James 5:14])*" **(Mk. 16:17-18).**

DAVID, ANOTHER GREAT EXAMPLE

The giant that David faced was a perfect example of what

we face in the spirit world. In the natural, there was no way that David could defeat such an enemy, but he did defeat him, and did so remarkably.

The Scripture says:

"Then said David to the Philistine, You come to me with a sword, and with a spear, and with a shield: but I come to you in the Name of the LORD of Hosts, the God of the armies of Israel, Whom you have defied *(as Goliath cursed David by his gods, David now invokes the 'Name of the LORD of Hosts'; so, in effect, it is Jehovah against 'Dagon').*

"This day will the LORD deliver you into my hand *(as stated, the Lord had already told him what to do)*; and I will smite you, and take your head from you; and I will give the carcases of the host of the Philistines this day unto the fowls of the air, and to the wild beasts of the Earth; that all the Earth may know that there is a God in Israel. *(David wasn't dealing from presumption, but rather, from a sure Word of the Lord; hence, he could boast!)*"

THE MANNER OF THE LORD

"And all this assembly shall know that the LORD saves not with sword and spear: for the battle is the LORD's, and He will give you into our hands. *(To be sure, the 'battle is the LORD's'; however, we have to function against the giants which come against us according to God's Prescribed Order, or else we will lose the conflict. That 'Order' is Christ and what He did for us at the Cross, which must ever be the Object of our Faith. That being the case, the Holy Spirit will then take our part, exactly as He did for David, and we are assured of Victory [Rom. 8:1-2, 11].)*

"And it came to pass, when the Philistine arose, and

came, and drew near to meet David, that David hasted, and ran toward the army to meet the Philistine *(Faith does not retreat, but rather, runs toward its foe).*"

THE PHILISTINE DEFEATED

"And David put his hand in his bag, and took thence a stone, and slang it, and smote the Philistine in his forehead, that the stone sunk into his forehead; and he fell upon his face to the earth. *(This was a Type of what Jesus would ultimately do to Satan. It had been predicted by the Lord immediately after the Fall, when He said to Satan through the serpent, 'And I will put enmity between you and the woman, and between your seed and her Seed; it [He] shall bruise your head, and you shall bruise His heel' [Gen. 3:15].)*

"So David prevailed over the Philistine with a sling and with a stone, and smote the Philistine, and killed him; but there was no sword in the hand of David. *(God is not limited as to what He can use to bring about Victory. In this case, He would use 'a sling and a stone,' but possessed by a boy who had Faith.)*"

CUT OFF HIS HEAD

"Therefore David ran, and stood upon the Philistine *(the Christian is meant to stand upon his Goliaths, and not them standing upon him)*, and took his sword *(the Sword of the Spirit)*, and drew it out of the sheath thereof, and killed him, and cut off his head therewith. And when the Philistines saw their champion was dead, they fled" (I Sam. 17:45-51).

Properly understanding what we are facing in the spirit world as Believers, we should realize that it's a hopeless endeavor to try to obtain Victory in any manner other than

God's Way. That Way is, as stated, *"Jesus Christ and Him Crucified"* (I Cor. 1:23). Any other way is doomed to failure!

SELF-RIGHTEOUSNESS

The church is at the same time the greatest organism on the face of the Earth and, as well, the most evil. I will remind the reader that it was not the drunks, the gamblers, the thieves, the immoral, etc., who crucified Christ, but rather, the church of His Day.

The Pharisees of His Day were the fundamentalists of that time, meaning that they claimed to believe all the Bible. Incidentally, the Bible then consisted of all the Books from Genesis to Malachi. The Sadducees, who, by and large, controlled the Priesthood, were what would be considered in today's terminology the modernists. They didn't actually believe much of anything. These two groups normally hated each other, but in opposition to Christ, they joined together.

Jesus faced these people constantly. Of all the many things He said, the following was probably the hardest. He said:

"... Verily I say unto you, That the publicans and the harlots go into the Kingdom of God before you *(He said this to their faces, and before the people; He could not have insulted them more, putting them beneath publicans, whom they considered to be traitors, and harlots).*

"For John *(John the Baptist)* came unto you in the way of righteousness, and you believed him not *(speaking to the religious leaders)*: but the publicans and the harlots believed him: and you, when you had seen *it,* repented not afterward, that you might believe him *(they saw the changed lives as a result of John's Gospel, but still wouldn't believe)*" (Mat. 21:31-32).

All Righteousness comes from God. It is made available to the Believer on simple Faith, but it must be Faith in Christ and what Christ did at the Cross. If one's faith is not anchored solely in Christ and the Cross, and for the totality of life and living, the end result is self-righteousness. In fact, it was self-righteousness which nailed Christ to the Cross. We must never forget that!

THE GREATEST DECISION I EVER MADE

When one is down and the people can do anything negative to him that they so desire and not fear being reprimanded, but rather, applauded, then one quickly finds out as to exactly how many good Christians there really are. There aren't many!

At a time of extreme crisis in this Ministry, and above all, my personal life, as well, with Frances, Donnie, and several friends with me, I laid my Bible on the table and said, *"I don't know the answer to a victorious life in Christ, but I do know the answer is in the Bible, and by the Grace of God I'm going to find it."* As stated, that was the greatest decision I ever made! That night in prayer, and again with a few friends, the Spirit of God moved mightily and said through Prophecy, *"I'm not a man that I should lie, neither the son of man that I should repent. What I have blessed, nothing can curse."* The next morning the Lord spoke to my heart, instructing me to begin two prayer meetings a day.

PRAYER

My Grandmother taught me to pray when I was but a child. I'll never forget one of the statements that she used to make to me. She said, *"Jimmy, God is a big God, so ask big!"* That little statement and what it means has helped me to touch this world for Christ. I set out to do exactly what the Lord told me to do. For ten years a group of us met every morning at about 10:00 a.m. and at 6:30 p.m. each evening, with the exception of Service nights. In fact, personally, I have continued to hold to that regimen of two prayer meetings each day and do so unto this hour.

At any rate, the Lord spoke to me and said, *"Do not seek Me so much for what I can do, but rather for Who I Am."* I knew that He was telling me that it was *"relationship"* that must be improved. He didn't tell me that I couldn't ask Him for things, but to not make it a priority.

In these prayer meetings, which we began immediately, other than what I have said, I didn't even really know that for which I was seeking. I wanted the answer to a Victorious Life, that is, how we could have Victory over the world, the flesh, and the Devil, to use a phrase coined by the Early Church Fathers. Other than that, I did not really know as to exactly that for which I was seeking.

I WILL HEAL YOU AND I WILL
HEAL THIS MINISTRY

A little less than a month after the prayer meetings began, on a Friday night while seeking the Lord, the Lord moved upon me greatly, giving me a tremendous Promise. There were only four or five of us present that evening, but what the Lord said to my heart, little by little I have seen it come to pass.

Just before we went to prayer that evening, I read a short Passage of Scripture from the Second Chapter of II Kings. It pertained to the great Prophet Elisha and took place very soon after the translation of Elijah. It concerned the city of Jericho and the healing there of the poisoned water. The Scripture says:

"And the men of the city said unto Elisha, Behold, I pray you, the situation of this city is pleasant, as my lord sees: but the water is naught *(poisoned)*, and the ground barren *(because of the poisoned water. Jericho is the city of the curse, and by God at that, simply because of its heathen worship in the days of Joshua. As well, the world is cursed, because of sin. In fact, it could be, as Jericho, a pleasant place; but instead, the water is poisoned and the ground barren)."*

A NEW CRUSE

"And he said, Bring me a new cruse *(this is symbolic of the sinless Body of the Lord Jesus Christ, because the cruse was made of clay)."*

SALT

"And put salt therein *(the 'salt' in it — a type of the incorruptible Word of God, that in its plentitude dwelt in Him — was the vehicle of this great healing power).* **And they brought it to him."**

CAST THE SALT IN THE POISONED WATERS

"And he went forth unto the spring of the waters, and cast the salt in there *(the Word of God must be cast into the poisoned spring; there is no other answer; that's the reason that it is imperative that this great Gospel of Jesus Christ be taken to the whole world [Mk. 16:15]),* **and said, Thus says the LORD, I have healed these waters; there shall not be from thence anymore death or barren land** *(Christ Alone can heal the broken heart, can set the captive free [Lk. 4:18-19])."*

HEALING

"So the waters were healed unto this day, according to the saying of Elisha which he spoke *(it was not a mere temporary, but a permanent benefit which Elisha bestowed upon the town; when Christ comes in, there is 'no more death or barren land')"* **(II Ki. 2:19-22).**

I commented on the Passage for a few moments, and then

we went to prayer.

THE WORD OF THE LORD TO ME

I had not been praying but just a few moments when the Spirit of God came upon me powerfully so. I began to weep with sobs being more akin to what was taking place in my heart.

The Lord spoke to me saying, *"As I healed the poisoned waters of Jericho, I will heal you, and I will heal this Ministry."*

After we finished seeking the Lord and retired for bed, I awakened at about midnight. The Spirit of the Lord continued to be on me even at that late hour. In fact, it remained until about noon the next day. Even though the Lord began immediately to do what He had said, it was a gradual process, which in my thinking, continues unto this hour, and perhaps will ever continue, at least until the Lord comes or calls me home. However, the greatest step taken was that which I wish to relate. It took place in 1997, and it was the Revelation of the Cross.

DISCOURAGEMENT

Knowing what the Lord had spoken to my heart, I remember seeking His Face, asking as to why it was taking so long, at least as it regarded that which I believed He had promised to me? If I remember correctly, the year was 1992. I then had so very, very much to learn. I had to learn that the Holy Spirit cannot fully have His Way until all hope of the flesh dies. Abraham and Sarah were some twenty-five years waiting on the Lord before the answer finally came. Then Isaac was born. With Jacob it was some twenty years before the change came. With Moses it was forty years. With David it was approximately fifteen years. With Paul it was at least several years, even though a number is not given. As stated, all hope of the flesh must die before the Lord can begin fully to have His Way in one's life. That time does not come quickly or easily.

PRECEPT UPON PRECEPT, LINE UPON LINE

I don't remember as to exactly how long I importuned the Lord regarding an answer, but at a point in time I ceased to pray about the matter, actually forgetting it. Again, I think it was a Friday night. About ten or fifteen of us had gathered for the prayer meeting.

The Lord brought to my mind the petition I had made of Him some weeks before, asking as to why it was taking so long. He instantly brought it all back to my heart and then said, *"This is my answer to you."*

"For precept must be upon precept, precept upon precept; line upon line, line upon line; here a little, and there a little" (Isa. 28:10).

This was the strangest Passage, but this is what the Lord gave me.

The Hebrew word for *"precept"* is *"tsab"* and means *"injunction"* or *"commandment."* The second *"precept"* is from the Hebrew word *"tsavah,"* which means *"to enjoin"* or *"to appoint, charge, set in order."*

The Hebrew word for *"line"* is *"qav,"* which means *"a rule, measuring cord, here a little and there a little."*

The idea is that everything must be measured by the Word of God. No other *"measurement"* will be accepted.

I knew the Lord had spoken to me. It was very, very obvious. I also felt that I knew what He was saying, and I still believe these years later that I had understood Him correctly.

I believe that He was telling me that night that every single thing in my life and Ministry must line up perfectly with the Word of God. There must not be any deviation whatsoever. I also believe that He was telling me that the *"healing"* would come *"here a little, and there a little."* And that's exactly the way that it has taken place. I had no idea at the time that it would be five more years, 1997, before this prayer would be answered. But, of course, the Lord knew exactly what everything would be and when everything would be. He gave me another Passage from the Word of God to encourage me.

EVERYONE WHO ASKS RECEIVES

I think it was early spring of 1992. Once again, it was in one of the night prayer meetings.

As we went to prayer that night, I began to seek the Lord, as I did each day, about particular things, etc. At a given point in time, the Holy Spirit drew my mind to the Eleventh Chapter of Luke. It concerned the Parable of the three loaves. Jesus said:

". . . Which of you shall have a friend, and shall go unto him at midnight, and say unto him, Friend, lend me three loaves *(a meager request)*;

"For a friend of mine in his journey is come to me, and I have nothing to set before him? *(We as Believers must give the Message of Eternal Life to all of mankind, but the truth is, within ourselves, we have nothing to give.)*"

A NEGATIVE ANSWER

"And he from within shall answer and say, Trouble me not: the door is now shut, and my children are with me in bed; I cannot rise and give to you *(an obvious denial)*.

"I say unto you, Though he will not rise and give him, because he is his friend, yet because of his importunity he will rise and give him as many as he needs *(the argument of this Parable is that if a sufficiency for daily need can, by importunity, i.e., 'persistence,' be obtained from an unwilling source, how much more from a willing Giver, which and Who is the Lord)*."

A PROMISE FROM THE LORD

"And I say unto you *(telling us how to approach the*

Lord for whatever we need), **Ask, and it shall be given you; seek, and you shall find; knock, and it shall be opened unto you** *(all of this speaks of persistence and guarantees a positive answer, at least if it's in the Will of God)*.

"**For everyone who asks receives; and he who seeks finds; and to him who knocks it shall be opened** *(He says 'everyone,' and that includes you!)*.

"**If a son shall ask bread of any of you who is a father, will he give him a stone? or if** *he ask* **a fish, will he for a fish give him a serpent?**

"**Or if he shall ask an egg, will he offer him (an egg containing) a scorpion?**

"**If you then, being evil, know how to give good gifts unto your children** *(means that an earthly parent certainly would not give a child a stone who has asked for bread, etc.)*: **how much more shall** *your* **Heavenly Father give the Holy Spirit to them who ask Him?** *(This refers to God's Goodness, and the fact that everything from the Godhead comes to us through the Person and Agency of the Holy Spirit; and all that He does for us is based upon the Cross of Christ, and our Faith in that Finished Work)*" **(Lk. 11:5-13).**

WHAT THE LORD WAS TELLING ME

The Lord in His Own Way was telling me that the time in which my request was being made was not exactly that which was appointed. In other words, I was asking for something out of due season. In the Parable it was midnight, and the answer was pure and simple, *"No!"*

However, through the man's insistence, he was able to get exactly what he needed. So, the Lord was telling me that I should *"ask, seek, and knock."* I was assured of an answer irrespective of the inopportune time.

I have gone back to that Promise again and again and, as

always, the Lord did not fail, as the Lord cannot fail.

1997

It was an early morning hour, a little bit before daylight. I always go to the office a little bit before our morning program over Sonlife Radio begins. This morning was to be no exception.

I don't remember what I was teaching over the radio, but I do know that I was studying in the Book of Romans, actually the Sixth Chapter.

I picked up a small book by a particular Greek scholar, as it regarded this great Sixth Chapter of Romans. To be frank, at that time I did not really know how great this Chapter actually was, but I was soon to find out.

In reading the comments by this Greek scholar, I found that most of the meaning of this great Sixth Chapter pertains to the sin nature. I had read the term *"sin nature"* before and had possibly even read this very Chapter in this Book, but this morning everything was to be different.

The Lord took the explanation the dear Brother gave, which I knew was right when I read it, and literally implanted it on my heart. In just a few minutes time, I understood what the sin nature was. I understood how that if it's not addressed properly, it can cause the Believer untold problems. Strangely and oddly enough, the dear Brother did not give any solution in his explanation for this difficulty and problem. The Lord was to give me that a few days later.

As the Lord implanted upon my heart the meaning of the sin nature, I then knew the cause of failure. As I have previously stated in the Introduction to this Volume, it's a terrible thing to fail when you are fighting with all of your strength not to fail, and then not know the reason for the failure. As I have also stated, no Christian wants to fail the Lord. Sin is abhorrent to any and every true Child of God. I knew the Lord had spoken to me, and I knew that He had revealed to me a great Truth.

WHAT IS THE SIN NATURE?

The sin nature pertains to the nature of the individual. Before the Fall of Adam and Eve in the Garden of Eden, their very nature was permeated by the Spirit of God. When they fell, they fell from a position of total God-consciousness down to the far, far lower level of total self-consciousness. Their very nature then became one of sin, transgression, iniquity, etc. In other words, the sin nature ruled them twenty-four hours a day, in totality. Consequently, every human being born thereafter, for we are all born in the likeness of Adam, is born with a human nature and a sin nature. If you will look back at your life before coming to Christ, you will have to admit that you were controlled by the sin nature in totality. That's the reason that it was said of Christ:

"And, behold, one came and said unto Him, Good Master *(addressed Him merely as a teacher)*, what good thing shall I do, that I may have eternal life? *('Doing' is not the answer, but rather, 'believing' [Jn. 3:16].)*
"And He said unto him, Why do you call Me good? *(You don't recognize Me as God.)* there is none good but One, *that is*, God *(Jesus wasn't saying that He wasn't good; in fact, He definitely was good, because He is God)* . . ." (Mat. 19:16-17).

That's the reason that man has to be Born-Again. In fact, the Lord does not rehabilitate anyone. That word is not even found in the Bible. He makes of us a New Creation (II Cor. 5:17).

Every Believer, in essence, has three natures. They are:
1. A human nature;
2. A sin nature; and,
3. The Divine Nature (II Pet. 1:4).

WHY DOESN'T THE LORD REMOVE
THE SIN NATURE AT CONVERSION?

He doesn't remove the sin nature at conversion for several

reasons. Some of them are:

• The sin nature serves as a measure of discipline. It makes us realize, even on a daily basis, that we must look to the Lord constantly in order to be what we ought to be in Christ.

• Our physical body is not yet Glorified, which it shall be at the First Resurrection of Life. As such, the sin nature remains, at least until the trump sounds.

• Paul said:

"For this corruptible *(sin nature)* must put on incorruption *(a Glorified Body with no sin nature)*, and this mortal *(subject to death)* must put on immortality *(will never die)*.

"So when this corruptible *(sin nature)* shall have put on incorruption *(the Divine Nature in total control by the Holy Spirit)*, and this mortal *(subject to death)* shall have put on immortality *(will never die)*, then shall be brought to pass the saying that is written, Death is swallowed up in Victory *([Isa. 25:8], the full benefits of the Cross will then be ours, of which we now have only the Firstfruits [Rom. 8:23])*" (I Cor. 15:53-54).

THE SIXTH CHAPTER OF ROMANS

One might say, and I think not be Scripturally wrong, that the entirety of the Word of God strains toward the Sixth Chapter of Romans. This, in essence, is the meaning of the New Covenant, at least as it regards Believers and our living for God. The following is a brief compendium of the great Book of Romans, which has been referred to as the Magna Carta of the Child of God.

• Romans, Chapter 1: This deals with the Gentile world and their desperate need of the Lord.

• Romans, Chapters 2 and 3: These two Chapters deal with the Jewish question and conclude with all, both Jews and Gentiles, in desperate need of a Redeemer. That Redeemer is the Lord Jesus Christ.

• Romans, Chapters 4 and 5: These two Chapters point to the answer to man's dilemma. It is Justification by Faith.

• Romans, Chapter 6: Now that Chapters 4 and 5 tell us how to be Saved Chapter 6 tells us how, as sincere Believers, we are to live for God. As stated, it just might be the most important Chapter in the entirety of the Bible.

• Romans, Chapter 7: This Chapter portrays the Believer being ruled by the sin nature. It's not a very pretty picture.

• Romans, Chapter 8: Someone has said that Chapter 6 presents the Mechanics of the Holy Spirit, while Chapter 8 presents the Dynamics of the Holy Spirit. In other words, this Chapter tells us what the Holy Spirit can do in our lives once we understand how He does it.

• Romans, Chapters 9-11: Many Believers think that Paul has suddenly changed the direction of his teaching to Prophecy. While these three Chapters contain some Prophecy, that's not the intent of the Holy Spirit. The intent is, if the church ignores the Cross of Christ, which is the only avenue of Righteousness, then the church will be cut off exactly as Israel was cut off. It is a solemn warning!

• Romans, Chapters 12-16: These Chapters give us the practical aspects of Christianity, in other words, how a Christian should conduct himself, which can only be done correctly if we understand Chapters 6, 7, and 8.

"SIN"

Paul mentions *"sin"* some seventeen times in the Sixth Chapter of Romans alone. When he originally wrote this Chapter, plus the entirety of all of his Epistles, he at times put before certain words what is now referred to as *"the definite article."* In other words, some fifteen times, when he used the word sin, he placed the word *"the"* in front of sin, making it read *"the sin."* I suppose the reason that the King James translators left it out is because it's somewhat clumsy in English. And again, had they translated it exactly as he wrote it, no doubt, millions would have wondered as to what sin he was talking about, in other words, a particular act of sin. He wasn't speaking of acts of sin at all, except in the Fifteenth Verse. He was speaking of the sin principle, or the sin nature. In the Fourteenth Verse he didn't use the definite article, but, inasmuch as he used the word *"sin"* as a noun instead of a verb, it means the same thing, the sin nature. The only place that he used the word *"sin"* as an act of sin is in Verse 15. He said, *"What then? Shall we sin, because we are not under the Law but under Grace?"*

His answer to that was very stringent, *"God forbid!"*

As the Lord began to reveal to me that early morning hour the meaning of the sin nature, it all became so very clear. But, of course, when the Lord does something, if He wants it to be clear, then it most definitely is. To know what has happened is one thing; to know why it has happened is something else altogether. I now knew why the failure! But, as stated, the Lord did not see fit that morning to give me the solution to the problem; nevertheless, I was so elated, so overjoyed, that it was almost like I had been let out of prison. And in a sense, that was true.

THE ANSWER FOR WHICH YOU SEEK
IS FOUND IN THE CROSS

I was continuing to rejoice over this most excellent Revelation given to me by the Lord from Romans, Chapter 6, on that particular morning when about six or seven of us went to prayer. Little did I realize that the Lord was about to give a second installment as it regarded this great Revelation. In essence, He once again took me back to the Sixth Chapter of Romans. So, this means that all that the Lord gave me was not new at all, but rather, that which had originally been given to the Apostle Paul and, no doubt, to many others down through the centuries. At any rate, when we went to prayer that morning, little did I realize what was about to happen.

I suppose we had been seeking the Lord for ten to fifteen minutes when, once again, the Spirit of God began to move upon me. Very simply and very quietly the Lord spoke to my heart as it regarded the solution to the sin nature, in fact, His Solution, is the only solution. He said three things to me, all very similar:

1. The answer for which you seek is found in the Cross.
2. The solution for which you seek is found in the Cross.
3. The answer for which you seek is found only in the Cross.

It was like waves of glory that flowed over my soul. I knew that I had the answer, but there was one nagging thing that bothered me. If the answer I sought was found only in the Cross, where did that leave the Holy Spirit? I had looked to the Leading and Guidance of the Holy Spirit all of my life. He had helped me touch much of this world for Christ, seeing literally hundreds of thousands brought to a Saving knowledge of Jesus Christ, and I exaggerate not. Yet, the Lord had said to me that the answer was found only in the Cross. Some days later, the Lord was to graphically give me the answer to that question.

There is no way that I have the vocabulary to express that which I felt in my soul as the Lord gave me this great Revelation. I, along with others, and especially Frances and Donnie, had been seeking the Lord day and night for some six years, and now He had gloriously answered. It was like I was walking on clouds!

THE DOOR MUST REMAIN OPEN

That morning, as the Lord began to pour into my heart that which I have stated, I instinctively knew that what He was giving me was only the beginning. I requested of Him that He continue to enlarge upon this Revelation, in other words, to keep the door open. That's exactly what He has done for the years that have passed. He has enlarged upon this Revelation, always according to the Word of God, over and over again, on a continuous basis. In fact, it is impossible to exhaust the meaning of the New Covenant, for that is actually what the Lord had given me. That's why Paul referred to it as *"The Everlasting Covenant"* (Heb. 13:20).

HOW THE HOLY SPIRIT WORKS

What I'm now going to give you in this part of this Chapter will be, without a doubt, one of the greatest Truths that anyone ever had the privilege to impart. To be frank, other than this Truth given to the Apostle Paul and perhaps others down through the centuries, but not at the present, I personally feel that it will be brand-new to the modern church. In all of my years of study, I've never read anything as to how the Holy Spirit works within our lives. Most Christians simply take Him for granted, and most Pentecostals go little farther than speaking with other Tongues. While the latter is of extreme significance, still, speaking with other Tongues, or even the Gifts of the Spirit, have absolutely nothing to do with the manner in which the Holy Spirit works within our lives.

AUTOMATIC?

Most Believers think the Work of the Holy Spirit, that is, if they think about it at all, is simply automatic within our lives. It isn't! If, in fact, what the Holy Spirit did within us and for us were automatic, there would never be another failure on the part of a single Child of God. No Believer would ever sin again, but always, would grow in Grace and the knowledge of the Lord; however, we all know that isn't true. Christians are failing right and left! Please note the following carefully, because I think it is the norm for most modern Christians.

A PERSONAL EXPERIENCE

I can recall in my own life and living countless times I've

held my head in my hands, asking the Lord as to why He did not help me. This was even during the time when the Lord was using me to touch much of this world with the Gospel, in fact, seeing literally hundreds of thousands brought to a Saving knowledge of Jesus Christ, He was helping me to preach to millions around the world! He was helping me to see hundreds of thousands Saved! He was helping me to see multiple thousands baptized with the Holy Spirit! So, why would He not help me to live victoriously over the powers of darkness as it regarded my own life and living? How many tears did I shed?! How many times did my heart break?! No, this is not an automatic thing. Far from it!

At this very moment as you read these lines in this book, millions of Christians are going through the same thing I went through. Even many, who are being mightily used of God, are suffering the same defeat. These are not hypocrites! Now, many would ask the following question:

HOW CAN GOD USE SOMEONE WHO IS AT THE SAME TIME FAILING?

If He didn't use those who are failing, to be frank, there would be precious few, if any, to use. The Lord did not wait until Abraham was perfect before He called him for the task at hand. The same could be said for Jacob and David, etc. The same could be said for the Apostle Paul and Simon Peter! And yet, we hear the words of Paul when he said, *"O wretched man that I am! Who shall deliver me from the body of this death?"* (Rom. 7:24). Paul was not a hypocrite. The simple fact was, which we will deal with later to a greater degree, he simply did not know how to live for God. Of course, this was before the Lord gave him the meaning of the New Covenant, which was and is the meaning of the Cross.

THE BAPTISM WITH THE HOLY SPIRIT

Many, who believe in the Baptism with the Holy Spirit with

the evidence of speaking with other Tongues, believe that once this great Gift is experienced in one's life, it is the answer and the solution to Victory over the world, the flesh, and the Devil. However, that is Scripturally incorrect as well!

There are millions of Christians right now who are baptized with the Holy Spirit with the evidence of speaking with other Tongues and practicing this great Gift almost on a daily basis, which they should, but who are living a life of spiritual failure, no matter how hard they try otherwise! While the Baptism with the Holy Spirit is of tremendous benefit to the Child of God, it is not the answer to living a victorious life and is not meant to be.

TRY HARDER!

I stood before a congregation of preachers some time back, possibly four or five hundred in attendance, and I asked them the question, *"When one of the members of your church comes to you and confides in you that he or she is living in spiritual bondage in some way, what do you say to them?"*

A silence hung over the crowd so deafening that it was almost embarrassing. I knew the answer to the question. They did not know what to tell the people. In fact, most of those preachers sitting there were struggling with the same problems themselves in one way or the other.

Preachers commonly give the usual jargon, *"Consecrate oneself to a greater degree,"* or *"Be more faithful to church,"* or *"Try harder!"*

That, *"Try harder,"* is probably the greatest degree of advice given.

A PERSONAL EXPERIENCE

There are some things that stay cemented in one's mind, and it's because the Holy Spirit wants it to be a lesson to us.

The time to which I refer was before the Lord gave me the

Revelation of the Cross. It must have been about 1995. At any rate, Frances and I had gone to another Church in our city to hear a particular Brother, who was a friend.

That night after the Service, scores of people gathered around us and were so gracious and kind. After I had shaken hands with only the Lord knows how many, and after the crowd had finally thinned out, I noticed a dear Brother who was hanging back somewhat, but finally approached me. I shook hands with him, and he quietly said, *"Brother Swaggart, I need help!"*

I did not know the man and stood there waiting for him to relate to me what the problem was. He said, *"I know I'm Saved and baptized with the Holy Spirit, but I'm struggling with a problem, and I think I'm losing the fight."* I quietly said to him, *"My Brother, what is the problem?"*

He said, *"I'm struggling with homosexuality!"*

I laid my hand on his shoulder and basically said the same thing that untold thousands of preachers say, *"You've got to pray more," "You've got to study the Word more," "You've got to 'try harder'."* He dropped his head and said, *"I'll try!"*

When I walked away from him, I had a sick feeling in the pit of my stomach. Instinctively, I knew that what I had told him would not help, but I did not know what else to say!

I never did see the man again and have no idea as to the outcome of the situation; however, I do know that millions are struggling with sin in one form or the other exactly as was that dear Brother, and they are not winning the Victory but are actually losing the fight. And, please believe me, this problem is not indicative only to the laity but includes preachers as well! And, I'm speaking of all kinds of sins, whatever they might be! The Lord has a Way of Victory, but the modern church, sadly and regrettably, at least for the most part, does not know that Way despite the fact that, in actuality, this is the story of the Bible.

DESPERATION BEFORE REVELATION

Someone has well said that all Revelation is preceded by

desperation. Perhaps that is true! It was with me! To fully relate that which the Lord gave to me as to how the Holy Spirit works, I have to go back to March of 1988.

My whole world had collapsed. As previously stated, the largest Evangelistic effort in the world lay in ruins, and I was to blame! Yet, even though I definitely was to blame, I did not know how I was to blame. I would not learn that until 1997, as I've already related, when the Lord gave me the great Revelation of the Cross.

At any rate, that particular morning I had gone out at the back of our property and was seeking the Lord as I often did. Our house, along with Donnie's, sits on twenty acres of land outside the city limits of Baton Rouge.

That morning as I began to pray, I experienced the oppressive powers of darkness as perhaps I had never experienced them in my life. I can still remember where I was standing near the fence. I still remember the awful feeling.

The Devil began to speak to me and say the following:

"You have disgraced your family, your Church, the millions of people who believe in you, and above all, you have disgraced the Work of the Lord," all of which was true. He continued, *"Why don't you take what money you have in the bank,"* which, if I remember, was eight hundred dollars, *"and simply disappear."* He continued, *"If you do that, you'll be doing God a service!"*

I remember leaning up against the fence sobbing and saying to the Lord, *"You promised that You would not put anything on us any harder than we can bear."* I then said, *"But Lord, no human being can stand this, please help me."*

One moment it seemed like there were a thousand pounds on my shoulders with no reason to live and no reason to go forward, and then, all of a sudden, it happened.

THE OPERATION OF THE HOLY SPIRIT

The Spirit of God came all over me. It was like the Lord reached down and said to Satan, *"That's enough!"* I felt like

I was floating on clouds with not a problem in the world, even though the problems, as would be obvious, remained.

Then the Lord spoke again to my heart, saying, *"I'm going to show you some things about the Holy Spirit you do not now know."* It was that simple, that short, that to the point!

Thoughts instantly flooded my mind. The Holy Spirit is God, and there are all kinds of things about Him that I don't know, nor any other human being. Yet, I instinctively knew that the Lord was addressing the problem at hand. Nothing else was said, just the statement, *"I'm going to show you things about the Holy Spirit you do not now know."*

I knew the Lord had spoken, and there was no doubt about that. However, days came and went, and there was nothing that I could put my finger on that was an answer to that which He had promised. In fact, the days went into weeks, the weeks into months, and the months into years, with nothing given, at least, as it regarded that which the Lord had said.

And now I come back to 1997. The Lord, that early morning hour, had graciously shown me the meaning of the sin nature. And then, some days later, had told me that the Cross was the solution to the problem. I then wondered, as stated, how the Holy Spirit figured in all of this. I knew that He did, but if the Cross alone were the answer to the dilemma, which the Lord had told me it was, then again, where did that leave the Holy Spirit?

To be sure, I sought the Lord earnestly the next few days because I knew there was something else there that I had not received.

I don't know the exact time, but it must have been several weeks later. At any rate, I was coming to the end of our Daily Radio Program, *"A Study In The Word"*. Loren Larson was on the program with me. He had been speaking and said something about the Holy Spirit.

Without premeditation, without thinking of what I was saying, and because I had never heard the statement before in my life, I blurted out, *"The Holy Spirit works exclusively within the parameters of the Finished Work of Christ, and will not work outside of those parameters."*

I sat there stunned for a few moments, asking myself, *"Where did that come from?"*

I had never done that before or since. It was not something I had read in a book or heard anyone preach. In fact, I had never heard the statement made in all of my life.

I paused for a moment, and Loren spoke up and said, *"Can you give me a Bible reference for that?"*

Once again and, as stated, this was not something I had studied. It was not something I had ever heard. It was not something I personally knew myself, yet, I had just made this statement, *"The Holy Spirit works entirely within the parameters of the Finished Work of Christ and, in fact, will not work outside of those parameters."*

As he asked me the Scriptural validity of this statement, I paused for a moment. And then, just as quickly, the Holy Spirit came on me again. I looked down at my Bible, and there it was. It was opened to the very Passage in question, which I had not even yet read. It stated:

"For the Law of the Spirit of Life in Christ Jesus has made me free from the Law of Sin and Death" (Rom. 8:2).

I instinctively knew that the Scripture I had given was correct! In fact, I was to learn in the following months what Romans 8:2 actually did mean. In other words, the Lord continued to open it up to me in a greater and greater measure which, in fact, He continues unto this hour.

THE LORD SPOKE TO MY HEART

The program ended a few moments later, and I remember getting up from the table, turning to my right, and then all of a sudden, the Spirit of God again began to envelop me. I stopped, my eyes filling with tears. And then the Lord spoke to me and said, *"Do you remember that day in March of 1988 when I told you, 'I'm going to show you things about the Holy*

Spirit you do not now know'?" Of course, I remembered it.

He then said to me, *"What I have just given you is the fulfillment of the Promise I made to you. I have shown you how the Holy Spirit works within the heart and life of the Believer."*

THE CROSS OF CHRIST

It is the Cross of Christ, as the Lord continued to open it to me, which gives the Holy Spirit the legal right and Means to do all that He does within us. Before the Cross, the Holy Spirit was very limited as to what He could do with Believers. The reason was simple, *"It is not possible that the blood of bulls and of goats should take away sins"* (Heb. 10:4). In other words, animal blood was insufficient to take away sins. Cover them, yes! Take them away, no! That's why John the Baptist, when introducing Christ, said:

"Behold the Lamb of God, Who takes away the sin of the world" (Jn. 1:29).

With animal blood insufficient, meaning the sin debt remained, this limited the Holy Spirit greatly. While He could come into the hearts and lives of a few individuals, such as the Prophets, etc., and help them perform their tasks, there is no indication that the Holy Spirit at all aided them in the Sanctification process. In fact, Sanctification before the Cross was mostly an external affair, but when Jesus died on the Cross, He atoned for all sin, past, present, and future, at least for all who will believe (Jn. 3:16), making it possible then for the Holy Spirit to come into our hearts and lives, and there to abide forever. A few hours before Calvary, Jesus said to His Disciples:

"And I will pray the Father, and He shall give you another Comforter *('Parakletos,' which means 'One called to the side of another to help')*, that He may abide with you forever *(before the Cross, the Holy Spirit, as stated, could only help a few individuals, and then only for a period of time; since the Cross, He lives in the hearts and lives of all Believers, and does so forever)*" **(Jn. 14:16).**

It is the Cross of Christ which has made possible the Advent of the Holy Spirit within our lives, which means the following:

THE DEMAND OF THE SPIRIT

The Holy Spirit doesn't demand very much of us, but He most definitely does demand one thing, and on this He will not bend. It is that our Faith be exclusively in Christ and the Cross, and that it be maintained exclusively in Christ and the Cross. The Cross is what gives Him the legal right and Means to do all that He does within our hearts and lives. So, that's where our Faith must be placed, and that's where our Faith must remain (Rom. 6:1-14; 8:1-2, 11; I Cor. 1:17-18, 21, 23; 2:2; Gal., Chpt. 5; 6:14; Eph. 2:13-18; Col. 2:14-15). The Revelation that the Lord gave me, which, as I've repeatedly stated, was not new, but actually that which was given to the Apostle Paul, and which he gave to us in his fourteen Epistles, can be summed up in three stages:
1. The meaning of the sin nature, of which we will have more to say later.
2. The only answer for sin is the Cross of Christ.
3. The Holy Spirit, Who Alone can make us what we ought to be, works entirely within the parameters of the Finished Work of Christ, which demands that our Faith be exclusively in Christ and the Cross at all times.
In all of this I have learned, and I am learning, that the things of God are not learned easily or quickly.
The great Patriarch Abraham had to experience some seven personal surrenders in his own life before he finally understood the Ways of the Lord, at least, as he should have understood those ways. Those surrenders are:
1. He first of all surrendered his native land (Gen. 12:1-3).
2. He surrendered his family (Gen. 12:1; 13:5-13).

3. He surrendered the vale of Jordan (Gen. 13:10).

4. He then surrendered the riches of Sodom (Gen. 14:21-24).

5. He surrendered self, which just might have been the hardest surrender of all (Gen. 15:6).

6. He then surrendered Ishmael (Gen. 21:9-14).

7. And finally, he surrendered Isaac. Each painful surrender was followed by increased Spiritual wealth (Gen. 22:1-14).

THE DISPOSSESSION OF ISHMAEL, WHO WAS A TYPE OF THE FLESH

All of that which the Lord does within our hearts and lives is so that we may learn the helplessness of the flesh, and that we depend totally upon Him. This is not an easy thing to do, nor do we come to this place quickly. Ishmael in Abraham's life was a work of the flesh and, as such, it would bring difficulties to Abraham and Sarah, in fact, difficulties in the form of the religion of Islam, which plagues the world unto this hour.

ISHMAEL, A WORK OF THE FLESH

"And Sarah saw the son of Hagar the Egyptian, which she had born unto Abraham, mocking. *(The effect of the birth of Isaac, a work of the Spirit, was to make manifest the character of Ishmael, a work of the flesh. The end result of the 'mocking' was that Ishmael actually desired to murder Isaac [Gal. 4:29]. Ishmael was probably eighteen to twenty years old at this time.)*"

CAST OUT THE BOND WOMAN AND HER SON

"Wherefore she *(Sarah)* said unto Abraham, Cast out this bondwoman and her son: *(Isaac and Ishmael symbolize the new and the old natures in the Believer. Hagar and Sarah typify the two Covenants of works and*

Grace, of bondage and liberty [Gal., Chpt. 4]. The birth of the new nature demands the expulsion of the old. It is impossible to improve the old nature. How foolish, therefore, appears the doctrine of moral evolution!) **for the son of this bondwoman shall not be heir with my son, even with Isaac.** *(Allowed to remain, Ishmael would murder Isaac; allowed to remain, the flesh will murder the Spirit. The Divine way of holiness is to 'put off the old man,' just as Abraham 'put off' Ishmael.*

"Man's way of holiness is to improve the 'old man,' that is, to improve Ishmael. The effort is both foolish and hopeless.)"

THE STRUGGLE

"And the thing was very grievous in Abraham's sight because of his son. *(It is always a struggle to cast out this element of bondage, that is, salvation by works, of which this is a type. For legalism is dear to the heart. Ishmael was the fruit, and, to Abraham, the fair fruit of his own energy and planning, which God can never accept.)*

AND THE LORD SAID . . .

"And God said unto Abraham, Let it not be grievous in your sight because of the lad, and because of your bondwoman; in all that Sarah has said unto you, hearken unto her voice; for in Isaac shall your seed be called. *(It is labor lost to seek to make a crooked thing straight. Hence, all efforts after the improvement of nature are utterly futile, so far as God is concerned. The 'flesh' must go, which typifies the personal ability, strength, and efforts of the Believer. The Faith of the Believer must be entirely in Christ and what Christ has done at the Cross. Then, and then alone, can the Holy Spirit have latitude to work in our lives, bringing forth perpetual Victory*

*[Rom. 6:14]. It must ever be understood, 'in Isaac [in Christ] shall your seed be called.')***"**

SPIRITUAL ADVANCEMENT

"And also of the son of the bondwoman will I make a nation, because he is your seed *(out of this 'work of the flesh' ultimately came the religion of Islam, which claims that Ishmael is the promised seed, and not Isaac).*

"And Abraham rose up early in the morning, and took bread, and a bottle of water, and gave it unto Hagar, putting it on her shoulder, and the child, and sent her away: and she departed, and wandered in the wilderness of Beer-sheba. *(This moment marks a distinct advance in the spiritual experience of Abraham. From this moment onwards all is strength and Victory. He casts out the bondwoman and her son; he no longer fears the prince of this world [Abimelech], but reproves him; and now that the heir is come, Christ in Type, he knows himself to be the possessor of Heavenly as well as earthly promises)***"* **(Gen. 21:9-14).**

"Oh, spotless Lamb, I come to Thee,
"No longer can I from You stay;
"Break every chain, now set me free,
"Take all my sins away."

"My hungry soul cries out for Thee,
"Come, and forever seal my breast;
"To Your dear Arms at last I flee,
"There only can I rest."

"Weary I am of inbred sin,
"Oh, will You not my soul release?
"Enter and speak me pure within,
"Give me Your Perfect Peace?"

"I plunge beneath Your Precious Blood,
"My hand in Faith takes hold of Thee,
"Your Promises just now I claim,
"You are enough for me."

CHAPTER TWO

The Foundation Of The Gospel

THE FOUNDATION OF THE GOSPEL

While one can certainly refer to the Message of the Cross, i.e., the Cross of Christ, as a Doctrine, in reality, it is far more than that. In fact, it is the foundation of all Doctrines in the Bible. This means that whatever Doctrine there is, as it regards the Word of God, it must be built squarely, so to speak, on the Foundation of the Cross of Christ.

It is this, the Foundation of the great Plan of God for the human race, simply because it is the very first Doctrine, so to speak, implemented by the Godhead.

The Holy Spirit through Simon Peter said, and concerning this very thing:

"**Forasmuch as you know that you were not redeemed with corruptible things,** *as* **silver and gold** *(presents the fact that the most precious commodities [silver and gold] could not redeem fallen man)***, from your vain conversation** *(vain lifestyle)* ***received*** **by tradition from your fathers** *(speaks of original sin that is passed on from father to child at conception)***;**

THE CROSS

"**But with the Precious Blood of Christ** *(presents the payment, which proclaims the poured out Life of Christ on behalf of sinners)***, as of a Lamb without blemish and without spot** *(speaks of the lambs offered as substitutes in the Old Jewish economy; the Death of Christ was not an execution or assassination, but rather a Sacrifice; the Offering of Himself presented a Perfect Sacrifice, for He was Perfect in every respect [Ex. 12:5])***:"**

BEFORE THE WORLD WAS CREATED

"**Who verily was foreordained before the foundation**

of the world *(refers to the fact that God, in His Omniscience, knew He would create man, man would Fall, and man would be redeemed by Christ going to the Cross; this was all done before the universe was created; this means the Cross of Christ is the Foundation Doctrine of all Doctrine, referring to the fact that all Doctrine must be built upon that Foundation, or else it is specious)*, **but was manifest in these last times for you** *(refers to the invisible God Who, in the Person of the Son, was made visible to human eyesight by assuming a human body and human limitations)*,"

FAITH

"Who by Him do believe in God *(it is only by Christ and what He did for us at the Cross that we are able to 'Believe in God')*, **Who raised Him** *(Christ)* **up from the dead** *(His Resurrection was guaranteed insomuch as He atoned for all sin [Rom. 6:23])*, **and gave Him Glory** *(refers to the exaltation of Christ)*; **that your Faith and Hope might be in God.** *(This speaks of a heart Faith in God, Who Saves sinners in answer to our Faith in the Resurrected Lord Jesus Who died for us)*" **(I Pet. 1:18-21).**

FALSE DOCTRINE

Let us say it again simply because it is so very, very important. The way all false doctrine begins is by having a false interpretation of the Cross, or ignoring the Cross, or denying its veracity altogether (I Cor. 1:17; 2:2; Gal. 6:14). In fact, in the First Chapter of the Gospel according to John, the great Apostle tells us Who Jesus actually is and was, and at the same time, the purpose of His Mission. He said:

THE DEITY OF CHRIST
THE CREATOR

"The same was in the beginning with God *(this very Person was in eternity with God; there's only one God, but manifested in three Persons — God the Father, God the Son, God the Holy Spirit).*

"All things were made by Him *(all things came into being through Him; it refers to every item of Creation one by one, rather than all things regarded in totality)*; and without Him was not anything made that was made *(nothing, not even one single thing, was made independently of His cooperation and volition)."*

LIFE AND LIGHT

"In Him was Life *(presents Jesus, the Eternal Logos, as the first cause)*; and the Life was the Light of men *(He Alone is the Life Source of Light; if one doesn't know Christ, one is in darkness).*

"And the Light shines in darkness *(speaks of the Incarnation of Christ, and His coming into this world; His 'Light,' because it is derived from His Life, drives out 'darkness')*; and the darkness comprehended it not *(should have been translated, 'apprehended it not'; it means that Satan, even though he tried with all his might, could not stop 'the Light'; today it shines all over the world, and one day soon, there will be nothing left but that 'Light')."*

THE WORD WAS MADE FLESH

"And the Word was made flesh *(refers to the Incarnation, 'God becoming man')*, and dwelt among us *(refers to Jesus, although Perfect, not holding Himself aloft from all others, but rather lived as all men, even a peasant),* **(and we beheld His Glory, the Glory as of the Only Begotten of the Father,)** *(speaks of His Deity, although hidden from the eyes of the merely curious; while Christ laid aside the expression of His Deity, He never lost the possession of His Deity)* **full of Grace and Truth** *(as 'flesh,' proclaimed His Humanity, 'Grace and Truth' His Deity)"* **(Jn. 1:2-5, 14).**

THE LAMB OF GOD

We are told that Jesus is God, and that He was made flesh, and it was for the purpose of going to the Cross. John the Baptist, in his introduction of Christ to the Ministry, proclaims this tremendous Truth. The Scripture says:

"The next day *(refers to the day after John had been questioned by the emissaries from the Sanhedrin)* **John sees Jesus coming unto him** *(is, no doubt, after the Baptism of Jesus, and the temptation in the wilderness),* **and said, Behold the Lamb of God** *(proclaims Jesus as the Sacrifice for sin, in fact, the Sin-Offering, Whom all the multiple millions of offered lambs had represented),* **which takes away the sin of the world** *(animal blood could only cover sin, it could not take it away; but Jesus offering Himself as the Perfect Sacrifice took away the sin of the world; He not only cleansed acts of sin, but, as well, addressed the root cause [Col. 2:14-15])"* **(Jn. 1:29).**

WAS IT WHO HE WAS OR WHAT HE DID?

Generally, those who ask this question are in some way attempting to denigrate the Cross. They are claiming that the Cross was incidental, in other words, just another incident along the way with very little Spiritual Meaning. They declare that Him being God manifest in the flesh was what redeemed

mankind. Well, the answer to all of this is very simple.

It was both, *"Who He was, and what He did!"* However, there is something we must remember in all of this.

Jesus Christ has always been God. As God, He was unformed, uncreated, unmade, had no beginning because He ever was, and ever shall be. When He became man in order to redeem the human race, even though He took upon Himself human flesh, He never for a moment ceased to be God. As someone said, while at this time He *"laid aside the expression of His Deity, He never for a moment lost possession of His Deity."* Concerning this, the Scripture says:

IN THE LIKENESS OF SINFUL FLESH

"For what the Law could not do, in that it was weak through the flesh *(those under Law had only their willpower, which is woefully insufficient; so despite how hard they tried, they were unable to keep the Law then, and the same inability persists presently; any person who tries to live for God by a system of laws is doomed to failure, because the Holy Spirit will not function in that capacity)*, God sending His Own Son *(refers to man's helpless condition, unable to save himself and unable to keep even a simple Law and, therefore, in dire need of a Saviour)* in the likeness of sinful flesh *(this means that Christ was really human, conformed in appearance to flesh which is characterized by sin, but yet sinless)*, and for sin *(to atone for sin, to destroy its power, and to save and Sanctify its victims)*, condemned sin in the flesh *(destroyed the power of sin by giving His Perfect Body as a Sacrifice for sin, which made it possible for sin to be defeated in our flesh; it was all through the Cross)*" **(Rom. 8:3).**

DEITY AND THE CROSS

God cannot die, so, in order to pay the price on Calvary's

Cross, which meant that He had to die, God would have to become human flesh, which He did. It is referred to as the *"Incarnation."* As stated, the very reason that God became flesh was to go to the Cross. This was decided, as we've already stated, in the high councils of Heaven from even before the foundation of the world.

Inasmuch as Jesus was always God, still, we must remember that not a single soul was Saved because of Who He was, although it was absolutely necessary for Him to be Who He was. No one but God could have done this thing, and for Him to bring about the Plan of Redemption, He would have to become Man, *"The Man Christ Jesus."* Let's start at the beginning:

• Jesus has always been God, and if that's all it took for man to be redeemed, then He would not have had to come down here and die on a Cross.

• The Conception of Christ by the Holy Spirit in the womb of Mary was absolutely necessary; however, had it stopped there, no one would have ever been redeemed.

• Jesus was Virgin-Born, which had never taken place with any other human being and will never take place with any other human being; still, had it stopped there, not one single soul would have been Saved.

• The Perfect Life of Christ was absolutely necessary. In other words, as our Substitute, He could not fail in word, thought, or deed. He had to be Perfect in His Life and Living, and in every respect. This He did, but had it ended there, not one single soul would have ever been Saved.

• His Healings and Miracles were absolutely necessary for they proved beyond the shadow of a doubt that He was the Son of God, Israel's Messiah, the fulfillment of all the prophetic predictions. But, as wonderful as all the Miracles were, had it stopped there, not one single soul would have been Saved.

• For man to be redeemed, the Holiness of God would have to be satisfied. This could be done in no other way except God becoming Man for the express purpose of going to the

Cross. That He did, offering Himself as a Perfect Sacrifice, the Sin-Offering, which satisfied the demands of a thrice-Holy God. That and that alone, the Cross of Christ, satisfied the demands of Heaven that whosoever will may come and take of the Water of Life freely (Rev. 22:17).

Again we state the fact that it was absolutely necessary that He be Who He was, the Son of the Living God, but still, He had to go to the Cross in order for man to be redeemed. That was His Purpose; that was the reason He came!

GOD'S PLAN

It seems that it has always been hard for man to grasp, even the Apostles, the fact that Jesus had to die on the Cross. They had pictures in their minds of grandeur and greatness; consequently, they were shocked at this statement that He made. The Scripture says:

"**From that time forth began Jesus to show unto His Disciples, how that He must go unto Jerusalem, and suffer many things of the Elders and Chief Priests and Scribes, and be killed, and be raised again the third day** *(His sufferings, and the glories that should follow, are always associated in Scripture [I Pet. 1:11; 4:13]; the Cross was ever His destination, the very reason He came; the Resurrection was never in doubt)*."

SIMON PETER

"**Then Peter took Him, and began to rebuke Him** *(Peter chides Jesus for speaking of suffering and death; regrettably, many preachers continue to do the same, as they reject the Cross)*, **saying, Be it far from You, Lord: this shall not be unto You** *(at that time Peter, nor any of the Disciples, understood the Cross as it regarded its necessity)*."

SATAN REBUKED

"**But He turned, and said unto Peter** *(respects strong action; would be the sternest of rebukes)*, **Get thee behind Me, Satan** *(Jesus used nearly the same words in rebuking Peter and the other Disciples that He had used to the Devil, and His temptation [Mat. 4:10]; all denial of the Cross in any form is of Satan)*: **you are an offence unto Me** *(speaks directly to Peter, because he is now being used by Satan)*: **for you savor not the things that be of God, but those that be of men** *(if it's not the Cross, then it's of men, which means it is of Satan)*."

THE CROSS

"**Then said Jesus unto His Disciples, If any** *man* **will come after Me, let him deny himself** *(not asceticism, but rather the denial of one's own strength and ability)*, **and take up his cross** *(the benefits of the Cross, what Jesus did there [Col. 2:14-15])*, **and follow Me** *(if Christ is not followed by the Means of the Cross, He cannot be followed at all)*."

THE FINDING OF LIFE

"**For whosoever will save his life shall lose it** *(tries to live his life outside of Christ and the Cross; it can only be lived in Christ through the Cross)*: **and whosoever will lose his life for My sake shall find it** *(lose his life to Christ, which means to give his life to Christ, which can only be done through the Cross; he then finds 'Newness of Life' [Rom. 6:3-5])*" **(Mat. 16:21-25).**

• **The only way to the Father is through Jesus Christ (Jn. 14:6).**
• **The only way to Jesus Christ is through the Cross (Lk. 14:27).**

• The only way to the Cross is by a denial of self (Lk. 9:23).

THE STORY OF THE BIBLE

The Story of the Bible is the Story of *"Jesus Christ and Him Crucified."* The first three Chapters of the Bible deal with the Creation of man and his Fall. The balance of the Bible, all the way from Genesis, Chapter 4, through to Revelation 22:21, pertains to the Redemption of mankind, which was done by and through Jesus Christ and what He did for us at the Cross. In fact, at the very dawn of time, immediately after the Fall of Adam and Eve in the Garden of Eden, the Lord instituted the Sacrificial system, portrayed in Genesis, Chapter 4. This was a way, despite man's fallen condition, that he could have forgiveness of sins and communion with the Lord. It would be by the means of the slain lamb, which would be a symbol of the coming Redeemer, the Lord Jesus Christ. In fact, when the Law was given to Moses, at the very heart of that Law was the Sacrificial system. Had it not been for that system, the human race could not have survived. All of that, the millions upon millions of lambs offered up in sacrifice, was a Type of the coming Redeemer, the Lord Jesus Christ. We find the pages of the Old Testament stained with blood, even a river of blood that never ceased to flow, all pointing toward the One Who was to come. He would shed His Life's Blood, giving His Life, which would effect the Salvation of mankind, at least for all who would believe (Jn. 3:16). While sacrifices were carried out from the very first page of human history, we must never forget that every lamb that was offered up in sacrifice by Israel, all and without exception, was a Type of the coming Redeemer, and meant to be so! It is virtually impossible for any person to read the Bible and not come away with the conclusion of God's Redemptive Plan, which was the Sacrifice of Christ.

One of the greatest examples is the deliverance of the Children of Israel from Egyptian bondage. The Scripture says:

"WHEN I SEE THE BLOOD, I WILL PASS OVER YOU"

"And the blood shall be to you for a token upon the houses where you are *(the blood applied to the doorposts meant that their Faith and trust were in the Pascal Lamb; the blood then applied was only a 'token,' meaning that it was then but a symbol of One Who was to come, Who would redeem mankind by the shedding of His Life's Blood)*: and when I see the blood, I will pass over you *(this is, without a doubt, one of the single most important Scriptures in the entirety of the Word of God; the lamb had taken the fatal blow; and because it had taken the blow, those in the house would be spared; it was not a question of personal worthiness, self had nothing whatever to do in the matter; it was a matter of Faith; all under the cover of the blood were safe, just as all presently under the cover of the Blood are safe; this means that they were not merely in a savable state, but rather that they were 'Saved'; as well, they were not partly Saved and partly exposed to Judgment, they were wholly Saved, and because there is no such thing as partial Justification; the Lord didn't say, 'When I see you,' or, 'When I see your good works,' etc., but, 'When I see the blood'; this speaks of Christ and what He would do at the Cross in order that we might be Saved, which pertained to Him giving Himself in Sacrifice, which necessitated the shedding of His Precious Blood [I Pet. 1:18-19])*, and the plague shall not be upon you to destroy you, when I smite the land of Egypt. *(Salvation from the 'plague' of Judgment is afforded only by the shed Blood of the Lamb, and Faith in that shed Blood.)*"

FOREVER

"And this day shall be unto you for a memorial; and you shall keep it a feast to the LORD throughout your generations; you shall keep it a feast by an ordinance

forever. *(The Passover is continued in the Lord's Supper [I Cor. 5:7-8]. In this way, the Passover may be regarded as still continuing unto Christianity, and is intended to continue, at least throughout the Kingdom Age, which is yet to come. The Passover per se is not continued, simply because it represented the Type, which was carried out through the offering of clean animals. Now that Christ has come and fulfilled the Type, it would not be proper to eat the Passover as it once was celebrated, and because all that is symbolized or represented was fulfilled in Christ)"* **(Ex. 12:13-14).**

However, most definitely, we are to understand that everything we have from the Lord, and forever, is because of what Jesus did at the Cross, and only because of what Jesus did at the Cross.

THE OFFENSE OF THE CROSS

Paul plainly told us that the Cross of Christ would offend some people. He said:

"And I, Brethren, if I yet preach Circumcision, why do I yet suffer persecution? *(Any message other than the Cross draws little opposition.)* then is the offence of the Cross ceased. *(The Cross offends the world and most of the church. So, if the preacher ceases to preach the Cross as the only way of Salvation and Victory, then opposition and persecution will cease. But so will Salvation!)*" (Gal. 5:11).

Actually, this problem did not begin with the Apostle Paul, and neither did it stop with the Apostle Paul. It began on the first page of human history and continues unto this very hour. There is an offense to the Cross.

How in the world could this be? What is it about the Cross

of Christ that offends people? Worse yet, how in the world can Christians be offended by the Cross?

The answer to that is multifold. As stated, this opposition began at the very dawn of time. The first account is given in the Fourth Chapter of Genesis, in fact, immediately after the Fall of the First Family. The Lord was to show them, despite their fallen condition, how they could have forgiveness of sins and fellowship with Him. It would be by virtue of the slain lamb, which would be a substitute, if you will, for the One Who would eventually come, actually, the Lord Jesus Christ.

We have in the Fourth Chapter of Genesis the very first occasion recorded of the sacrifice being offered and its results. In that episode, the stage was set for acceptance of what the Lord had said, i.e., the Cross, and for the opposition. Both came from the same family. I will portray it directly from THE EXPOSITOR'S STUDY BIBLE.

CAIN AND ABEL

"And Adam knew Eve his wife *(is the Biblical connotation of the union of husband and wife in respect to the sex act)*; and she conceived, and bore Cain *(the first child born to this union, and would conclude exactly as the Lord said it would, with 'sorrow')*, and said, I have gotten a man from the LORD *(by Eve using the title 'LORD,' which means 'Covenant God,' and which refers to the 'Seed of the woman,' [Gen. 3:15], she thought Cain was the Promised One; she evidently didn't realize that it was impossible for fallen man to bring forth the Promised Redeemer)*.

"And she again bore his brother Abel *('Abel' means 'vanity;' Cain being the oldest, this shows that Eve by now had become disillusioned with her firstborn, undoubtedly seeing traits in him which she knew could not be of the Promised Seed; she was losing faith in God)*. And Abel was a keeper of sheep, but Cain was a tiller of the ground *(both were honorable professions).*"

THE FRUIT OF THE GROUND

"**And in process of time it came to pass** *(the phrase used here refers to a long indefinite period)***, that Cain brought of the fruit of the ground an offering unto the LORD.** *(This was probably the first offering that he brought, even though the Lord had explained to the First Family the necessity of the Sacrificial system, that is, if they were to have any type of communion with God and forgiveness of sins. There is evidence that Adam, at least for a while, offered up sacrifices. Cain knew the type of sacrifice that the Lord would accept, but he rebelled against that admonition, demanding that God accept the labor of his hands, which, in fact, God could not accept. So we have, in the persons of Cain and Abel, the first examples of a religious man of the world and a genuine man of Faith.)*"

THE FIRSTLINGS OF HIS FLOCK

"**And Abel, he also brought of the firstlings of his flock and of the fat thereof** *(this is what God demanded; it was a blood sacrifice of an innocent victim, a lamb, which proclaimed the fact that Abel recognized his need of a Redeemer, and that One was coming Who would redeem lost humanity; the Offering of Abel was a Type of Christ and the price that He would pay on the Cross of Calvary in order for man to be redeemed).* **And the LORD had respect unto Abel and to his offering:** *(As stated, this was a Type of Christ and the Cross, the only Offering which God will respect. Abel's Altar is beautiful to God's Eye and repulsive to man's. Cain's altar is beautiful to man's eye and repulsive to God's. These 'altars' exist today; around the one that is Christ and His atoning Work, few are gathered, around the other, many. God accepts the* *slain lamb and rejects the offered fruit; and the offering being rejected, so of necessity is the offerer.)*"

ANGER

"**But unto Cain and to his offering He had not respect** *(let us say it again, God has no respect for any proposed way of Salvation, other than 'Jesus Christ and Him Crucified' [I Cor. 1:23; 2:2])*. **And Cain was very angry, and his countenance fell** *(that which filled Abel with peace filled Cain with wrath; the carnal mind displays its enmity against all this Truth which so gladdens and satisfies the heart of the Believer)*."

WHY?

"**And the LORD said unto Cain** *(God loves Cain, just as He does Abel, and wishes to bless him also)*, **Why are you angry** *(Abel's Altar speaks of Repentance, of Faith, and of the Precious Blood of Christ, the Lamb of God without blemish; Cain's altar tells of pride, unbelief, and self-righteousness, which always elicits anger)*? **and why is your countenance fallen** *(anger, in one form or the other, accompanies self-righteousness, for that is what plagued Cain; God's Righteousness can only come by the Cross, while self-righteousness is by dependence on works)*?"

ACCEPTANCE?

"**If you do well, shall you not be accepted** *(if you bring the correct sacrifice and, thereby, place your Faith)*? **and if you do not well, sin** *(a Sin-Offering)* **lies at the door** *(a lamb was at the door of the Tabernacle)*. **And unto you shall be his desire, and you shall rule over him** *(the Lord promised Cain dominion over the Earth of that day, if he would only offer up, and place his trust in, the* *right sacrifice; He promises the same presently to all who trust Christ [Mat. 5:5]).*

CAIN MURDERS ABEL

"And Cain talked with Abel his brother: and it came to pass, when they were in the field, that Cain rose up against Abel his brother, and killed him *(the first murder; Cain's religion was too refined to kill a lamb, but not too cultured to murder his brother; God's way of Salvation fills the heart with love; man's way of salvation inflames it with hatred; 'Religion' has ever been the greatest cause of bloodshed).*"

AM I MY BROTHER'S KEEPER?

"And the LORD said unto Cain, Where is Abel your brother? *(Adam sins against God and Cain sins against man. In their united conduct, we have sin in all its forms, and that on the first page of human history.)* **And he said, I know not: Am I my brother's keeper** *(He showed himself a 'liar' in saying, 'I know not'; 'wicked and profane' in thinking he could hide his sin from God; 'unjust' in denying himself to be his brother's keeper; 'obstinate and desperate' in not confessing his sin)*?"

YOUR BROTHER'S BLOOD

"And He *(God)* **said, What have you done** *(this concerns man's sins, the fruit of his sinful nature)*? **The voice of your brother's blood cries unto Me from the ground.** *(There is some Scriptural evidence that Cain cut his brother's throat. Thus, with the first shedding of human blood, that ominous thought sprang up, divinely bestowed, that the Earth will grant no peace to the one who has wantonly stained her fair face with the life-stream of man.)*"

THE CURSE

"**And now are you cursed from the Earth** *(Cain repudiated the Cross, murdered his brother, and is now cursed by God; this is the first curse leveled by God against a human being)***, which has opened her mouth to receive your brother's blood from your hand** *(was the beginning of what has proven to be a saturation; from then until now, the Earth has been soaked with the blood of innocent victims)*" **(Gen. 4:1-11).**

THE STAGE WAS SET

We find in this episode man addressing God's Plan of Redemption. Abel accepted it, thereby, offering up the required lamb, the innocent victim, which was a Type of Christ. Cain, although he knew the right way and even admitted that God deserved a sacrifice, still proceeded to offer up a sacrifice of his own making and not that which was demanded by God. In doing so, he, in essence, was claiming that he did not need a Redeemer, which has been the attitude of most of the human race ever since.

The world has ever tried to manufacture another god, while the church, sadly, has ever tried to manufacture another sacrifice.

Why?

God's Way, and His only Way, is *"Jesus Christ and Him Crucified"* (I Cor. 1:23).

Most of the church world rejects the Cross of Christ out of hand. In fact, they reject the Bible as being the very Word of God, thereby, devising their own religiosity. Unfortunately, over half of that which refers to itself as *"Christianity"* falls into that category. Then, there is a great segment of the church, virtually about half, which believes in the Cross of Christ as it regards Salvation, and rightly so; however, beyond that, they do not realize or understand the part the Cross of Christ plays in one's Sanctification. So, while trusting Christ for Salvation by the means of the Blood of the Lamb, they, at the same time, attempt to sanctify themselves by their own personal efforts. This means they are condemned to live a life of spiritual failure.

There is a small segment of the Church which understands the Cross of Christ, not only as it refers to Salvation but, as well, to Sanctification. Unfortunately, those who accept the Christ of the Cross referring to Salvation do not easily come into the arena of the Cross of Christ referring both to Salvation and Sanctification. As a result, every type of proposed scheme that comes to the mind of man is ventured as the way to *"live for God."* Many of the things proposed are right in their own capacity, in other words, Scriptural, but grossly out of context when used as a means of victory in the Lord. Let me give some examples.

THE LORD'S SUPPER

A short time ago I was listening to a preacher over television, a man, incidentally, with whom I was not acquainted.

In the things I will relate, I do not question his motives, his efforts, which I will later name, or the preachers who are proposing such. I will have to accept their sincerity, whether correct or not; however, irrespective of sincerity, wrong direction will never lead to the right place. In other words, those preachers, and those who listen to them, are going to suffer the terrible bondage of sin and all of its fallout because of such wrong direction.

The young preacher in question, who I have later learned pastors a very large church, was telling the people, in essence, that if they would take the Lord's Supper each day or week, whatever time frame he proposed, this would ensure their prosperity, healing, victory, etc.

Now, while the Lord's Supper is most definitely Scriptural, when it is placed in such a posture as addressed here, such direction is wrong. The ceremony of the Lord's Supper will not bring about victory over sin, or anything else, for that matter. When used, however, in the manner in which it was originally intended, which is to keep in memory that which the Lord did for us at Calvary's Cross, this will be in obedience to the Word of God, and any obedience to the Word brings blessings (I Cor. 11:23-31).

FASTING

It is obvious that fasting is Scriptural; however, fasting will not help one to overcome sin, as some are claiming. In other words, to fast a certain number of days, as helpful as it will be, does not cause one to gain victory over sin. When we do these things, we have turned these viable Scriptural Ordinances into law, which God can never accept.

I read where a particular preacher had made the statement in one of the articles that he had written that he was going to go into a room in his house and stay there until he had total victory over whatever problem he was facing. It was a problem of sin in some manner. Now, while I admire his consecration, still, he could stay in that room and do without food until they could pull him through a keyhole, and he wouldn't get victory over sin.

A PARTNER TO HELP YOU

This one has been borrowed from the world of psychology. Once again, let me state that I did not know the preacher that I am about to mention but only saw him over television. I overheard this particular preacher make the statement that the manner and way of victory in the world was to get someone in whom one could confide and the two pray together. He stated that this would help one to overcome sin, thereby, to live the life that ought to be lived.

While I greatly desire the prayers and Biblical counsel of my brothers and sisters in the Lord, still, this particular method will not help. Think about it a moment. If one could get Victory over sin in this fashion, Jesus would not have had to come down to this world and die on the Cross of Calvary. Paul said:

"If Righteousness come by the Law, then Christ is dead in vain" (Gal. 2:21).

MANIFESTATIONS

I had a dear lady tell me once that if Christians would experience the Power of God to such an extent that they would *"fall out under the power,"* this would solve their problems, whatever the problems were.

Now, I definitely believe that at times the Lord uses His Mighty Power to knock a person off his feet, so to speak, but still, as valuable as that might be in its own right, it will not give one victory over sin. Jesus didn't say that if one falls out under the Power, such will make one free. He rather said, *"And you shall know the Truth, and the Truth shall make you free"* (Jn. 8:32).

Here is the problem with the dear lady's statement. If one doesn't know the Truth, which is *"Jesus Christ and Him Crucified"* (I Cor. 1:23), even if one is truly knocked off one's feet by the Power of God, he will get up in the same manner he fell. In other words, Satan will be attacking that person again very shortly.

DEMON POSSESSION

When Christians have problems of one sort or the other, and especially with sin, some preachers are very quick to say that the person has a *"demon of . . ."* whatever it might be. In other words, if they are bothered by lust, it is said that they have a demon of lust. If they're bothered with an uncontrollable temper, they have a demon of uncontrollable temper, etc. To be sure, wherever sin is involved, one can be certain that demon spirits are involved as well; however, as it regards whatever problem a Believer might have, it's not a demon spirit that's in that person that's causing the problem. That's unscriptural. We don't find anywhere in the Bible where Jesus or the Apostles cast demons out of Believers. They, at times, rebuked demons which were oppressing Believers, but that's as far as it went.

It's very easy for Believers to believe that demon spirits are causing their problems simply because they have tried so hard to overcome the problems, whatever they might be, and have not been able to do so.

The reason they have been unable to do so is that they do not know God's Prescribed Order of Victory, which is Christ and what He did at the Cross. Our Faith must be exclusively in that Finished Work, which then gives the Holy Spirit the latitude to work within our hearts and lives.

THE FAMILY CURSE

Another proposed solution for the problems of Christians is for a preacher who understands these things to rebuke the family curse. What is the family curse?

It is claimed that if one's relative several generations removed did some terrible thing and was cursed by God, the curse can pass down to the Christian, who will then need to have it rebuked, as stated, by a preacher who understands these things. Such is derived from the following Verse:

"You shall not bow down yourself to them, nor serve them: for I the LORD your God am a jealous God, visiting the iniquity of the fathers upon the children unto the third and fourth generation of them who hate Me" (Ex. 20:5).

If it is to be noticed, it states, *"of them who hate Me."* When a person comes to the Lord, he certainly no longer hates the Lord, so that nullifies the claim of the family curse.

To be sure, there are all types of curses in the world, which most definitely are upon many, many people. However, when a person comes to Christ, the Scripture plainly tells us, *"Therefore if any man be in Christ, he is a new creature: old things are passed away; behold, all things are become new"* (II Cor. 5:17).

The teaching of the family curse, at least as it's taught in many circles, is an insult to the Finished Work of Christ at the Cross. To be sure, it is a Finished Work, which means it leaves nothing hanging. Believers who have fear instilled in their hearts because they believe that some dreaded thing is upon them because of something a great, great grandfather did many years ago can be sure that the fear that is there was placed there by man or the Devil, or both, and not by God. Paul plainly wrote:

"For God has not given us the spirit of fear; but of Power, and of love, and of a sound mind" (II Tim. 1:7).

We do not deny that Christians have problems, and some of them are very severe. However, the reason for the lack of victory over these problems is that they do not know or understand what Jesus did for them on the Cross of Calvary. Therefore, they do not know how to avail themselves of the great Victory He has purchased all on our behalf.

THE LAUGHING PHENOMENON

In the early 1990's, the laughing phenomenon swept the Church. People were taught that if they would believe the Lord, He would give them a spirit of laughter, which would fill their hearts with joy, with some of them rolling on the floor and laughing for hours on end. While the Lord at times most definitely does cause one to laugh accordingly, still, that is not the answer for sin. Such will not break bondages of darkness and will not set the captive free. Once again, if we believe such, then we are repudiating Calvary, which makes the Cross of Christ less, much less, than it really is. I can assure all and sundry that the Lord is most displeased with such thinking.

THE PURPOSE DRIVEN LIFE SCHEME

While the Purpose Driven Life scheme deals mostly with church growth, which most definitely is not Spiritual Growth, still, it is being touted, as well, as an avenue for victory over sin. While this is dealt with very little as it regards this problem, many have thought it was the answer.

We received a letter sometime back and, more than likely, many such as this, which stated, *"Brother Swaggart, I've just finished the Forty Days of Purpose, now what do I do?"* At the risk of being blunt allow me to say:

The Purpose Driven Life scheme is not of the Lord. It was devised totally and completely by men, which means that it's something with which the Lord cannot bless. Instead of it leading one closer to the Lord, it will have the opposite effect.

One night when this thing began, Frances handed me this particular book and asked me to read it and tell her what I thought.

I read a few pages and laid it down.

She came back a little bit later and asked me, *"Did you read the book?"* Of course, enough time had not passed for me to have read the book.

I said to her, *"I read a few pages, but I don't have to read any more. I know it's not of the Lord."* The reason I knew that was because that whatever it was they were promoting, it most definitely was not the Cross of Christ, and if it's not the Cross of Christ, it's not going to do anyone any good.

If the truth be known, it's the problem of Cain all over again. As stated earlier, he did not deny that there was a God. He did not deny the need for an Altar. He did not deny the need for a sacrifice. He rather denied the type of sacrifice which God demanded, which was the slain lamb, which would be a substitute for the Lamb of God Who would take away the sin of the world (Jn. 1:29). So, he offered the sacrifice of his own making, and that has been the sin of religion from the very dawn of time, and it continues unto this hour.

Paul said:

"For I determined not to know anything among you, save Jesus Christ, and Him Crucified" (I Cor. 2:2).

Paul was well educated. He could easily have discussed the

great philosophies of the world of that day, because he knew those philosophies. However, he also knew that any discussion in that capacity, plus any other direction that could be taken, while possibly titillating to the ears, would not set anyone free. *"Jesus Christ and Him Crucified"* must be the Message, and the only Message, because that alone will set the captive free.

"Fill thou my life, O Lord my God,
"In every part with praise,
"That my whole being may proclaim,
"Your Being and Your Ways."

"Naught for the lip of praise alone,
"Nor e'vn the praising heart,
"I ask, but for a life made up,
"Of praise in every part:"

"Praise in the common things of life,
"It's goings out and in;
"Praise in each duty and each deed,
"However small and mean."

"Fill every part of me with praise;
"Let all my being speak,
"Of You and of Your Love, O Lord,
"Poor though I be and weak."

"So shall You, Lord from me, even me,
"Receive the glory due;
"And so shall I begin on Earth,
"The song forever new."

"So shall no part of day or night,
"From sacredness be free;
"But all my life, in ever step,
"Be fellowship with Thee."

CHAPTER THREE

The Cross Of Christ And The Sin Nature

THE CROSS OF CHRIST AND
THE SIN NATURE

An understanding of the sin nature according to the Word of God is at least one of the single most important Doctrines that the Believer could ever learn and know. Unfortunately, most of the modern church has little knowledge or no knowledge at all concerning this most important subject. As a result, and this is the tragic part, most modern Believers, and we speak of those who truly love the Lord and are truly trying to serve Him to the best of their ability, are being ruled by the sin nature in some way.

Many would immediately ask, *"If this subject is so important, why isn't it taught in the Churches?"*

It should not come as a surprise that Satan will do everything within his power to hinder the True Gospel, while at the same time, even aiding and abetting the message which will lead people astray. As I've already stated, the pattern for this of which I speak begins in the Fourth Chapter of Genesis with the episode of Cain and Abel. That battle has raged from then until now. Listen to Paul:

I AM CRUCIFIED WITH CHRIST

"I am Crucified with Christ: nevertheless I live; yet not I, but Christ lives in me: and the life which I now live in the flesh I live by the Faith of the Son of God, Who loved me, and gave Himself for me" (Gal. 2:20).

The verb *"crucified"* is in the perfect tense, which speaks of a past, completed action having present results. Paul uses it to show that his identification with Christ at the Cross was a past fact, and that the Spiritual Benefits that have come to him through his identification are present realities with Him. By this statement he also shows how he died to the Law, namely by dying with Christ, Who died under its penalty (Rom. 6:3-5). The Law's demands were satisfied and, therefore, have no more hold on Paul, or any Believer, at least one whose Faith is exclusively in Christ and what Christ did at the Cross.

DEATH TO SELF

To Paul, being thus crucified with Christ also meant death to self. When Paul died with Christ, it was the Pharisee Saul who died. As far as he was concerned, what he was and did up to that time had passed away. Saul was buried and the old life with him. The dominating control of the Adamic nature (the sin nature) had its power over him broken.

THE CHRIST-CENTERED LIFE

Consequently, it is no longer a self-centered life that he lives but a Christ-centered one. His new life is a Person, the Lord Jesus, through the Person of the Holy Spirit, living in Paul, and through the Ministry of the Holy Spirit, the Lord Jesus is manifest in his life. The new life is no longer like the former one, dependent upon the ineffectual efforts of a man attempting to draw near to God by his own works. The new life is a Person, namely Christ, within a person, living out His Life in that person. Instead of attempting to live his life in obedience to a set of rules in the form of the legal enactments of the Mosaic Law, Paul now yields to the indwelling Holy Spirit and cooperates with Him in the production of a life pleasing to God, which is energized by the Divine Life resident in him through the regenerating Work of the Spirit, all made possible by the Cross.

THE RELIGION OF MAN

However, man, even believing man, somewhat balks at this position given here by the Holy Spirit through Paul. Man likes to have some credit and some position. He likes that which he can see and handle. He refuses to be treated as vile and incapable of good and is angered that he and his religious efforts should be condemned to annihilation.

SELF TRYING TO SANCTIFY SELF

Oh, yes! Man will willingly practice efforts to annihilate himself, for that ministers to his own importance. However, to accept the absolute judgment of death upon his nature, his religious energies, and his moral virtues, and to be commanded to be silent and as a dead sinner, to trust the Life-giving Saviour, finding in Christ all that is needful for Righteousness and worship, is distasteful and repelling, hence, the offense of the Cross. But this is the Doctrine of Galatians 2:20.

THE CROSS

When Paul mentioned, *"living by the Faith of the Son of God,"* he was once again taking the Believer to the Cross. With the first phrase, *"I am Crucified with Christ,"* he takes the Believer to Romans 6:3-5. There the Believer was baptized into the Death of Christ, buried with Him by baptism into death, and raised with Him in Newness of Life. No! This is not speaking of Water Baptism but the Crucifixion of Christ. The Believer gains this place and position in Christ by simply having Faith in Christ and what Christ did at the Cross.

In fact, Paul opens this great statement of Galatians 2:20 by taking the Believer to the Cross. He said, *"I am Crucified with Christ."* He closed this great Scripture also with the Cross by saying, *"I live by the Faith of the Son of God, Who loved me, and gave Himself for me."* So, he opens with the Cross, and he closes with the Cross. Only the Holy Spirit in such brief terminology could give the actual meaning of the New Covenant in this one Passage. And, He most definitely did!

Going back to the statement we previously made, *"Believing man will willingly practice efforts to annihilate himself, for that ministers to his own importance,"* presents itself as the bane of Believers. In other words, this is where the rubber meets the road. So, what am I telling you?

I am telling you that within our own ability, our own personal strength, and our own personal efforts, we cannot hope to gain victory over the sin nature. It's simply not possible. It can only be done by the Power of the Holy Spirit, and He carries out such by our Faith being placed supremely in Christ and what Christ has done for us at the Cross. The Holy Spirit will work in no other way and, in fact, can work in no other way. It is the Cross of Christ that has given Him the legal Means to do all that He does within our hearts and lives.

WHAT IS THE SIN NATURE?

Even though we touched on this in Chapter 1, it is so important, the sin nature and how it functions, that I want to make certain that all bases are covered, at least to the degree of my knowledge. There will be some repetition regarding this subject and, in fact, through the entirety of this Volume, as it regards the Cross. In a sense, it is impossible to do otherwise inasmuch as certain truths overlap themselves.

The sin nature, or it might be referred to as the evil nature, was what happened to Adam and Eve immediately after the Fall. They fell from a position of total God-consciousness down to the far, far lower level of total self-consciousness. Whereas before the Fall they had been dominated by the Divine Nature, now the Divine Nature is no more. They are totally and completely dominated by the sin nature. This means that their very nature became that of sin, of transgression, of iniquity, of disobedience to the Word of God, etc. Due to the fact that every human being who has ever lived was in the loins of Adam, so to speak, this means that what he was, a fallen creature, every child born was and is controlled by the sin nature. That's the reason that Jesus had to be Virgin Born. Had he been born by natural procreation, as all other human beings, He would have been born in original sin, which means that He would not have been a suitable sacrifice. But, His Birth was totally unlike any other human birth that ever was, or ever would be, simply because man had absolutely nothing to do with that birth.

Concerning His Birth, the great Prophet Isaiah said:

"Therefore the Lord Himself shall give you a sign; Behold, a virgin shall conceive, and bear a Son, and shall call His Name Immanuel" (Isa. 7:14).

In Hebrew, the word *"virgin"* is *"hallmah,"* which means *"the virgin — the only one that ever was or ever will be a mother in this way."*

The *"Son"* Who would be born would be the *"Son of God."* The word *"Immanuel"* means *"God with us."* Such was fulfilled in Christ.

SONS OF GOD

The original intention of God was that human beings would bring sons and daughters of God into the world. However, due to the Fall, man can succeed only in bringing sons and daughters into the world in the *"likeness of Adam"* (Gen. 5:3).

As stated, the sin nature dominates unbelievers in totality, meaning twenty-four hours a day, seven days a week. Everything the unredeemed person does is from the position of the sin nature. Even the so-called good things they do are motivated from a wrong impulse. That's the reason that a person has to be *"Born-Again,"* and that's the reason the Lord does not attempt to rehabilitate anyone. There is nothing good in man that can be rehabilitated. So, to be what he ought to be, he has to be Born-Again, i.e., *"become a new creature,"* which can only be done in Jesus Christ (II Cor. 5:17).

THREE NATURES

Redeemed man has three natures. They are:
1. Human nature: Christ, as well, had a human nature.
2. The sin nature: Due to being Virgin Born, Christ had

no sin nature.

3. The Divine Nature.

As would be obvious, the unredeemed individual does not have a Divine Nature, that being possible only by the Born-Again experience. Peter said:

"**Whereby are given unto us exceeding great and Precious Promises** *(pertains to the Word of God, which alone holds the answer to every life problem)*: **that by these** *(Promises)* **you might be partakers of the Divine Nature** *(the Divine Nature implanted in the inner being of the believing sinner becomes the source of our new life and actions; it comes to everyone at the moment of being 'Born-Again')*, **having escaped the corruption that is in the world through lust.** *(This presents the Salvation experience of the sinner, and the Sanctification experience of the Saint)*" **(II Pet. 1:4).**

While the Lord does not remove the sin nature from the Believer at conversion, because it serves to discipline the Believer, still, He has given us in His Word the Means by which we can have Victory over this ever present problem.

THE FIRST TRUTH REGARDING THE BELIEVER AS IT WAS GIVEN TO PAUL

In the Revelation of the Cross, which the Lord gave to me in 1997, He showed me what the sin nature is and how it functions. A few days later he gave me the solution to the sin nature, which is the Cross of Christ. In both cases He took me to the Sixth Chapter of Romans.

I learned later that this was the first Truth given to Paul by the Lord as it regards Believers. How did He show me that?

He showed me that by taking me to the Word. Chapters 5 and 6 of Romans deal with the manner in which the believing sinner comes to Christ, in other words, how a person is Saved.

Believing sinners are justified by Faith, which refers to Faith in Christ, and Faith in Christ alone! So, this tells us how that man is Born-Again. As stated, that is dealt with in Chapters 4 and 5 of Romans.

Now, when we come to the Sixth Chapter of Romans, it is very obvious that this is given to Believers, in other words, telling us how to live for God. To do that, he deals with the sin nature, which is the first subject addressed regarding Believers. In other words, how we live for God.

Seventeen times in the Sixth Chapter of Romans alone Paul deals with sin. Fifteen of those times, in his original Text, he used in front of the word *"sin"* what is now referred to as the definite article, making it read *"the sin."* Let me give you an example:

"What shall we say then? Shall we continue in (the) *sin, that Grace may abound? God forbid. How shall we, who are dead to* (the) *sin, live any longer therein?"* (Rom. 6:1-2). In other words, in these Verses he is not talking about acts of sin, but rather, the root of sin, the sin principle, the sin nature. In Verse 14, he doesn't use the definite article in front of the word *"sin,"* but he does use it as a noun instead of a verb. So, it means the same thing, *"the sin nature."*

Verse 15 is the only Verse in this Chapter where he is speaking of acts of sin. He said, *"What then? shall we sin, because we are not under the Law, but under Grace?"* (Rom. 6:15).

So, the question longs to be asked as to why the King James translators did not translate it exactly as Paul wrote it.

I really cannot answer that; however, quite possibly they reasoned that had they placed the definite article in front of the word *"sin"* every time that Paul used it, it might have made the subject even more confusing. For instance, had they translated, *"let not the sin therefore reign in your mortal body . . ."* people would have probably wondered what type of sin was Paul dealing with. By him putting the definite article before the word *"sin"* tells us that he wasn't speaking of acts of sin, but rather, the very nature of sin, hence, the *"sin nature."* He tells us in this Sixth Chapter how to have Victory over the sin nature so that it would not cause us any problem. But unfortunately, precious few Christians, even preachers, know what Paul was saying. Momentarily we will give exactly what the great Apostle told us, but first, I want to deal with the manner in which the church presently addresses this subject.

IGNORANCE

Virtually the entirety of the modern church is totally ignorant of the sin nature. They don't have the slightest idea as to what it is, and to be sure, such ignorance will guarantee that the person is going to be controlled by the sin nature in some way, which makes life miserable, to say the least, and greatly hinders our progress in the Lord.

Before the Lord gave me this great Truth, in looking back, and in all of my years of study, and I've always been an avid reader, I don't remember one single message that I ever read regarding the sin nature. I don't remember hearing one single sermon regarding the sin nature. The word was mentioned here and there in some of the sermons I read, but no explanation was ever given. In this case, and to be sure, ignorance is not bliss, but rather, the very opposite.

The reader should understand that ignorance is no escape from the result of the ruling power of the sin nature. This means that the Believer, irrespective of the lack of knowledge concerning this all-important subject, will still suffer the results of what the sin nature can do, which, as stated, makes life miserable.

Most of the time when we hear of Believers who fail the Lord, it is because the sin nature was ruling that person, driving them deeper and deeper into this morass of evil, and despite all of their efforts, they are unable to break the bondage. Now, don't misunderstand, while sin originates in the heart, it is carried out, even as Paul explains to us in this Sixth Chapter of Romans, through the physical members of the body. I speak of the eyes, sexual organs, tongue, hands, feet, etc. That's why the great Apostle said:

THE PHYSICAL BODY

I will quote both Text and notes directly from THE EXPOSITOR'S STUDY BIBLE, which we will do throughout the entirety of this Volume.

"**Let not sin** *(the sin nature)* **therefore reign** *(rule)* **in your mortal body** *(showing that the sin nature can once again rule in the heart and life of the Believer, if the Believer doesn't constantly look to Christ and the Cross; the 'mortal body' is neutral, which means it can be used for Righteousness or unrighteousness)*, **that you should obey it in the lusts thereof** *(ungodly lusts are carried out through the mortal body, if Faith is not maintained in the Cross [I Cor. 1:17-18])*."

RIGHTEOUSNESS OR UNRIGHTEOUSNESS

"**Neither yield you your members** *(of your mortal body)* **as instruments of unrighteousness unto sin** *(the sin nature)*: **but yield yourselves unto God** *(we are to yield ourselves to Christ and the Cross; that alone guarantees Victory over the sin nature)*, **as those who are alive from the dead** *(we have been raised with Christ in 'Newness of Life')*, **and your members** *as* **instruments of Righteousness unto God** *(this can be done only by virtue of the Cross and our Faith in that Finished Work, and Faith which continues in that Finished Work from day-to-day [Lk. 9:23-24])*" **(Rom. 6:12-13).**

DENIAL

Many preachers claim that the Believer doesn't have a sin nature. While they might have had one, they say, before conversion, after they come to Christ, there is no more sin nature.

My answer to that is simple: as stated, Paul in the great Sixth Chapter of Romans is writing exclusively to Believers. In fact, it would do no good to write to unbelievers simply because they would not understand what was being said (I Cor. 14). So, if Paul is writing to Believers, as he most definitely is, and if the sin nature is no more, then why in the world did he spend so much time and space explaining something that doesn't exist? Let's say it in a little different way:

Why would the Holy Spirit, Who was telling Paul what to write, deal with this subject to such a great extent, if it no longer exists?

We should know and understand that the Holy Spirit does not waste words. No, He gave all of this instruction in Romans, Chapter 6, regarding the sin nature, because it is a problem that continues. In fact, the Believer will not be rid of such until the Trump of God sounds or the Lord calls us Home. When the Trump sounds, the Scripture plainly says what will happen.

"For this corruptible *(sin nature)* must put on incorruption *(a Glorified Body with no sin nature)*, and this mortal *(subject to death)* **must** put on immortality *(will never die)*" (I Cor. 15:53).

Furthermore, John the Beloved wrote:

"If we say that we have no sin *(refers to 'the sin nature')*, we deceive ourselves *(refers to self-deception)*, and the Truth is not in us. *(This does not refer to all Truth as it regards Believers, but rather that the Truth of the indwelling sinful nature is not in us)*" (I Jn. 1:8).

While John did not use the definite article in front of the word *"sin,"* he is using it as a noun instead of a verb. So, it means the same thing. He is not speaking of acts of sin, but rather, the indwelling sin nature.

LICENSE

There are some few who do have a modicum of understanding

as it regards the sin nature, but who use that knowledge for license. What do we mean by that?

In other words, they excuse their constant sinning by blaming it on the sin nature. Paul addressed this very thing. He said:

> "What shall we say then? *(This is meant to direct attention to Rom. 5:20.)* Shall we continue in sin, that Grace may abound? *(Just because Grace is greater than sin doesn't mean that the Believer has a license to sin.)*
>
> "God forbid *(presents Paul's answer to the question, 'Away with the thought, let not such a thing occur').* How shall we, who are dead to sin *(dead to the sin nature)*, live any longer therein? *(This portrays what the Believer is now in Christ)*" (Rom. 6:1-2).

We must never forget that the Lord saves us from sin, not in sin! So, those who use the little knowledge they have of the sin nature as a license to keep doing wrong are only deceiving themselves.

STRUGGLE

Oddly enough, the word *"struggle"* probably fits good Christians, those who are the most consecrated, more than all. Not understanding the sin nature, they have come to believe that their great struggle with sin, in order to overcome it, is part and parcel of the Christian experience. Consequently, they make a degree of holiness out of that struggle. In other words, *"I've struggled more than you, etc."* But, the sadness is, it doesn't really matter how much they struggle, they're not going to overcome the sin nature by that means.

Sometime back the Lord dealt with me about this very thing. There is something in believing man that thinks that by great effort, a great exhibition of Faith, sin can be overcome in this manner. We even go so far as to think that this pleases the Lord. In other words, if we could in our struggles finally say, *"I have overcome,"* this would greatly please the Lord.

It won't!

In fact, it will have the exact opposite result. The following is what I believe the Lord spoke to my heart.

It doesn't matter how great our struggle is, how much effort we put into it, or what we try to do to be an overcomer, we will not succeed. Now, let me show you why!

"**And if Christ** *be* **in you** *(He is in you through the Power and Person of the Spirit [Gal. 2:20])*, **the body** *is* **dead because of sin** *(means that the physical body has been rendered helpless because of the Fall; consequently, the Believer trying to overcome by willpower presents a fruitless task)*; **but the Spirit** *is* **Life because of Righteousness** *(only the Holy Spirit can make us what we ought to be, which means we cannot do it ourselves; once again, He performs all that He does within the confines of the Finished Work of Christ)*" **(Rom. 8:10).**

We are plainly told in this Passage, as stated, that the Fall in the Garden of Eden rendered the physical body of man ineffective. As it regards overcoming sin by willpower, by personal strength, we can't do it because *"the body is dead because of sin,"* i.e., the Fall.

Then the Lord spoke to my heart and said, *"Even if one could do such a thing, that is, to overcome sin by our own personal efforts, the latter end would still be worse than ever."*

How?

Then the Believer would look to his *"great faith,"* which would tend to do nothing except glorify the individual instead of the Lord, thereby, producing pride, which is man's basic problem. In other words, it would only add to the problem instead of removing the problem.

WILLPOWER!

Most modern Believers, and again we are speaking of those

who truly love the Lord, are trying to live for God by the means of *"willpower."* **Many Christians even think that before they were Saved, they didn't have the willpower to say** *"no"* **to sin, but now that they are Saved, their willpower has been greatly strengthened, enabling them to say** *"no"* **to sin, etc. None of that is correct!**

Listen again to Paul. He said:

"**For I know that in me, (that is, in my flesh,) dwells no good thing** *(speaks of man's own ability, or rather the lack thereof, in comparison to the Holy Spirit, at least when it comes to spiritual things)*: **for to will is present with me** *(Paul is speaking here of his willpower; regrettably, most modern Christians are trying to live for God by means of willpower, thinking falsely that since they have come to Christ, they are now free to say 'no' to sin; that is the wrong way to look at the situation; the Believer cannot live for God by the strength of willpower; while the will is definitely important, it alone is not enough; the Believer must exercise Faith in Christ and the Cross, and do so constantly; then he will have the ability and strength to say 'yes' to Christ, which automatically says, 'no' to the things of the world)*; **but** *how* **to perform that which is good I find not** *(outside of the Cross, it is impossible to find a way to do good)*" **(Rom. 7:18).**

THE LAW OF THE MIND AND THE LAW OF GOD

Paul again tells us:

"**For I delight in the Law of God** *(refers to the moral Law of God ensconced in the Ten Commandments)* **after the inward man** *(refers to the spirit and soul of man which has now been regenerated)*" **(Rom. 7:22).**

Paul tells us here in this Verse that when people come to

Christ, they now delight in the Law of God, meaning they want to obey it, and desire to do so with all of their strength.

He then said:

"**I thank God through Jesus Christ our Lord** *(presents Paul revealing the answer to his own question; Deliverance comes through Jesus Christ and Christ Alone, and more particularly what Jesus did at Calvary and the Resurrection).* **So then with the mind I myself serve the Law of God** *(the 'will' is the trigger, but it within itself can do nothing unless the gun is loaded with explosive power; that Power is the Cross)*" **(Rom. 7:25).**

So this tells us that most Believers are trying to satisfy the *"Law of God"* with the *"Law of the Mind."* But then, Paul said:

THE LAW OF SIN AND DEATH

"**But I see another Law in my members** *(the Law of Sin and Death desiring to use my physical body as an instrument of unrighteousness)*, **warring against the Law of my mind** *(this is the Law of desire and willpower)*, **and bringing me into captivity to the Law of sin** *(the Law of Sin and Death)* **which is in my members** *(which will function through my members, and make me a slave to the Law of Sin and Death; this will happen to the most consecrated Christian if that Christian doesn't constantly exercise Faith in Christ and the Cross, understanding that it is through the Cross that all powers of darkness were defeated [Col. 2:14-15])*" **(Rom. 7:23).**

So, in these Passages Paul tells us that the Law of the Mind, meaning the desire to obey the Law of God, while necessary and commendable, still, within itself is not enough. In other words, *"the Law of Sin and Death"* is stronger than the Law of the Mind, but regrettably, that's the way that most modern

Believers are attempting to live for God. It is by the Law of the Mind.

There is only one Law that is greater and more powerful than the Law of Sin and Death, and that is *"the Law of the Spirit of Life in Christ Jesus"* (Rom. 8:2). We'll deal with that in a later Chapter.

FIGHT THE GOOD FIGHT OF FAITH

There is only one fight in which we are to be engaged, and that is, *"the good fight of Faith."* Paul also said:

"**Fight the good fight of Faith** *(in essence, the only fight we're called upon to engage; every attack by Satan against the Believer, irrespective of its form, is to destroy or seriously weaken our Faith; he wants to keep our Faith in things other than the Cross, and if it's in the Cross, to push it from the Cross to other things)*, **lay hold on Eternal Life** *(we do such by understanding that all Life comes from Christ, and the Means is the Cross)*, **whereunto you are also Called** *(Called to follow Christ)*, **and have professed a good profession before many witnesses.** *(This does not refer to a particular occasion, but to the entirety of his life for Christ)*" (I Tim. 6:12).

SIN?

In a sense, if we're fighting a battle with sin of any nature, then we're fighting the wrong battle. That battle was fought and won at Calvary nearly two thousand years ago. The struggle is with Faith, as it always is with Faith.

What do we mean by that?

Paul said, ". . . *I live by the Faith of the Son of God, Who loved me, and gave Himself for me*" (Gal. 2:20).

The phrase, *"The Faith of the Son of God,"* refers to the Faith that's made possible by what Christ did for us at the

Cross. We are to have Faith in Christ and what He did for us at the Cross, understanding that He is always the Source while the Cross is always the Means.

CONTINUING IN THE FAITH

That's why Paul said:

"**If you continue in the Faith** *(at the same time says it is possible not to continue in the Faith; 'the Faith' is 'Christ and Him Crucified')* **grounded and settled** *(the Foundation of the Faith, which Object must always be the Cross)***, and** *be* **not moved away** *(moved away from the Cross)* **from the Hope of the Gospel, which you have heard** *(pertains to the fact that they had been brought in right)***,** *and* **which was preached to every creature which is under Heaven** *(the Message of the Cross is the same for all)***; whereof I Paul am made a Minister** *(the meaning of the New Covenant was actually given to Paul, which is the meaning of the Cross [Gal. 1:11-12])*" **(Col. 1:23).**

To sum up, while there definitely is a struggle, it is to be with Faith and not sin.

GRACE

Of all the things we've named, ignorance, denial, license, and struggle, Grace is the only Means by which Victory can be won over the sin nature.

In simple terms, *"Grace"* is simply the Goodness of God extended to undeserving Saints. But, we must ever understand, it is the Cross of Christ which makes all Grace possible.

God doesn't have any more Grace today than He did three thousand years ago. The problem then was that the blood of bulls and goats was insufficient to take away sins (Heb. 10:4). Inasmuch as the sin debt remained, so to speak, this limited

God as to the degree of Grace that He could bestow upon individuals. However, since the Cross, which atoned for all sin, the Lord can bestow Grace fully on all who will believe, which He most definitely does.

So, understanding that, how do we have Victory over the sin nature?

UNPLUGGED, SO TO SPEAK

The moment the believing sinner comes to Christ, at that moment the sin nature, one might say, although not removed, is unplugged. It is somewhat like an electric power saw. If it's plugged in, it can cause people a lot of grief if it's not handled very correctly, but, if it's unplugged, it's not dangerous at all.

So, when the believing sinner comes to Christ, as stated, the sin nature is disconnected, but the problem is, it doesn't stay disconnected.

Even though the new Christian now hates sin, still, he finds very shortly that he has failed the Lord in some way. This comes as a shock to him because, as stated, he now despises sin in all of its forms.

Having failed the Lord in some way, which characterizes every Believer who has ever lived, the Believer now sets about to stop a recurrence of the same failure. While the sin committed, whatever it was, would not cause the sin nature to become active again, what now follows most definitely will.

To keep from failing again, the Believer now formulates a set of rules to see to it that there is no recurrence of the problem. These are rules which he has devised himself or borrowed from someone else. Consequently, he places his faith in these rules and his keeping them, which activates the sin nature.

While the *"rules"* may be very Scriptural and good in their own right, still, this is not God's Way. What happens is this:

Whatever we are to do in Christ, whatever we are to be in Christ, it cannot be done without the leading, guidance, and empowerment of the Holy Spirit. The problem is that the Holy

Spirit will not work with us regarding these rules, whatever they might be. He works exclusively, as stated, within the parameters of the Finished Work of Christ, and will not work outside of those parameters. This requires that our Faith be exclusively in Christ and the Cross and not in the rules or something else. Let me give you an example.

PRAYER

There is no privilege the Believer has that is greater than that of prayer. It is the Means of fellowship with the Lord and the Means of communion with Him. As such, prayer is a must for every Believer. In fact, and, as stated, without a proper prayer life, there can be very little growth in the Lord; however, it is quite possible for the Believer to turn prayer into a law, which God cannot accept. Let me explain!

My grandmother taught me to pray when I was but a child. Over and over again she would tell me, *"Jimmy, God is a big God, so ask big."* That little simple advice has helped me to touch the world for Christ, literally seeing hundreds of thousands brought to a Saving knowledge of our Redeemer. So, from the very beginning, I have always had a very strong prayer life.

I thought that I could overcome sin, could overcome the powers of darkness, and could overcome Satan himself, by having a proper prayer life. I remember increasing it from an hour a day to two hours a day.

In fact, for the second hour, I would get up at 1 a.m. or 2 a.m. and stagger around the house, trying to pray. I almost drove myself to a nervous breakdown, but the simple truth was that I did not know what else to do.

While the Lord would greatly bless me in these prayer times, even as He always had, still, one cannot pray oneself into Victory over sin. It's not possible, and it's not meant to be possible.

When we do such, we have turned prayer into a law, which

God cannot bless. Now, let me tell you why!

Every Victory was finished at Calvary. When Jesus said, *"It is finished,"* that simple statement covered more ground than you and I will ever know. It meant that Satan, every demon spirit, and every fallen Angel, all and without exception, were totally defeated by what Christ there did (Col. 2:14-15).

What He did was to atone for all sin, past, present, and future, at least for all who will believe (Jn. 3:16). Sin, being the legal right that Satan had to hold man captive, has been removed. In other words, since Calvary, Satan has no more right to hold anyone in bondage. Understanding that, our Faith must be exclusively in Christ and the Cross, which then gives the Holy Spirit latitude to work within our hearts and lives.

Trying to overcome the powers of darkness, I turned prayer into *"works."* Neither the *"work of prayer"* nor anything else of that nature is meant by the Lord to be used as a vehicle to overcome the powers of darkness. Again we state the fact that at the Cross all sin was atoned, and every power of darkness was defeated (Rom. 6:1-14; 8:1-2, 11; I Cor. 1:17-18, 23; 2:2; Col. 2:14-15).

While prayer, as well as every other Biblical privilege, has its place, and a wonderful place it is, still, we must ever understand that it was at the Cross that all Victory was won. Channeling prayer in the right direction is the greatest blessing that one could ever be afforded; however, if we treat any of the Biblical Disciplines in a wrong manner, trying to make them function in a way they were never intended, this frustrates the Grace of God.

FRUSTRATING THE GRACE OF GOD

Paul said:

"I do not frustrate the Grace of God *(if we make anything other than the Cross of Christ the Object of our Faith, we frustrate the Grace of God, which means we stop its action, and the Holy Spirit will no longer help us)*: **for if Righteousness** *come* **by the Law** *(any type of Law)*, **then Christ is dead in vain.** *(If I can successfully live for the Lord by any means other than Faith in Christ and the Cross, then the Death of Christ was a waste)*" **(Gal. 2:21).**

In fact, *"frustrating the Grace of God,"* which means to hinder its action, is perhaps the greatest sin that any and all of us have committed, and to a great extent, still commit. The moment, as stated, that we place our Faith in anything except the Cross of Christ, at that moment we frustrate the Grace of God. Please allow me to give this little formula once again, as I will possibly do two or three other times in this Volume as well.

FOCUS: The Lord Jesus Christ (Jn. 14:6).

OBJECT OF FAITH: The Cross of Christ (Rom. 6:3-5; I Cor. 1:17-18, 23; 2:2).

POWER SOURCE: The Holy Spirit (Rom. 8:1-2, 11).

RESULTS: Victory (Rom. 6:14).

Now, let me give this formula once again but in the manner in which it is generally practiced.

Focus: Works!

Object of faith: Our performance.

Power source: Self.

Results: Defeat!

Now, look at the two formulas very carefully and very closely. The first one guarantees Victory, while the latter, which is mostly where the modern church is, brings nothing but defeat.

God has many wonderful and great things to give to us; however, He can only do it in one way, and that is by us understanding that Jesus Christ is the Source of all things we receive, and because He is the One Who has paid the price and did it all for us. We must, as well, understand that the Cross of Christ is the Means by which all of this is done, and the only Means. It's not one among several means, but the only Means, meaning that the Holy Spirit works exclusively within the Framework of the Finished Work of Christ and, in fact, will work no other way.

If the Believer doesn't place his Faith exclusively in Christ and the Cross, understanding this is God's Way, he will find the sin nature ruling him. And, despite every effort made otherwise, he will find himself failing the Lord over and over again with the problem, whatever it is, getting worse almost by the day. In fact, this can go on for many years. Actually, and, as stated, most modern Believers are ruled by the sin nature in some way, meaning they live in the Seventh Chapter of Romans for the entirety of their lives. To be sure, it's not very pleasant. Once again we quote Paul:

"**O wretched man that I am!** *(Any Believer who attempts to live for God outside of God's Prescribed Order, which is 'Jesus Christ and Him Crucified,' will, in fact, live a wretched and miserable existence. This life can only be lived in one way, and that is the way of the Cross.)* **Who shall deliver me from the body of this death?** *(The minute he cries 'Who,' he finds the path of Victory, for he is now calling upon a Person for help, and that Person is Christ; actually, the Greek Text is masculine, indicating a Person)*" **(Rom. 7:24).**

GOD'S PRESCRIBED ORDER OF VICTORY

As we have already said elsewhere in this Volume, Paul begins Chapter 6 of the great Book of Romans by telling us that the problem is sin (Rom. 6:1-2). And then, he quickly gives us the solution. It is the Cross of Christ and the Cross of Christ alone!

He said:

"**Know you not, that so many of us as were baptized into Jesus Christ** *(plainly says that this Baptism is into Christ and not water [I Cor. 1:17; 12:13; Gal. 3:27;*

Eph. 4:5; Col. 2:11-13]) **were baptized into His Death?**
(When Christ died on the Cross, in the Mind of God, we died with Him; in other words, He became our Substitute, and our identification with Him in His Death gives us all the benefits for which He died; the idea is that He did it all for us!)"

NEWNESS OF LIFE

"**Therefore we are buried with Him by baptism into death** *(not only did we die with Him, but we were buried with Him as well, which means that all the sin and transgression of the past were buried; when they put Him in the Tomb, they put all of our sins into that Tomb as well)***:** **that like as Christ was raised up from the dead by the Glory of the Father, even so we also should walk in newness of life** *(we died with Him, we were buried with Him, and His Resurrection was our Resurrection to a 'Newness of Life')*."

THE LIKENESS OF HIS DEATH

"**For if we have been planted together** *(with Christ)* **in the likeness of His Death** *(Paul proclaims the Cross as the instrument through which all Blessings come; consequently, the Cross must ever be the Object of our Faith, which gives the Holy Spirit latitude to work within our lives)*, **we shall be also** *in the likeness* **of** *His* **Resurrection** *(we can have the 'likeness of His Resurrection,' i.e., 'live this Resurrection Life,' only as long as we understand the 'likeness of His Death,' which refers to the Cross as the Means by which all of this is done)*" **(Rom. 6:3-5).**

"More holiness give me,
"More sweetness within,
"More patience in suffering,

"More sorrow for sin:
"More Faith in my Saviour,
"More sense of His Care,
"More joy in His Service,
"More freedom in prayer."

"More gratitude give me,
"More trust in the Lord,
"More zeal for His Glory,
"More hope in His Word;
"More tears for His Sorrows,
"More pain at His Grief,
"More meekness in trial,
"More praise for relief."

"More Victory give me,
"More strength to overcome,
"More freedom from earth-stains,
"More longing for Home;
"More fit for the Kingdom,
"More useful I'd be,
"More blessed and holy,
"More, Saviour, like Thee."

CHAPTER FOUR

What Is The Gospel?

WHAT IS THE GOSPEL?

The Greek word for *"Gospel"* is *"euaggelizo,"* and simply means *"good news or good tidings."* The manner in which that *"good news"* is brought about, the Holy Spirit through Paul gives to us in the following:

> "For Christ sent me not to baptize *(presents to us a Cardinal Truth)*, but to preach the Gospel *(the manner in which one may be Saved from sin)*: not with wisdom of words *(intellectualism is not the Gospel)*, lest the Cross of Christ should be made of none effect. *(This tells us in no uncertain terms that the Cross of Christ must always be the emphasis of the Message)*" (I Cor. 1:17).

In other words, if the preacher is not preaching the Cross, then whatever it is he is preaching is not the Gospel of Jesus Christ.

Now, some are claiming at this present time that while they believe in the Cross, they don't preach the Cross because, in their words, *"it may offend people."*

We must understand that the feelings of people aren't our objective. Preaching the True Gospel is. The fallen sons of Adam's lost race can be Saved in only one manner, and that is by the preaching of the Cross. Paul also made this statement:

> "But we preach Christ Crucified *(this is the Foundation of the Word of God and, thereby, of Salvation)*, unto the Jews a stumblingblock *(the Cross was the stumblingblock)*, and unto the Greeks foolishness *(both found it difficult to accept as God a dead Man hanging on a Cross, for such Christ was to them)*;"

CHRIST THE POWER OF GOD

> "But unto them who are called *(refers to those who*

accept the Call, for the entirety of mankind is invited [Jn. 3:16; Rev. 22:17]),* **both Jews and Greeks** *(actually stands for both 'Jews and Gentiles'),* **Christ the Power of God** *(what He did at the Cross atoned for all sin, thereby, making it possible for the Holy Spirit to exhibit His Power within our lives),* **and the Wisdom of God.** *(This Wisdom devised a Plan of Salvation, which pardoned guilty men and at the same time vindicated and glorified the Justice of God, which stands out as the wisest and most remarkable Plan of all time)*" **(I Cor. 1:23-24).**

NEVERTHELESS . . .

In effect, the Holy Spirit through the great Apostle is saying, *"I am sorry that the Message of the Cross offends people, whether Jew or Gentile, still, the Cross must be preached, because there is no other remedy."* Whether they liked it or not was not the question.

AN ILLUSTRATION

Sometime back I heard the promoter of the *"Seeker Sensitive"* church growth method being interviewed. His church supposedly runs some 20,000 people in attendance.

He stated that they had canvassed the area to ascertain what the people really wanted in a church. From that canvas they gathered that the people did not want anything said about sin, about the Blood of Jesus, about Hell, or about the Cross. So, he went on to state, this is what they had given the people. He also stated that the Cross was never mentioned in his church and neither was sin. He admitted that some of the old songs which pertained to the Cross were beautiful, still, his choirs did not sing them. The reason? It might offend people! That was some ten or more years ago that I heard that interview.

The other day I read an article which he had written. He

stated that a short time ago they had handed out question-
naires to all the many thousands of people in his church, asking very pointed, personal questions. The questionnaire was
anonymous, so the people could tell the truth and wouldn't
have to sign their names.

He went on to state that he was shocked at the results. He
found his church, according to the admittance of his people,
was full of homosexuals, lesbians, alcoholics, drug addicts,
gamblers, pedophiles, thieves, liars, etc.

He stated that they were going to have to rethink their
position because, evidently, what they were preaching, that is,
if you would call it preaching, simply was not working.

He was dead right. The gospel, so-called, he was preaching
was not working because it was not the Gospel.

THE PROBLEM

The problem is sin! You can label it anything you like or
call it anything you like, but it comes down to one fact, the
problem is sin. Man is a sinner, and there's only one remedy
for sin, not twenty, not ten, not even two, only one, and that is
what Paul said, *"Jesus Christ and Him Crucified."* If we don't
preach the Cross, then we might as well tell the people how to
play mumblety-peg.

The Gospel of Jesus Christ is not a proclamation of diplomacy. It is an ultimatum! As someone has well said, *"One
can be a spiritual leader, or one can be a Prophet, one cannot be
both."* Spiritual leaders, so-called, seek to appease men, while
Prophets proclaim the Truth, irrespective as to whether it is
liked or not.

Sometime back I was sent a questionnaire by a particular religious organization to which I then belonged, asking the
question as to what I believed the people wanted as it regarded
the Gospel.

I wrote them back a very kind note, but at the same time,
very straightforward. I said, *"I have little interest as to what*

the people want; rather, I want to know what God wants, and then ask Him to help me to deliver the Message, whatever that Message is."

THE APOSTLE PAUL

Before Paul went to the city of Corinth, sent there by the Holy Spirit, he first went to the great city of Athens. The Scripture says:

ATHENS

"Now while Paul waited for them at Athens, his spirit was stirred in him, when he saw the city wholly given to idolatry" (Acts 17:16).

As a result, he ministered in the Jewish synagogue, *"and in the market daily with them who met with him"* (Acts 17:17). He was then invited to preach *"in the midst of Mars' Hill"* (Acts 17:22). Part of his Message is recorded in the Seventeenth Chapter of Acts. While most rejected his Message, a few did believe (Acts 17:34). While his Message was par excellent, at the same time, the great Apostle did not preach the Cross. In relationship to that, as he went into Corinth, there is some evidence that he had been disappointed with the results in Athens. And now he was going to Corinth, one of the most jaded cities in the Roman Empire. It was noted for two things, vice and philosophy, in fact, Satan's two greatest weapons. The great Apostle may have been greatly troubled in his spirit, wondering how in the world he could break through this twin shell of vice and philosophy in Corinth. While Athens was bad, Corinth, if possible, was worse.

It is quite possible that the Holy Spirit whispered to his heart saying, *"Preach the Cross,"* and then He might have said, *"If the Message of the Cross will work in Corinth, it will work anywhere."* I say this simply because of what Paul himself said in his first Epistle to the Corinthians. He said:

DETERMINATION

"And I, brethren, when I came to you, came not with excellency of speech or of wisdom *(means that he depended not on oratorical abilities, nor did he delve into philosophy, which was all the rage of that particular day)*, declaring unto you the Testimony of God *(which is Christ and Him Crucified)*.

"For I determined not to know anything among you *(with purpose and design, Paul did not resort to the knowledge or philosophy of the world regarding the preaching of the Gospel)*, save Jesus Christ, and Him Crucified *(that and that alone is the Message, which will save the sinner, set the captive free, and give the Believer perpetual Victory)*" (I Cor. 2:1-2).

The word *"determined"* in the Greek is *"krino,"* and means, *"to decide mentally or judicially, to conclude."* It is a strong word, in a sense meaning, *"I will go to court before I change my views."*

The idea is that the great Apostle was fully and totally convinced that the Message of the Cross was the only Message that would set the captive free.

To be sure, Paul was one of the most educated men to be used by the Holy Spirit to pen the Gospel. He wrote almost half of the New Testament. He was probably more knowledgeable in the Law of Moses, having studied under the great scholar Gamaliel (Acts 22:3), than anyone of his time. In addition, it is believed by some modern scholars that Paul also attended the university at Tarsus, one of the most noted of its day. Irrespective of all that, he brushed it aside, knowing that no matter how cleverly or glibly that he could deliver great philosophical meanderings, having people then remark as to how brilliant he was, such effort, he knew, would be worthless. Intellectualism, as stated, would never set the captive free. He found that the Holy Spirit would only anoint the Message of the Cross. So, he determined not to know anything else except that Message.

WHAT DOES IT MEAN TO PREACH THE CROSS?

When we mention the Cross, we aren't speaking of the wooden beam on which Jesus died, but rather, what He there did. He offered Himself as a Sacrifice on the Cross, which satisfied the demands of a thrice-Holy God, thereby, paying the price for man's Redemption. Concerning this, Paul said:

ONE MEDIATOR

"For *there is* one God *(manifested in three Persons — God the Father, God the Son, and God the Holy Spirit)*, and one Mediator between God and men, the Man Christ Jesus *(He can only be an adequate Mediator Who has sympathy with and an understanding of both parties, and is understandable by and clear to both; in other words, Jesus is both God and Man, i.e., 'Very God and Very Man')*;"

A RANSOM

"Who gave Himself a ransom for all *(refers to the fact that our Lord's Death was a spontaneous and voluntary Sacrifice on His Part; the word 'ransom' refers to the price He paid, owed by man to God, which was His Precious Blood [I Pet. 1:18-20])*, to be testified in due time. *(This refers to the planning of this great Work, which took place 'before the Foundation of the world' [I Pet. 1:18-20], unto the 'due time' of its manifestation, which refers to when Christ was Crucified)*" (I Tim. 2:5-6).

EVERY DOCTRINE MUST BE BUILT ON THE FOUNDATION OF THE CROSS

That to which we have already alluded, the great Plan of Redemption, which, in effect, is *"Jesus Christ and Him Crucified,"* was formulated in the Mind of the Godhead from before the foundation of the world (I Pet. 1:18-20). In fact, any doctrine that is formulated on any other source can be concluded as to being specious, i.e., *"false."*

THE CROSS OF CHRIST IS THE MEANS OF ALL THINGS WE RECEIVE FROM GOD!

As we've said over and over again, while our Lord is the Source of all things we receive from God, the Cross of Christ is the Means by which those things are given to us. Without the Cross of Christ, God couldn't even look our way. We must understand that! When we go to Him in prayer, we must go in the Name of Jesus (Jn. 16:26), because it's our Lord and what He did for us at the Cross that opens up to us the very Throne of God. The Cross of Christ made everything possible, and the Cross of Christ is what makes everything possible. The Preacher of the Gospel must be fully convinced of that.

THE NEW JERUSALEM

When we go to the last two Chapters of the Bible, Chapters 21 and 22 of the Book of Revelation, some seven times in those two Chapters, the Holy Spirit refers to our Lord as *"the Lamb."* Why does He do this, considering the fact that during this particular time, which, in effect, will last forever, there is no more Satan, as he, along with his demon spirits and fallen Angels, have all been pressed into the Lake of Fire? In fact, at this time there is no more sin, no more disobedience, nothing that steals, kills, and destroys, and yet, the Holy Spirit refers to Jesus seven times as *"the Lamb"* (Rev. 21:9, 14, 22-23, 27; 22:1, 3).
Why?
The Holy Spirit refers to Jesus seven times in these two Chapters in order that we may know that this great and glorious Forever is all made possible by the Lord Jesus Christ and what He did for us at the Cross.
The name or word *"Lamb"* is mentioned seven times because

seven is God's Number of totality, universality, completion, and perfection. In other words, that which Jesus Christ perfected at the Cross was perfect, meaning it will never have to be changed or amended. That's why the Holy Spirit through Paul referred to this great Covenant as *"the Everlasting Covenant"* (Heb. 13:20).

THE PREACHER MUST PREACH THE CROSS NOT ONLY FOR SALVATION, BUT, AS WELL, FOR SANCTIFICATION!

The modern church has at least a modicum of understanding as it regards the Cross respecting Salvation, but almost none at all as it regards Sanctification, i.e., *"how we live for God."* That is tragic considering that almost all the emphasis by the Holy Spirit is placed on Sanctification as it regards the Cross of Christ. While, of course, the Cross of Christ respecting Salvation is far more important, simply because without Salvation, which is afforded by the Cross, one cannot have anything from God. But, as it regards instruction, information, teaching, and education, virtually the entirety of that which Paul taught regarding the Cross, almost all refers to Sanctification. So, what the Holy Spirit emphasizes, we should, as well, emphasize. That's why Paul told the Church at Corinth and, no doubt, all others, as well, *"For I determined not to know anything among you, save Jesus Christ and Him Crucified"* (I Cor. 2:2). The Cross is to be preached to the sinner for Salvation and to the Saint for Sanctification.

ALL VICTORY IS FOUND IN THE CROSS

Preaching the Cross (I Cor. 1:18) means that the Preacher proclaims the Scriptural Truth that all Victory comes by the Way of the Cross, and that it can be obtained in no other manner. Now, this is where the *"offense of the Cross"* comes in. As we have previously stated, *"Believing man will willingly practice efforts to annihilate himself, for that ministers to his own importance; but, to accept the absolute judgment of death upon his nature, his religious energies, and his moral virtues, and to be commanded to be silent, and, as a dead sinner, to trust the Life-giving Saviour, finding in Him all that is needful for Righteousness and Worship, is distasteful and repelling, hence, the offense of the Cross."*

The preacher must understand that all Salvation comes through the Cross; the Baptism with the Holy Spirit comes through the Cross; all Blessing comes through the Cross; all answer to prayer comes through the Cross; all of the Presence of God comes through the Cross; all Gifts of the Spirit come through the Cross; and, all Fruit of the Spirit comes through the Cross. In fact, every single thing we receive from God, the Cross of Christ is the Means by which all of these things are given to us. That's what it means to preach the Cross.

AN OLD TESTAMENT EXAMPLE

As an Old Testament example, the Holy Spirit in Hebrews 11:21 points to Jacob's action in the Forty-ninth Chapter of Genesis as the great Faith action of his life. Feeble and dying and having nothing except the staff on which he leaned and worshipped, he, yet, bestowed vast and unseen possessions on his grandsons.

First, he recited the Gift of the Land of Canaan to him by God (Gen. 49:3-4). Then, making Joseph his firstborn (Gen. 49:22), he adopted Joseph's two sons as his own (*"even as Reuben and Simeon, they shall be mine"*), and setting the younger above the elder, endowed them with the firstborn's double portion. It was a beautiful picture of a Faith that was Divine, intelligent, and triumphant.

THE DOUBLE PORTION

The double portion given to Joseph as the firstborn was a conquered portion (Gen. 49:22). The possession given by God to the Divine Firstborn among many Brethren, the Lord Jesus Christ, is also a conquered possession, i.e., it was done at the Cross, and it redeemed His People out of the land of the enemy — the Amorite, one might say.

Everything Jacob said came to pass, and everything our Heavenly Jacob has promised us will also come to pass. The Cross has made it all possible! (Rom. 6:1-14).

"On You my heart is resting,
"Ah, this is rest indeed:
"What else, Almighty Saviour,
"Can a poor sinner need?
"Your Light is all my wisdom,
"Your Love is all my stay;
"Our Father's Home in Glory,
"Draws nearer every day."

"My guilt is great, but greater,
"The Mercy You do give,
"Yourself, a Spotless Offering,
"Have died that I should live.
"With You, my soul unfettered,
"Has risen from the dust;
"Your Blood is all my treasure,
"Your Word is all my trust."

"Through me, You gentle, Master,
"Your purposes fulfill;
"I yield myself forever,
"To Your most Holy Will.
"What though I be but weakness?
"My strength is not in me;
"The poorest of Your People,
"Has all things, having Thee."

"When clouds are darkest round me,

"You, Lord, are then most near,
"My drooping faith to quicken,
"My weary soul to cheer.
"Safe nestling in Your Bosom,
"I gaze upon Your Face;
"In vain my foes would drive me,
"From You, my Hiding-place."

"Tis You have made me happy,
"Tis You have set me free;
"To Whom shall I give glory,
"Forever, but to Thee?
"Of earthly love and blessing,
"Should every stream run dry,
"Your Grace shall still be with me,
"Your Grace to live and die."

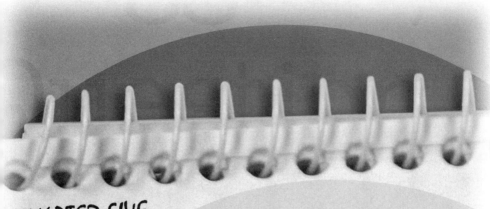

CHAPTER FIVE

What Jesus Said About The Cross

WHAT JESUS SAID ABOUT THE CROSS

Anything that Christ said or did, as should be obvious, was of the utmost significance; however, if one thing could be said to be more important than the other, then the following is of pronounced significance. He said:

"**The Son of Man must suffer many things** *(is mentioned apart from the glory that follows the sufferings)*, **and be rejected of the Elders and Chief Priests and Scribes** *(concerned the entirety of the religious leadership of Israel)*, **and be slain** *(refers to the Crucifixion of Christ; the religious leaders would be guilty of His Death)*, **and be raised the third day** *(the Resurrection, which was never in doubt; the purpose of God becoming man was to go to the Cross because this is the only way sin could be addressed, and sin is the problem)*.

DISCIPLESHIP

"**And He said to** *them* **all, If any** *man* **will come after Me** *(the criteria for Discipleship)*, **let him deny himself** *(not asceticism as many think, but rather, that one denies one's own willpower, self-will, strength, and ability, depending totally on Christ)*, **and take up his cross** *(the benefits of the Cross, looking exclusively to what Jesus did there to meet our every need)* **daily** *(this is so important, our looking to the Cross; that we must renew our Faith in what Christ has done for us, even on a daily basis, for Satan will ever try to move us away from the Cross as the Object of our Faith, which always spells disaster)*, **and follow Me** *(Christ can be followed only by the Believer looking to the Cross, understanding what it accomplished, and by that means alone [Rom. 6:3-5, 11, 14; 8:1-2, 11; I Cor. 1:17-18, 21, 23; 2:2; Gal. 6:14; Eph. 2:13-18; Col. 2:14-15])*."

THE SAVING OR LOSING OF ONE'S LIFE

"For whosoever will save his life shall lose it *(try to live one's life outside of Christ and the Cross)*: **but whosoever will lose his life for My sake, the same shall save it** *(when we place our Faith entirely in Christ and the Cross, looking exclusively to Him, we have just found 'more Abundant Life' [Jn. 10:10])*" **(Lk. 9:22-24).**

Jesus went on to say, which places even more emphasis on taking up the cross:

THE LORD MUST COME FIRST

"And there went great multitudes with Him *(proclaims Him having left the home of this Pharisee, and now continuing His journey toward Jerusalem)*: **and He turned, and said unto them** *(He was anxious now, at the end, clearly to make it known to all these multitudes what serving Him really signified)*,

"If any *man* come to Me *(no exceptions)*, **and hate** *(prefer)* **not his father, and mother, and wife, and children, and brethren, and sisters, yea, and his own life also** *(no affection, however strong, must be permitted to compete with or displace Christ)*, **he cannot be My Disciple** *(once again, no exceptions!)*."

THE CRITERIA FOR DISCIPLESHIP

"And whosoever does not bear his Cross *(this doesn't speak of suffering, as most think, but rather, ever making the Cross of Christ the Object of our Faith; we are Saved and we are victorious, not by suffering, although that sometimes will happen, or any other similar things, but rather by our Faith, but always with the Cross of Christ as the Object of that Faith)*, **and come after Me** *(one can follow*

Christ only by Faith in what He has done for us at the Cross; He recognizes nothing else), **cannot be My Disciple** *(the statement is emphatic!; if it's not Faith in the Cross of Christ, then it's faith that God will not recognize, which means that such people are refused)*" **(Lk. 14:25-27).**

WHAT DID JESUS MEAN?

When Jesus mentioned bearing the cross, His Disciples and all who heard Him must have been flabbergasted, to say the least. What did He mean?

The cross was one of, if not, the most hated instrument of torture ever devised by evil men. It was the favorite form of execution by the Romans, and incidentally, they did not execute Roman citizens on crosses, but rather gave them a nobler manner of dying. It was common to see at particular spots in every city in the Roman Empire men hanging on crosses, which took sometimes a week or even two for them to die, and all of that was a constant reminder that Roman peace was not to be trifled with.

So, when Jesus talked about taking up the cross, the Disciples must have wondered as to what He was talking about? He could not have used anything that would have been more shocking than a cross.

THE MEANING OF THE CROSS

Of course, our Lord knew exactly that of which He was speaking, and which His followers must learn. This was an absolute requirement.

AN ABSOLUTE REQUIREMENT

He made it very clear that anyone and everyone who was to follow Him had to take up the cross. If they did not do such, emphatically, even dogmatically, He stated, *"And whosoever does not bear his cross and come after Me, cannot be My Disciple."* So, the Way of the Cross is the only Way. Please allow me to once again use this little formula:

- The only way to God is through Jesus Christ (Jn. 14:6).
- The only way to Jesus Christ is by the Cross (Lk. 14:27).
- The only way to the Cross is a denial of self (Lk. 9:23).

All of this means that if the Way of the Cross is ignored, or another way is chosen, such a person cannot claim to be a follower of Christ. This tells us that the Cross of Christ is not one of several ways, it is the only Way.

In fact, this is not something new. It goes all the way back to the very dawn of time when the Lord told the First Family, despite being fallen, by the means of the slain lamb, which was a Substitute until Christ would come, they could have forgiveness of sins and communion with Him. However, they had to come by the way of the slain lamb, i.e., *"the Cross,"* or such would not be possible. So, the Disciples should have known what He was talking about; however, by the time of Christ, the Mosaic Law had been reduced to a mere ritual and ceremony with most of its true meaning lost. So, they did not know!

SELF-DENIAL

What exactly did Jesus mean when He said that one must *"deny himself,"* if he were to follow Him?

He was not speaking of asceticism. The word means *"a practicing of strict self-denial as a measure of personal and Spiritual Discipline. It refers to being austere in appearance, manner, and attitude."* Unfortunately, down through the centuries, many Christians have thought that was what Jesus was talking about. It wasn't!

When He spoke of self-denial, He was referring to the fact that Believers would have to deny the flesh, which refers to personal ambition, education, courage, fortitude, strength, ability, talent, knowledge, etc. In other words, the *"flesh"* refers to that, which is indicative of human beings, what we as human beings can do within our own strength and ability. He is telling us here that Righteousness and Holiness cannot be reached by personal efforts. While the *"will"* of an individual is definitely important, still, the human being within himself doesn't have the ability and strength to be what he ought to be in the Lord. That can be only in one way, and that is by the Believer placing his or her Faith exclusively in Christ and what Christ did for us at the Cross. With our Faith properly placed, meaning that the Cross of Christ is ever the Object of our Faith, then the Holy Spirit, Who Alone can make us what we ought to be, can work unhindered within our hearts and lives. However, when we attempt to live this life by personal strength, willpower, and ability, the Holy Spirit is greatly hindered, and this actually constitutes spiritual adultery (Rom. 7:1-4). That's what Jesus was addressing which, in fact, is the most serious difficulty of the Believer.

Most Christians don't have the slightest idea as to what the flesh actually is and, thereby, think that because they place some Scriptures around the flesh, then it becomes spiritual. It doesn't! Paul plainly told us the following concerning the flesh:

"There is therefore now no condemnation *(guilt)* to them which are in Christ Jesus *(refers back to Rom. 6:3-5 and our being baptized into His Death, which speaks of the Crucifixion)*, who walk not after the flesh *(depending on one's personal strength and ability or great religious efforts in order to overcome sin)*, but after the Spirit *(the Holy Spirit works exclusively within the legal confines of the Finished Work of Christ; our Faith in that Finished Work, i.e, 'the Cross,' guarantees the help of the Holy Spirit, which guarantees Victory)"* (Rom. 8:1).

WEAK THROUGH THE FLESH

"For what the Law could not do, in that it was weak through the flesh *(those under Law had only their willpower, which is woefully insufficient; so despite how hard they tried, they were unable to keep the Law then, and the same inability persists presently; any person who tries to live for God by a system of laws is doomed to failure, because the Holy Spirit will not function in that capacity)*, **God sending His Own Son** *(refers to man's helpless condition, unable to save himself and unable to keep even a simple Law and, therefore, in dire need of a Saviour)* **in the likeness of sinful flesh** *(this means that Christ was really human, conformed in appearance to flesh, which is characterized by sin, but yet sinless)*, **and for sin** *(to atone for sin, to destroy its power, and to save and Sanctify its victims)*, **condemned sin in the flesh** *(destroyed the power of sin by giving His Perfect Body as a Sacrifice for sin, which made it possible for sin to be defeated in our flesh; it was all through the Cross)***:"**

WALKING AFTER THE SPIRIT AND NOT THE FLESH

"That the Righteousness of the Law might be fulfilled in us *(the Law finding its full accomplishment in us can only be done by Faith in Christ, and what Christ has done for us at the Cross)*, **who walk not after the flesh** *(not after our own strength and ability)*, **but after the Spirit** *(the word 'walk' refers to the manner in which we order our life; when we place our Faith in Christ and the Cross, understanding that all things come from God to us by Means of the Cross, ever making it the Object of our Faith, the Holy Spirit can then work mightily within us, bringing about the Fruit of the Spirit; that is what 'walking after the Spirit' actually means!)*" **(Rom. 8:3-4).**

ARE YOU MINDING THE THINGS OF THE FLESH OR OF THE SPIRIT?

"For they who are after the flesh do mind the things

of the flesh *(refers to Believers trying to live for the Lord by means other than Faith in the Cross of Christ)*; **but they who are after the Spirit the things of the Spirit** *(those who place their Faith in Christ and the Cross, do so exclusively; they are doing what the Spirit desires, which alone can bring Victory)*" **(Rom. 8:5).**

PLEASING THE LORD

"**So then they who are in the flesh cannot please God** *(refers to the Believer attempting to live his Christian Life by means other than Faith in Christ and the Cross)*.

"**But you are not in the flesh** *(in one sense of the word is asking the question, 'Since you are now a Believer, and no longer depending on the flesh, why are you resorting to the flesh?')*, **but in the Spirit** *(as a Believer, you now have the privilege of being led and empowered by the Holy Spirit; however, He will do such for us only on the premise of our Faith in the Finished Work of Christ)*, **if so be that the Spirit of God dwell in you** *(if you are truly Saved)*. **Now if any man have not the Spirit of Christ, he is none of His** *(Paul is saying that the work of the Spirit in our lives is made possible by what Christ did at Calvary, and the Resurrection)*" **(Rom. 8:8-9).**

To say it again, the denial of ourselves is the placing of our Faith exclusively in Christ and what He did for us at the Cross, and not depending on our own strength and ability whatsoever. Then the Holy Spirit can work mightily within our lives.

TAKE UP HIS CROSS

As we said in some of the notes, most Christians think that Jesus was talking about suffering when He said that we must *"take up the Cross."* Even though they know that Christ made this statement, *"and take up his Cross,"* still, they don't want to get too much involved, simply because they think He is talking about suffering, and that's not something any sane person would desire to do.

No, Jesus was not talking about suffering. If suffering were the criteria, then most of the world would be Saved, i.e., Disciples of Christ, but we know that isn't so! So, what did He mean?

In fact, the privilege of taking up our cross is the greatest privilege, the greatest blessing, the most profound life and living, that one could ever begin to engage. It is the key to all Victory, the key to all blessing, and the key to all life. Instead of it being something to shy away from, it is that to which we must run toward, and gladly so.

When Jesus spoke of the Cross, He wasn't speaking of a wooden beam. In fact, for the sake of argument, if they actually found the Cross on which Jesus died and could prove that it was the same Cross, it would not do anyone any more good than any other piece of wood. It's not the Cross per se that He was addressing, but what would be done there and, in fact, what was done.

At the Cross, by the giving of Himself in Sacrifice, which means that He poured out His Precious Blood, this satisfied the demands of a thrice-Holy God, and it, thereby, atoned for all sin, past, present, and future, at least for all who will believe (Jn. 3:16). Paul said that Jesus at the Cross not only atoned for all sin, in other words, He took the penalty of the broken Law in our place, but in doing so, He ". . . *spoiled principalities and powers, and made a show of them openly, triumphing over them in it*" (Col. 2:14-15).

SIN AND THE LEGAL MEANS

It is sin that gives Satan the legal right to hold men captive. In this nation alone, there are some 20 million alcoholics and another 20 million problem drinkers, whatever that means. There are some 40 million gamblers and about 30 million drug addicts. As well, there are several millions of homosexuals and lesbians held in a terrible bondage of iniquity that drives many of them to suicide. In fact, all sin places man in bondage, in captivity, one might say, a captivity of *"guilt"* (Rom. 8:1). That's why a beautiful *"peace"* is given to every person who is Born-Again. It is sin that separates man from God, and with all sin removed, which it is by the believing sinner expressing Faith in Christ and what He did at the Cross, this brings a liberty, a Redemption, a peace.

So, when Jesus spoke of taking up the Cross, He was speaking of us placing our Faith and trust in that which was done at the Cross, and what was done constitutes Redemption. As stated, this is the greatest privilege that any individual could ever have, taking up the Cross and following Christ, i.e., *"trusting in what He there did for us."*

DAILY

Jesus said that this must be done, the taking up the cross, even on a daily basis. What did He mean by that?

He meant that we are to renew our Faith each and every day, so to speak, making certain that the Cross of Christ is the Object of such Faith.

Why should it be done on a daily basis?

Keeping our Faith in the Cross on a constant basis is the great struggle. This is where Satan attacks us. Please note the following:

Every single attack by Satan against us, whether it be in the realm of our finances, a physical attack, or Spiritual, it is for but one purpose, and that is to completely destroy our Faith or, at least, to seriously weaken it. If he can succeed in moving our Faith from the Cross of Christ to other things, the damage will be done. Whatever the other things might be doesn't make much difference.

As well, the idea is that Faith in the Cross of Christ is the only Faith that God will recognize. So, whatever we do, we are to make certain that it is anchored squarely in the Cross and nothing else. There is only one Way of Salvation, and that is Faith in Christ and what He did for us at the Cross. As well, there is only one Way of Victory over the world, the flesh and the Devil, and that is Faith in Christ and what He has done for us at the Cross. This tells us that the Means for both Salvation and Sanctification is the Cross.

Taking up the Cross daily doesn't mean that one has to go through some type of physical or spiritual regimen every morning, etc. It simply means that we are to understand that our Faith must be in the Cross of Christ, and it must be attended even on a daily basis. The Lord has no other way simply because no other way is needed, and it should be guarded closely.

FOLLOWING CHRIST

Plainly we are told in these Passages that the only way we can follow Christ is to *"deny ourselves, and take up the Cross daily."*

No doubt, at the time Jesus uttered these words, the Disciples didn't understand what in the world He was talking about. In fact, it would not be until the Lord gave to the Apostle Paul the meaning of the Cross, which, in essence, is the meaning of the New Covenant, that they then understood. Actually, Jesus did not even bother to explain what He said, knowing that before the fact, it would be useless. Several things had to happen before they could have understanding of this great Truth. They were:

• The Crucifixion.
• The Resurrection.
• The Ascension.
• The sending of the Holy Spirit in a new dimension.
• The explanation of all of this which was given to the Apostle Paul (Gal. 1:12).

As it regards the Holy Spirit, Who on the Day of Pentecost would come in a new dimension, meaning that the Cross had paid the sin debt, making all of this possible, Jesus said:

"But the Comforter *(Helper)***, *which is* the Holy Spirit** *(proclaims the Third Person of the Godhead)***, Whom the Father will send in My Name** *(because Jesus paid the price on the Cross, enabling the Holy Spirit to come in a completely new dimension)***, He shall teach you all things, and bring all things** *(proclaims the Holy Spirit as the Great Teacher of the Word of God, which is the only way one can learn the Word)* **to your remembrance, whatsoever I have said unto you** *(refers to the Holy Spirit helping the Apostles remember what Jesus had said and, as well, to understand what He had said)***" (Jn. 14:26).**

All of this means that if one doesn't understand the Cross of Christ as one should, and we are speaking of the Cross as it refers to Sanctification, that is a sure sign that the Holy Spirit is not having His Way in one's heart and life.

THE HOLY SPIRIT

Once again, Jesus speaks of the Holy Spirit and the great part that He plays in all of this. He said:

"And I will pray the Father, and He shall give you another Comforter *('Parakletos,' which means 'One called to the side of another to help')***, that He may abide with you forever** *(before the Cross, the Holy Spirit could only help a few individuals, and then only for a period of time; since the Cross, He lives in the hearts and lives of Believers, and does so forever)***;"

THE SPIRIT OF TRUTH

"*Even* the Spirit of Truth *(the Greek says, 'The Spirit of the Truth,' which refers to the Word of God; actually, He does far more than merely superintend the attribute of Truth, as Christ 'is Truth' [I Jn. 5:6])***; Whom the world**

cannot receive *(the Holy Spirit cannot come into the heart of the unbeliever until that person makes Christ his or her Saviour; then He comes in)*, **because it sees Him not, neither knows Him** *(refers to the fact that only Born-Again Believers can understand the Holy Spirit and know Him)*: **but you know Him** *(would have been better translated, 'but you shall get to know Him')*; **for He dwells with you** *(before the Cross)*, **and shall be in you** *(which would take place on the Day of Pentecost and forward, because the sin debt has been forever paid by Christ on the Cross, changing the disposition of everything)*" **(Jn. 14:16-17).**

WHAT THE HOLY SPIRIT WILL DO

In Saint John 14, Jesus told us of the fact of the Holy Spirit coming into the heart and life of the Believer after the Day of Pentecost and there to abide forever. Now, He tells us what the Holy Spirit will do for us:

"**Howbeit when He, the Spirit of Truth, is come** *(which He did on the Day of Pentecost)*, **He will guide you into all Truth** *(if our Faith is properly placed in Christ and the Cross, the Holy Spirit can then bring forth Truth to us; He doesn't guide into some truth, but rather 'all Truth')*: **for He shall not speak of Himself** *(tells us not only What He does, but Whom He represents)*; **but whatsoever He shall hear,** *that* **shall He speak** *(doesn't refer to a lack of knowledge, for the Holy Spirit is God, but rather, He will proclaim the Work of Christ only)*: **and He will show you things to come** *(pertains to the New Covenant, which would shortly be given)*."

THE HOLY SPIRIT WILL MAKE THINGS CLEAR

"**He shall glorify Me** *(will portray Christ and what Christ did at the Cross for dying humanity)*: **for He shall**

receive of Mine *(the benefits of the Cross)*, **and shall show *it* unto you** *(which He did, when He gave these great Truths to the Apostle Paul [Rom., Chpts. 6-8, etc.])*.**"**

THE BENEFITS OF THE CROSS

"All things that the Father has are Mine *(has always been the case; however, due to the Cross, all these things can now be given to the Believer as well)*: **therefore said I, that He shall take of Mine, and shall show *it* unto you** *(the foundation of all the Holy Spirit reveals to the Church is what Christ did at the Cross [Rom. 6:3-14; 8:1-2, 11; I Cor. 1:17-18, 21, 23; 2:2; Gal., Chpt. 5])*" **(Jn. 16:13-15).**

"Out of my bondage, sorrow, and night,
"Jesus, I come! Jesus, I come!
"Into Your Freedom, Gladness, and Light,
"Jesus, I come to Thee!
"Out of my sickness into Your Health,
"Out of my want and into Your Wealth,
"Out of my sin and into Your Self,
"Jesus, I come to Thee!"

"Out of my shameful failure and loss,
"Jesus, I come! Jesus, I come!
"Into the glorious gain of Your Cross,
"Jesus, I come to Thee!
"Out of earth's sorrows into Your Balm,
"Out of life's storm and into Your Calm,
"Out of distress to jubilant Psalm,
"Jesus, I come to Thee!"

"Out of unrest and arrogant pride,
"Jesus, I come! Jesus, I come!
"Into Your Blessed Will to abide,

"Jesus, I come to Thee!
"Out of myself to dwell in Your Love,
"Out of despair into raptures Above,
"Upward for aye on wings like a dove,
"Jesus, I come to Thee!"

"Out of the fear and dread of the tomb,
"Jesus, I come! Jesus, I come!
"Into the Joy and Light of Your Home,
"Jesus, I come to Thee!
"Out of the depths of ruin untold,
"Into the Peace of Your Sheltering Fold,
"Ever Your Glorious Face to behold,
"Jesus, I come to Thee!"

CHAPTER SIX

The Power Of The Cross

THE POWER OF THE CROSS

Paul said:

"**For the preaching** *(Message)* **of the Cross is to them who perish foolishness** *(Spiritual things cannot be discerned by unredeemed people, but that doesn't matter; the Cross must be preached just the same, even as we shall see)*; **but unto us who are Saved it is the Power of God.** *(The Cross is the Power of God simply because it was there that the total sin debt was paid, giving the Holy Spirit, in Whom the Power resides, latitude to work mightily within our lives)*" **(I Cor. 1:18).**

THE MEANING OF THE GREEK WORD TRANSLATED *"PREACHING"*

The Greek word translated *"preaching"* is *"Logos."* It means either *"Word"* or *"Message,"* and should have been translated accordingly.

The Greek word *"Logos"* actually cannot be separated from Christ.

Concerning the word *"Logos,"* Wuest says:

"John begins his testimony regarding Jesus of Nazareth with the statement, 'In the beginning was the Word, and the Word was in fellowship with God, and the Word was as to its essence, Deity' (Jn. 1:1). John uses the Greek word 'Logos' as a designation of Jesus of Nazareth. 'Logos' is from the root 'leg,' appearing in 'lego,' the primitive meaning of which is 'to lay:' then, 'to pick out, gather, pick up:' hence, 'together or put words together,' and so, 'to speak' hence, 'to gather or put words together,' and so, 'to speak.' Hence 'Logos' is first of all, a collecting or collection both of things in the mind, and of words by which they are expressed. It therefore signifies both the outward form by which the inward thought is expressed, and the inward thought itself. As signifying the outward form, it is never used in the merely

grammatical sense, as simply the name of a thing or act, but means a word as the thing referred to, the material, not the formal part; a word as embodying a conception or idea. As 'Logos' has the double meaning of thought and speech, so Jesus of Nazareth is related to God as the word to the idea, the word being not merely a name for the idea, but the idea itself expressed.

"The 'Logos' of John is the real, Personal God, the Word, Who was originally before the creation with God, and was God, one in essence and nature, yet Personally distinct; the revealer and interpreter of the hidden being of God; the reflection and visible image of God, and the organ of all His manifestations in the world. He made all things, proceeding Personally from God for the accomplishment of the act of creation, and became man in the person of Jesus of Nazareth, accomplishing the redemption of the world."[1]

THE CROSS AND THE LORD JESUS CHRIST

So, what does all of this mean?

It means that when one rightly preaches Jesus, one is rightly at the same time preaching the Cross. As well, when one rightly preaches the Cross, one is rightly at the same time preaching Jesus. The two cannot be separated. That's why Paul said, *"But we preach Christ Crucified"* (I Cor. 1:23).

FOOLISHNESS

When the Holy Spirit through Paul said, *"For the preaching (Message) of the Cross is to them who perish foolishness,"* he was at the same time saying that he knew this Message would not be popular, and that most would reject it.

The tragedy of all of this is that it is somewhat understandable as to the world rejecting the Message of the Cross, but it is tragic when the church rejects the Message of the Cross. The only proclamation of this great Word must come from the Church. If the church looks at the Cross as foolishness, then the last and only hope for man is lost. As previously stated, the only thing standing between man and Hell itself is the Cross of Christ. Presently, there are fewer preachers preaching the Cross than at any time since the Reformation. Thank God for the few who still hold the line, but it is not nearly enough. Those who know how to pray must seek the Face of the Lord that He will raise up others who, without fear or favor, will preach this Message.

THE CROSS OF CHRIST AND HUMANISTIC PSYCHOLOGY

I was raised in a particular Pentecostal Denomination, actually, the largest in the world. When I began in the 1950's, it was at the height of its Spiritual Power. In fact, its Missionaries touched the world for Christ. But, in the 1960's, some of the preachers began to dabble into humanistic psychology. Its Bible schools, which turned out Preachers of the Gospel, also embraced this religion of humanism. Soon they were little turning out Preachers, but rather, amateur psychologists.

In the 1980's, as the Lord began to bless our Ministry, and we began to enlarge our effort all over the world by television, I had little understanding as to what humanistic psychology really was. In fact, thinking it was just another way to help people, I hired two psychologists and put them on staff at our Church in Baton Rouge, Louisiana, which we were just beginning. Then the Ministry only owned two radio stations, with one of those stations being in Baton Rouge. I gave these two psychologists, a man and his wife, time over our station each day. Once again, knowing nothing about this particular subject, I was under the impression that they could help people.

After a period of time, one of our other Preachers asked me if I knew what these people were teaching. I didn't!

I tuned in the program and suddenly realized that whatever it was they were teaching was not the Gospel of Jesus Christ but something else altogether. I called them in and soon realized that this direction was hopeless. I had no choice but to terminate the both of them.

INVESTIGATION

I began to study everything I could get my hands on, as it regarded this particular subject of humanistic psychology, and soon found out that it was the total opposite of the Word of God. In other words, one could not mix the two.

At that time, I had no knowledge of the Cross of Christ as it regarded Sanctification. I preached the Cross strongly as it regarded Salvation, but had no knowledge otherwise. Yet, I knew that humanistic psychology was not of God. The more I studied the subject, the more I realized that this was a path that was carved out by Satan himself.

At that time, we had the largest television audience in the world as it regarded Gospel. I began to strongly stand up against the subject of psychology, proclaiming over our television network the error of this direction. It did not sit well at all with the powers that be in the particular denomination with which I was associated. I soon found out that they had embraced this direction in totality, and here I was over the largest Gospel network in the world proclaiming the fallacy of this false direction. As stated, it did not sit well at all! In fact, I soon learned the degree of their hatred.

In those days, I knew that humanistic psychology was wrong, but I did not understand the Gospel of Jesus Christ that would set the captive free. Tragically, I did not know anyone else who did! Looking back, after the Lord has given me this great Revelation of the Cross, there was then no one, at least to my knowledge, that correctly understood what the Apostle Paul taught us as it regards our everyday life and living, in other words, how that we could have victory over the world, the flesh, and the Devil. While one can be Saved and not understand this great Truth, it is certain that one cannot walk in victory without understanding this great Truth.

THE MEANING OF THE NEW COVENANT

If this great Truth had been only casually mentioned in the Bible, that would be something else, but considering that it makes up nine-tenths of Paul's teaching, then we begin to realize the significance placed on this subject by the Holy Spirit. As stated, the meaning of the Cross is the meaning of the New Covenant, but tragically, most preachers understand the Cross only as it refers to Salvation and not at all as it refers to Sanctification, and that is despite the fact that the latter makes up the bulk of the teaching of the Word of God. Satan has been very successful at keeping this great Truth from the church. Again, as stated, without an understanding of this Truth, while one can be Saved, one simply cannot walk in victory. Paul said, *"For if Righteousness come by the Law, then Christ is dead in vain"* (Gal. 2:21). In other words, if one can walk in victory without understanding the meaning of the Cross, *"then Christ is dead in vain."* That means that Jesus died for nothing! The truth is, that which the Apostle Paul gave us is the only manner in which one can successfully live for the Lord. Unfortunately, this all-important subject is *"foolishness"* to most!

HOW IS THE PREACHING OF THE CROSS
THE POWER OF GOD?

To be sure, there was no power in the wooden beam on which Jesus died. In fact, and as previously stated, if it were suddenly announced that the actual Cross on which Jesus died had been found in Jerusalem, and it could be ascertained that, indeed, this was the actual Cross, still, that particular wooden beam would not help anyone anymore than any other piece of wood. It's what He there did that sets the captive free.

As well, there was no power even in the Death of Christ. Concerning His Death Paul said, *"He was Crucified through weakness"* (II Cor. 13:4). Admittedly, it was a contrived weakness, meaning that He purposely did not use the Power that He had; nevertheless, there was no power in His Death. So, where is the Power?

THE HOLY SPIRIT

The Power is actually in the Holy Spirit. So, if it is in the Holy Spirit, how does that correlate with the preaching of the Cross?

The Holy Spirit works entirely within the parameters of the Finished Work of Christ. In other words, it is the Cross of Christ, what Jesus there did, that gives the Holy Spirit the legal means to do all that He does in our hearts and lives. That's why Paul referred to this as *"the Law of the Spirit of Life in Christ Jesus"* (Rom. 8:2).

Anytime that Paul uses the phrase *"in Christ Jesus,"* or one of its derivatives, such as *"in Christ,"* or *"in Whom,"* etc., he is, without fail, speaking of what Christ did at the Cross.

Before the Cross, and as previously stated, due to the fact that the blood of bulls and goats could not take away sins, which meant that the sin debt remained, this greatly limited the Holy Spirit as to what He could do. But, with the sin debt lifted, which it was at Calvary's Cross, at least for those who believe, this opened the door for the Holy Spirit to come into our hearts and lives and there abide forever (Jn. 14:16-17).

As also stated, the Holy Spirit doesn't require very much of us; however, He does require one thing, and on that He will not bend, and that is that our Faith ever be in Christ and what Christ did for us at the Cross. Now, that seems simple enough, doesn't it? Yet, it's the area of our Faith which Satan contests the most, and it's because he knows this is his defeat. However, if the Believer will place his Faith exclusively in the Cross of Christ and not allow it to be moved elsewhere, which constitutes *"fighting the good fight of Faith,"* he will find a Victory that he never knew existed. No, this will not stop the Evil One from making every effort to sidetrack our Faith, but it does guarantee Victory on the part of the individual who will persevere in this great task. This is the Gospel of Jesus Christ! This is the Power of God! Unfortunately, the modern church, at least for the most part, has opted for the wisdom of this world, which constitutes humanistic psychology. Regarding this, Paul also said:

THE WISDOM OF THE WORLD

"For it is written *(Isa. 29:14)*, I will destroy the wisdom of the wise, and will bring to nothing the understanding of the prudent *(speaks to those who are wise in their own eyes, in effect, having forsaken the Ways of the Lord)*.

"Where *is* the wise? *(This presents the first of three classes of learned people who lived in that day.)* where *is* the Scribe? *(This pertained to the Jewish Theologians of that day.)* where *is* the disputer of this world? *(This speaks of the Greeks, who were seekers of mystical and metaphysical interpretations.)* has not God made foolish the wisdom of this world? *(This pertains to what God did in sending His Son to Redeem humanity, which He did by the Cross. All the wisdom of the world couldn't do this!)*"

THE WORLD BY WISDOM KNEW NOT GOD

"For after that in the Wisdom of God the world by wisdom knew not God *(man's puny wisdom, even the best he has to offer, cannot come to know God in any manner)*, it pleased God by the foolishness of preaching *(preaching the Cross)* to save them who believe. *(Paul is not dealing with the art of preaching here, but with what is preached.)*

"For the Jews require a sign *(the sign of the Messiah taking the Throne and making Israel a great Nation once again)*, and the Greeks seek after wisdom *(they thought that such solved the human problem; however, if it did, why were they ever seeking after more wisdom?)*:"

CHRIST THE POWER OF GOD

"**But we preach Christ Crucified** *(this is the Foundation of the Word of God and, thereby, of Salvation)*, **unto the Jews a stumblingblock** *(the Cross was the stumblingblock)*, **and unto the Greeks foolishness** *(both found it difficult to accept as God a dead Man hanging on a Cross, for such Christ was to them)*;

"**But unto them who are called** *(refers to those who accept the Call, for the entirety of mankind is invited [Jn. 3:16; Rev. 22:17])*, **both Jews and Greeks** *(actually stands for both 'Jews and Gentiles')*, **Christ the Power of God** *(what He did at the Cross atoned for all sin, thereby, making it possible for the Holy Spirit to exhibit His Power within our lives)*, **and the Wisdom of God.** *(This Wisdom devised a Plan of Salvation which pardoned guilty men and at the same time vindicated and glorified the Justice of God, which stands out as the wisest and most remarkable Plan of all time.)*"

THE FOOLISH THINGS OF THE WORLD TO CONFOUND THE WISE

"**Because the foolishness of God is wiser than men** *(God achieves the mightiest ends by the humblest means)*; **and the weakness of God is stronger than men** *(refers to that which men take to be weak, but actually is not — the Cross)*.

"**For you see your calling, brethren** *(refers to the nature and method of their Heavenly Calling)*, **how that not many wise men after the flesh, not many mighty, not many noble, *are Called*** *(are Called and accept)*:

"**But God has chosen the foolish things of the world to confound the wise** *(the preaching of the Cross confounds* *the wise because it falls out to changed lives, which nothing man has can do)*; **and God has chosen the weak things of the world to confound the things which are mighty** *(the Cross is looked at as weakness, but it brings about great strength and power, regarding those who accept the Finished Work of Christ)*;

"**And base things of the world, and things which are despised, has God chosen** *(it is God working in the base things and the despised things, which brings about miraculous things)*, **yes, and things which are not, to bring to naught things that are** *(God can use that which is nothing within itself, but with Him all things become possible)*:"

GLORY IN THE LORD

"**That no flesh** *(human effort)* **should glory in His Presence.**

"**But of Him are you in Christ Jesus** *(pertains to this great Plan of God, which is far beyond all wisdom of the world; we are 'in Christ Jesus,' by virtue of the Cross — what He did there)*, **Who of God is made unto us Wisdom, and Righteousness, and Sanctification, and Redemption** *(we have all of this by the Holy Spirit, through Christ and what He did at the Cross; this means the Cross must ever be the Object of our Faith)*:

"**That, according as it is written** *(Jer. 9:23)*, **He who glories, let him glory in the Lord.** *(He who boasts, let him boast in the Lord, and not in particular preachers)*" **(I Cor. 1:19-31).**

"O Lamb of God, still keep me,
"Close to Your Wounded Side;
"Tis only there in safety,
"And peace I can abide."

"What foes and snares surround me,

"What lusts and fears within;
"The Grace that sought and found me,
"Alone can keep me clean."

"Tis only in You hiding,
"I feel myself secure;
"Only in You abiding,
"The conflict can endure;"

"Your Arm the victory gains,
"Over every hateful foe;
"Your Love my heart sustains,
"And all its care and woe."

"Soon shall my eyes behold Thee,
"With rapture face-to-face;
"One half truth not been told me,
"Of all Your Power and Grace;"

"Your Beauty, Lord, and Glory,
"The wonders of Your Love,
"Shall be the endless story,
"Of all Your Saints above."

CHAPTER SEVEN

The Necessity Of The Cross

THE NECESSITY OF THE CROSS

Paul in his first Epistle to the Church at Corinth said to them:

"And I, brethren, when I came to you, came not with excellency of speech or of wisdom *(means that he depended not on oratorical abilities, nor did he delve into philosophy, which was all the rage of that particular day)*, declaring unto you the Testimony of God *(which is Christ and Him Crucified)*.

"For I determined not to know anything among you *(with purpose and design, Paul did not resort to the knowledge or philosophy of the world regarding the preaching of the Gospel)*, save Jesus Christ, and Him Crucified *(that and that alone is the Message which will save the sinner, set the captive free, and give the Believer perpetual Victory)*" (I Cor. 2:1-2).

Now, we must note carefully what the great Apostle said to us.

The word *"determine"* in the Greek is *"krino,"* and means, *"to distinguish, to decide mentally or judicially."* The word is so powerful that it also means that one would sue at the law in order to maintain one's position. In other words, the position is no longer in question. Why was Paul so certain, so sure at this stage, of the Message of the Cross?

THE MESSAGE AT MARS' HILL

When Paul first came to Corinth, he came from the great city of Athens. He had remained there for a period of time, actually preaching the Gospel in the marketplace of that great city. Even though his Message was, by and large, rejected, still, it carried enough weight that he was called upon to minister to the Supreme Court of Athens, which constituted some of the wisest men of that city.

While Athens had long since lost the glory of previous years, still, even though living off of past reputation, it still carried weight. The Seventeenth Chapter of Acts carries the account of this meeting.

Those to whom Paul preached that day had no knowledge of the Lord whatsoever. They lived in heathenistic darkness despite their professed wisdom. Paul's Message basically consisted of the fact of the reality of God. In that Message he mentioned the Resurrection of Christ. The Scripture says concerning this:

"And when they heard of the Resurrection of the Dead, some mocked *(the 'mocking' was caused by sheer unbelief)*: and others said, We will hear you again of this **matter** *(many were touched by Paul's Message, but regrettably procrastinated)*.

"So Paul departed from among them *(they ascertained that he had broken none of their laws, so he was free to go, which he did!)*" (Acts 17:32-33).

CORINTH

The Scripture says:

"After these things Paul departed from Athens *(seems to imply that he departed alone, with Silas and Timothy joining him later at Corinth)*, and came to Corinth *(one of the great cities of the Roman Empire)*" (Acts 18:1).

Obviously, the Lord called Paul from Athens to the city of Corinth. The city was, in fact, one of the most jaded in the world. It had scores of temples dedicated to heathen gods, occupied by hundreds of temple prostitutes, both men and women. In fact, Corinth was so jaded that if individuals gave in to the excesses of Corinth, they were said to be *"Corinthianized."* This means that they had thrown aside all convention, giving themselves wholly to their evil passions. It was one of the most wicked cities in the world of its day.

Coupled with *"vice"* was the twin evil of heathenistic philosophy. In fact, Corinth had produced some of the most noted philosophers in the world of that day. So, Satan had employed in that city his two most powerful attractions, *"vice and philosophy."*

Paul probably went to Corinth by boat, which would have docked at Cenchrea, which was the port for Corinth. It was several miles from the heart of the great city.

After leaving the ship at Cenchrea, the great Apostle, more than likely, would have walked the distance of several miles to the heart of the city.

There is some indication that Paul at that time was a troubled man. He had not met with the success for which he had hoped at Athens. In fact, when he mentioned the Resurrection as he ministered on Mars' Hill, the crowd, which assembled there to hear him, actually booed him down. In other words, he didn't really finish the Message. While a few accepted Christ, still, I think the great Apostle was troubled at the turn of events.

THE HOLY SPIRIT

Knowing that the Lord had sent him to Corinth, and possibly disillusioned somewhat with the results at Athens, he must have wondered as to how he could break through the twin vices of the city of Corinth. He was possibly chagrined about Athens, and this certainly did not help his feelings as he came into the most wicked city of the Roman Empire. How could he penetrate these two vices of immorality and heathenistic philosophy?

How do we know that these thoughts could have plagued the great Apostle?

We know it from his statement, *"For I determined not to know anything among you, save Jesus Christ, and Him Crucified"* (I Cor. 2:2).

The word *"determined"* speaks of a great struggle that had gone on in his heart, and that he had made a conscious decision to go in a certain direction. That direction would be the Cross of Christ.

As he came from Cenchrea to Corinth, walking the several miles, he had plenty of time to think. No doubt, he was praying all the while. Considering Athens and what must have looked like failure to him, I'm sure he reasoned as to how in the world he could penetrate the powers of darkness in Corinth. At a given point in time, the Holy Spirit may have whispered to him, *"Preach the Cross!"* And, the Holy Spirit might have continued, *"If the Cross works at Corinth, it will work anywhere!"*

So, Paul would tell the Corinthians, incidentally, where a great Church would be built, *"I determined not to know anything among you, save Jesus Christ, and Him Crucified."*

It worked in Corinth, and to be sure, it has worked in untold other places as well. In fact, there is no power of darkness that can stand against the Message of the Cross.

PAUL AND PHILOSOPHY

Paul was one of the most educated men to be used by the Lord to pen the Holy Scriptures. In fact, he wrote almost half of the New Testament. He had studied for years under the great Law scholar Gamaliel (Acts 22:3). Before Paul was converted on the Road to Damascus, he was being groomed to take the place of Gamaliel as the leading voice of the Pharisees. So, as it regarded the Law of Moses, there was no scholar in Israel more knowledgeable concerning this subject than Paul.

As well, it is believed by some modern scholars that Paul, due to some of the things he said, attended the great university in his home town of Tarsus. If so, he would have been highly educated not only in Mosaic Law but, as well, in the philosophy of the Greeks, which was the noted rage of that time. So, he had the capacity to stand toe-to-toe, so to speak, with the most educated of his day. No doubt, the temptation was great to deal with these subjects in his preaching; however, he fought down that temptation, knowing that, while it may sound clever, it would not set anyone free. He found that the Message of the Cross alone would set the captive free, and we are speaking of Salvation for the sinner and Sanctification for the Saint. So, he determined in his mind and spirit not to go in these other directions but to preach the Cross. He found that it worked exactly as the Holy Spirit said that it would work.

THE MODERN CHURCH

The church of this present day should take a lesson from Paul. While the expanse of time noted is nearly two thousand years, still, the problem is the same, and it is sin. As well, the solution is the same, and it is the Cross of Christ. It doesn't matter what the nationality of the people might be; it doesn't matter their culture; it doesn't matter their educational background; and, it doesn't matter about their state, their place, or their position. The problem is sin, and the solution is the Cross of Christ. Paul found that out, and the modern church needs to find this same truth as well!

MODERN RELIGIOUS PHILOSOPHY

One particular psychologist in a major Pentecostal Denomination made the foolish statement that modern man was facing problems not addressed in the Bible. Accordingly, or so he gathered, both the Bible and psychology are needed to address these particular problems. How foolish can we get! Is what he said correct? Is modern man facing problems not addressed in the Word of God? Peter, under the inspiration of the Holy Spirit, had something to say about that. Attend carefully to his words.

SIMON PETER

"Simon Peter, a servant and an Apostle of Jesus

Christ (*the position of 'servant' is placed first; if one cannot be a true servant for the Lord, then one cannot be an Apostle; the Lord guides the Church by the Office of the Apostle through the particular Message given to the individual, which will always coincide directly with the Word of God; Apostles aren't elected, they are called of God*)**, to them who have obtained like Precious Faith with us** (*proclaims the Faith that Gentiles can now be Saved exactly as Jews, in fact, all coming the same way*) **through the Righteousness of God and our Saviour Jesus Christ** (*this Righteousness is obtained by the Believer exhibiting Faith in Christ and what He did at the Cross*)**:"**

ALL THINGS THAT PERTAIN
TO LIFE AND GODLINESS

"Grace and Peace be multiplied unto you through the knowledge of God, and of Jesus our Lord (*this is both Sanctifying Grace and Sanctifying Peace, all made available by the Cross*)**,**

"According as His Divine Power has given unto us all things (*the Lord with large-handed generosity has given us all things*) **that *pertain* unto life and godliness** (*pertains to the fact that the Lord Jesus has given us everything we need regarding life and living*)**, through the knowledge of Him Who has called us to Glory and Virtue** (*the 'knowledge' addressed here speaks of what Christ did at the Cross, which alone can provide 'Glory and Virtue'*)**:"**

THE DIVINE NATURE

"Whereby are given unto us exceeding great and Precious Promises (*pertains to the Word of God, which alone holds the answer to every life problem*)**: that by these** (*Promises*) **you might be partakers of the Divine**

Nature *(the Divine Nature implanted in the inner being of the believing sinner becomes the source of our new life and actions; it comes to everyone at the moment of being 'Born-Again'),* **having escaped the corruption that is in the world through lust.** *(This presents the Salvation experience of the sinner, and the Sanctification experience of the Saint)"* **(II Pet. 1:1-4).**

THE PROVISIONS OF THE HOLY SPIRIT

Now, the Holy Spirit through Peter will give us that which is provided to the Believer, and which addresses every phase of life and living. They are:

"And beside this *(Salvation),* **giving all diligence** *(refers to the responsibility we as Believers must show regarding the Christian life),* **add to your Faith Virtue** *(this is Faith in the Cross, which will bring 'Virtue'; the type of 'Virtue' mentioned here is 'energy' and 'power');* **and to Virtue knowledge** *(this is the type of knowledge, which keeps expanding);*
"And to knowledge temperance *(self-control);* **and to temperance patience** *(our conduct must honor God at all times, even in the midst of trials and testing);* **and to patience godliness** *(being like God);*
"And to godliness brotherly kindness *(carries the idea of treating everyone as if they were our own flesh and blood 'brother' or 'sister');* **and to brotherly kindness charity** *(love)."*

THE ATTRIBUTES OF THE HOLY SPIRIT

"For if these things be in you, and abound *(continue to expand),* **they make** *you that you shall* **neither** *be* **barren nor unfruitful in the knowledge of our Lord Jesus Christ.** *(Once again, this 'knowledge' refers to what Christ* *did at the Cross, all on our behalf.)*

"**But he who lacks these things is blind, and cannot see afar off** *(the reason one may lack these things is he is spiritually blind; in other words, such a one has made something other than the Cross the Object of his Faith)*, **and has forgotten that he was purged from his old sins.** *(Such a Believer is once again being ruled by the 'sin nature' exactly as he was before conversion, which is always the end result of ignoring the Cross.)*"

MAKE YOUR CALLING AND ELECTION SURE

"**Wherefore the rather, Brethren, give diligence to make your Calling and Election sure** *(this is what Jesus was speaking of when He told us to deny ourselves and take up the Cross daily and follow Him [Lk. 9:23]; every day the Believer must make certain his Faith is anchored in the Cross and the Cross alone; only then can we realize the tremendous benefits afforded by the Sacrifice of Christ)*: **for if you do these things, you shall never fall** *(presents the key to Eternal Security, but with the Promise being conditional)*:

"**For so an entrance shall be ministered unto you abundantly into the Everlasting Kingdom of our Lord and Saviour Jesus Christ.** *(The entrance into the Kingdom is solely on the basis of Faith evidenced in Christ and the Cross [Eph. 2:13-18; Jn. 3:16])*" **(II Pet. 1:5-11).**

EIGHT ATTRIBUTES FOR LIFE AND LIVING

As it regards life and living, the Holy Spirit lists eight attributes given to us by the Lord or, at least, made available. They, to be sure, will answer all situations. They are:

1. FAITH: This always pertains to Faith in Christ and what Christ has done for us at the Cross. In other words, the Cross of Christ must ever be the Object of our Faith (Rom. 6:3-5;

I Cor. 1:17-18, 23). This is the Faith, and this alone is the Faith, that God will recognize.

2. VIRTUE: The Greek word for *"Virtue"* is *"arête,"* and means, *"manliness,"* or, as stated, *"energy and power."* Upon the individual being Saved and baptized with the Holy Spirit, power becomes a part of their persona (Acts 1:8).

3. KNOWLEDGE: The Greek word for *"knowledge"* is *"gnosis,"* and means, *"to be aware of, to know, to perceive, to be sure, to understand."* All true knowledge comes from the Word of God and the Word of God alone!

4. TEMPERANCE: The Greek word for *"temperance"* is *"egkrateia,"* and means, *"self-control."* This can be done only by the Believer placing his Faith exclusively in Christ and the Cross, which then gives the Holy Spirit latitude to work within his life, which gives him Victory over the passions of the flesh (Rom. 8:1-2).

5. PATIENCE: The Greek word for *"patience"* is *"hupomone,"* and means, *"to stay under, to endure, to cheerfully wait"* (James 5:11).

6. GODLINESS: The Greek word for *"godliness"* is *"eusebeia,"* and means, *"Holiness."* As Believers, we have no personal holiness; however, a perfect, pure, spotless Holiness is supplied to every Child of God, all made possible by the Cross (Heb. 12:10).

7. BROTHERLY KINDNESS: The Greek word for brotherly kindness is *"philadelphia,"* and means, *"love of the Brethren"* (I Jn. 3:11).

8. CHARITY: The Greek word for *"charity"* is *"agape,"* and means, *"the God kind of love"* (Jn. 3:16).

If all of these attributes are properly understood, we should know and realize that everything we need to live this life, and to live it abundantly so, even in this modern age, is found in these attributes. So, for someone to say that modern man is facing problems not addressed in the Bible is, in effect, saying that God, the Holy Spirit, is lacking in knowledge. Such a statement is stupid, even if I have to be blunt!

THE SOURCE AND THE MEANS

Please allow me to repeat myself:

• Jesus Christ is the Source of all things that we receive from God (Jn. 14:6).

• The Cross of Christ is the Means by which these things come to us (Rom. 6:3-5; I Cor. 1:17-18, 23; 2:2).

• The Cross of Christ must at all times be the Object of our Faith (Gal. 6:14).

• With our Faith properly placed, the Holy Spirit, Who works exclusively within the parameters of the Finished Work of Christ, will then grandly help us to be what we ought to be (Rom. 8:1-2, 11).

"One with You, Thou Son eternal,
"Joined by Faith in spirit one,
"Share we in Your Death inclusive,
"And Your Life, O God the Son."

"One with You, Thou Son Beloved,
"Part of You become through Grace,
"Heirs with You of our one Father,
"We're Your Spirit's dwelling place."

"One with You, Thou Son incarnate,
"Born with You, the Man of worth,
"We, the members of Your Body,
"Sojourn with You here on Earth."

"One with You, Thou Son anointed,
"Sharing too the Spirit's Power,
"We in full cooperation,
"Labor with You hour by hour."

"One with You, Thou Son forsaken,
"Judgment and the curse we've passed;

"We to sin are dead forever,
"Hell beneath our feet is cast."

"One with You in Resurrection,
"Death can never us oppress,
"Live we in Your New Creation,
"Bearing Fruits of Righteousness."

"One with You, Thou Son ascended,
"Seated with You on the Throne,
"Your Authority we share and,
"Rule with You, Your Rank we own."

"One with You, Thou Son returning,
"Glorified with You we'll be,
"E'er to manifest Your Beauty,
"One with You eternally."

How To Walk After The Spirit

HOW TO WALK AFTER THE SPIRIT

"*There is* therefore now no condemnation *(guilt)* to them which are in Christ Jesus *(refers back to Rom. 6:3-5 and our being baptized into His Death, which speaks of the Crucifixion)*, who walk not after the flesh *(depending on one's personal strength and ability or great religious efforts in order to overcome sin)*, but after the Spirit *(the Holy Spirit works exclusively within the legal confines of the Finished Work of Christ; our Faith in that Finished Work, i.e., 'the Cross,' guarantees the help of the Holy Spirit, which guarantees Victory)*" (Rom. 8:1).

In the Verse quoted, Paul set side by side "*walking after the flesh*" and "*walking after the Spirit.*" So, we will study them in that order.

THE WORD "*WALK*"

The word "*walk,*" as Paul here used it, in the Greek is "*peripateo,*" and means, "*the manner in which we order our behavior or conduct.*" In other words, in a sense, it is how we live for God. In fact, nothing could be more important than the meaning of this word "*walk.*" The simple but tragic truth is, most modern Believers simply do not know how to live for the Lord. I realize that statement will not be too readily accepted; however, it is true.

Let the Believer understand that there is nothing one can do to stop the attacks of Satan. No matter who we are and no matter what we do, Satan is going to continue to attack, continue to hinder, and continue to do everything within his power to destroy our Faith or, at least, seriously weaken it. That's a given. Peter said the following:

THE FIERY TRIAL

"Beloved, think it not strange concerning the fiery

trial which is to try you *(trials do not merely happen; they are designed by wisdom and operated by love; Job proved this)*, **as though some strange thing happened unto you** *(your trial, whatever it is, is not unique; many others are experiencing the same thing!)*:

"But rejoice *(despite the trial)*, **inasmuch as you are partakers of Christ's sufferings** *(refers to suffering for Righteousness' sake)*; **that, when His Glory shall be revealed** *(refers to His Second Coming)*, **you may be glad also with exceeding joy.** *(There will be great joy in the heart of every Saint when we come back with the Lord at the Second Coming.)*

"If you be reproached for the Name of Christ, happy are you *(should have been translated, 'since you are reproached')*; **for the Spirit of Glory and of God rests upon you** *(refers to the Holy Spirit)*: **on their part He is evil spoken of, but on your part He is glorified.** *(This refers to the fact that the world, and even the apostate church, reproaches this sacred influence of the Holy Spirit by their treatment of true Christians. But if we conduct ourselves correctly, the Lord is Glorified in our lives)*" **(I Pet. 4:12-14).**

GOD'S PRESCRIBED ORDER OF VICTORY

However, despite the fact of the Evil One continuing to come against us, continuing to tempt, and continuing to harass us, still, the Lord has given us His Prescribed Order of Victory. That Prescribed Order, in brief, is Christ and what He has done for us at the Cross and our Faith in that Finished Work. It is all wrapped up in Christ and what He did for us. In fact, that's what this Book is all about, to show us, according to the Word of God, how to live this life and how to walk in Victory, and we speak of Victory over the world, the flesh, and the Devil, to use a phrase coined by the Early Church Fathers. Even then, if one perfectly understands that which the Holy Spirit through Paul and the Apostles has given to us, still, it won't be easy.

However, the Believer can come to the place, and is meant to come to the place, that *"sin shall not have dominion over you"* (Rom. 6:14). As previously stated, Paul is not here teaching sinless perfection because the Bible does not teach such; however, the Holy Spirit through him is definitely teaching Victory over sin. The Lord did not Save us in sin, but rather, from sin, but sad to say, and even as we stated in the Introduction to this Book, most modern Christians are in bondage to sin in some way. To be sure, as sin always does, the situation continues to get worse, which is exactly what Satan intends. We must always remember that we are not wrestling *"against flesh and blood, but against principalities, against powers, against the rulers of the darkness of this world, against spiritual wickedness in high places"* (Eph. 6:12).

THE FLESH

To which we've already addressed in this Volume, but because of its great significance, please allow me to repeat myself.

The *"flesh,"* as Paul used the word again and again, refers to that which is indicative of human beings. In other words, it speaks of our own personal talent, strength, motivation, education, ability, efforts, etc. Within themselves, these things aren't wrong. But emphatically, the Apostle Paul tells us that if we try to live for God by means of the *"flesh,"* which refers to our own human ability, we will fail every time. It simply cannot be done that way, but that's the way that most of us try to live.

We Christians are very fond of telling the unsaved that they cannot trust in their merit or good works, etc., but that they must trust Christ, and that is exactly correct. However, then we turn right around and try to live for God by the very means that we tell the unconverted will not save them. In other words, the Believer is Saved by Faith but then tries to sanctify by the means of self. In fact, that's why Paul wrote the entirety of the Epistle to the Galatians. False teachers had come into the Churches established in that area and were telling the Galatians that along with accepting Christ, they had to also keep the Law. That's why Paul said the following, and strongly so.

ANOTHER GOSPEL

The great Apostle said:

"I marvel that you are so soon removed from Him *(the Holy Spirit) Who* called you into the Grace of Christ *(made possible by the Cross)* unto another gospel *(anything which doesn't have the Cross as its Object of Faith)*:
"Which is not another *(presents the fact that Satan's aim is not so much to deny the Gospel, which he can little do, as to corrupt it)*; but there be some who trouble you, and would pervert the Gospel of Christ *(once again, to make the Object of Faith something other than the Cross)*."

ACCURSED!

"But though we *(Paul and his associates)*, or an Angel from Heaven, preach any other gospel unto you than that which we have preached unto you *(Jesus Christ and Him Crucified)*, let him be accursed *(eternally condemned; the Holy Spirit speaks this through Paul, making this very serious)*.
"As we said before, so say I now again *(at some time past, he had said the same thing to them, making their defection even more serious)*, If any *man* preach any other gospel unto you *(anything other than the Cross)* than that you have received *(which Saved your souls)*, let him be accursed *('eternally condemned,' which means the loss of the soul)*."

PLEASING MEN OR PLEASING GOD

"For do I now persuade men, or God? *(In essence, Paul is saying, 'Do I preach man's doctrine, or God's?')* **or do I seek to please men?** *(This is what false apostles do.)* **for if I yet pleased men, I should not be the Servant of Christ** *(one cannot please both men and God at the same time)***" (Gal. 1:6-10).**

To be sure, the great Apostle was not here merely venting his spleen, so to speak. Was he angry? Yes, he was; however, it is high time that some modern preachers get angry, also!

As well, Paul was not on an ego trip. The great Revelation of the New Covenant, which, in effect, is the Revelation of the Cross, was given to the Apostle Paul by the Lord Jesus Christ (Gal. 1:12). Even though the great Apostle did not plainly state such, it is my personal belief that he received this Revelation when he was taken to what he referred to as *"the third Heaven."* He said:

VISIONS AND REVELATIONS OF THE LORD

"It is not expedient for me doubtless to glory *(but necessary!)*. **I will come to Visions and Revelations of the Lord** *(refers to that given to Paul by the Lord)*.

"I knew a man in Christ above fourteen years ago *(speaking of himself)*, **(whether in the body, I cannot tell; or whether out of the body, I cannot tell: God knows;)** *(He doesn't know if he was actually taken to Heaven in his physical body, or only saw these things in a Vision.)* **such an one caught up to the third Heaven.** *(The first heaven is the clouds, etc. The second heaven is the starry space. The third Heaven is the Planet Heaven, the Abode of God)*" **(II Cor. 12:1-2).**

At any rate, the Lord gave to the Apostle the meaning of

the New Covenant, which, as stated, is the meaning of the Cross, which is the Means by which we receive all things from the Lord. He knew if false apostles preached any other type of gospel, anything other than the Cross of Christ, it would wreck the Faith of the people and would cause some of them to be eternally lost. So, that which he was addressing was and is the single most important thing on the face of the Earth.

MODERN FALSE APOSTLES

Where does that leave the modern church? How many preachers presently are preaching the same Message preached by the Apostle Paul? Paul emphatically stated, *"We preach Christ Crucified"* (I Cor. 1:23). If one studies Paul at all, one must come to the concrete conclusion that the Apostle *"preached the Cross."* He preached it as the only Means of Salvation and the only Means of Sanctification. To be sure, all of this tells us that the Lord doesn't have ten ways of Salvation and Sanctification, not five ways, not even two ways, but only one way. That one way is the Cross of Christ (Rom. 6:1-14; 8:1-2, 11; I Cor. 1:17-18, 21, 23; 2:2; Gal., Chpt. 5; 6:14; Eph. 2:13-18; Col. 2:14-15).

The modern presentation could be broken down in three ways. They are:

1. There are preachers who do not preach the Cross of Christ at all, neither for Salvation nor Sanctification. These of whom we speak, which characterizes the far greater majority, recognize the Cross of Christ not at all. Whatever it is they preach is a humanitarian gospel, so-called, or at best, a motivational message. They preach a type of evolutionary morality. Under such a message no one is Saved, and no lives are changed, so it constitutes as being no more than a waste of time.

2. There are preachers who preach the Cross of Christ for Salvation, and rightly so. However, they do not preach the Cross for Sanctification simply because they are ignorant of this which Paul taught, or else they simply do not believe what Paul taught. If it's ignorance only, the Holy Spirit can

ultimately bring them into all that the great Apostle gave to us. If it's unbelief, meaning that they simply do not believe that the answer to all sin and all perversion is found solely in the Cross of Christ, they will soon cease to preach the Cross regarding Salvation. If Light is rejected, Light is then withdrawn!

3. There are preachers who proclaim the Cross of Christ as the Means of Salvation and the Cross of Christ as the Means of Sanctification as well! Regrettably, this number is few and far between.

The ones preaching the Cross for Salvation, and Salvation only, will see some people Saved, and thank the Lord for that; however, neglecting to preach the Cross regarding Sanctification, they simply do not know how to tell Believers to live for God.

THE SPIRIT

The Spirit, as here used by Paul, and as should be obvious, is the Holy Spirit. Without His Work within our lives, there will be no Spiritual Growth whatsoever. In fact, the Holy Spirit functions in every aspect of one's Salvation and one's Sanctification.

He is the One Who anoints the Preacher to preach the Message that the sinner needs to hear, or the singer to sing the song the sinner needs to hear, etc. When the Word is given, and in whatever form, it is the Holy Spirit who convicts the sinner of sin, of Righteousness, and of Judgment. Without this Conviction, the person cannot be Saved and, in fact, will have no desire to be Saved.

Also, the Holy Spirit grants to every believing sinner a measure of Faith in order that he might believe and, thereby, be Saved. Without the Holy Spirit granting such Faith, the person wouldn't even have the capacity to believe (Rom. 12:3). We must understand that all sinners are *"dead in trespasses and sins"* (Eph. 2:1). This means spiritually dead, dead to all things that pertain to God. And, we must understand, as well, that *"dead"* is *"dead."* That's how one arrives at the doctrine of total depravity. In this dead state the sinner can have no correct thoughts of God and cannot desire God, at least in the right way, so, the Holy Spirit has to provide to such a person everything that he needs in order to accept Christ.

A TEMPLE OF THE HOLY SPIRIT

At the moment the person gives his or her heart to Christ, the Holy Spirit comes in to the heart and life of the individual, and does so to abide forever (Jn. 14:16).

Then the Believer needs to go on and be baptized with the Holy Spirit, which is always accompanied by the individual speaking with other Tongues (Acts 2:4; 8:14-17; 10:44-46; 19:1-7).

This is so necessary, the Baptism with the Holy Spirit, that Jesus, in essence, told His Followers, which was just before His Ascension, that they should not go testify about Him, should not preach the Gospel or, in fact, do anything until they were first baptized with the Holy Spirit. In fact, the Scripture says:

"And, being assembled together with *them* (speaks of the time He ascended back to the Father; this was probably the time of the 'above five hundred' [I Cor. 15:6]), Commanded them (not a suggestion) that they should not depart from Jerusalem (the site of the Temple where the Holy Spirit would descend), but wait for the Promise of the Father (spoke of the Holy Spirit which had been promised by the Father [Lk. 24:49; Joel, Chpt. 2]), which, said *He*, you have heard of Me (you have also heard Me say these things [Jn. 7:37-39; 14:12-17, 26; 15:26; 16:7-15])."

THE BAPTISM WITH THE HOLY SPIRIT

"For John truly baptized with water (merely symbolized the very best Baptism Believers could receive before *the Day of Pentecost)*; **but you shall be baptized with the Holy Spirit not many days hence** *(spoke of the coming Day of Pentecost, although Jesus did not use that term at that time)*" **(Acts 1:4-5).**

THE POWER

Our Lord went on to say:

"**But you shall receive power** *(Miracle-working Power)*, **after that the Holy Spirit is come upon you** *(specifically states that this 'Power' is inherent in the Holy Spirit, and solely in His Domain)*: **and you shall be witnesses** *(doesn't mean witnessing to souls, but rather, to one giving one's all in every capacity for Christ, even to the laying down of one's life)* **unto Me** *(without the Baptism with the Holy Spirit, one cannot really know Jesus as one should)* **both in Jerusalem, and in all Judaea, and in Samaria, and unto the uttermost part of the Earth** *(proclaims the Work of God as being worldwide)*" **(Acts 1:8).**

Still, one must realize that even though baptized with the Holy Spirit with the evidence of speaking with other Tongues, this within itself, although a tremendous help, will not guarantee at all a victorious life. In fact, and regrettably, there are millions who have been baptized with the Holy Spirit, with some greatly used of God, who still do not and, in fact, cannot live the life they ought to live unless they understand God's Prescribed Order of Victory. The Power of the Holy Spirit is most definitely meant to help us in respect to our life and living. While the Holy Spirit definitely will not leave, and thank the Lord for that, still, if we ignore the Cross, He is very limited as to what He can do for us, at least, as it regards our everyday life and living. But, please understand, it is the Holy Spirit Alone Who can make us what we ought to be, give us the Victory that we should have and, thereby, live the life we ought to live. He does it all through the Cross.

WALKING AFTER THE FLESH

What was Paul talking about when he used the term, *"walking after the flesh"*?

In simple terms, he was meaning that the Believer's faith is placed in something other than Christ and the Cross. It really doesn't matter too very much what else it might be, or how good the other thing may be in its own right, still, if it's not the Cross that's the object of our faith, such is constituted by the Lord as trying to live this life by the means of the *"flesh."* Let's give an example that should be very easy to understand.

PRAYER

Prayer is one of the greatest privileges that the Believer has. To be able to take our needs to the Lord, to thank Him, and to have communion with Him are the greatest things that can happen to a Child of God. In fact, there can be precious little relationship if the Believer doesn't have a proper prayer life. However, as wonderful as prayer is, as needful and necessary that it is, still, prayer within itself will not bring about victory in our lives over the world, the flesh, and the Devil. If we try to use it in that fashion, we, in effect, turn it into a law, which the Lord cannot honor, at least, in the capacity that we desire.

Let's ask a question!

How much prayer is enough to bring about victory over sin? Would thirty minutes a day be enough? Perhaps it might take an hour a day.

No, it doesn't really matter how much we pray, how sincere we might be, and how dedicated we might be. While we definitely will be blessed in our prayer and praying, still, we will find that our efforts in this capacity to give us victory over sin will not bring fruitful results.

AN ILLUSTRATION

Years ago I read a particular statement made by a preacher

concerning this very thing. He did not tell what the problem was in his life, but he made the statement, *"I'm going to go into a room, lock the door, and stay there in faith and prayer until the Lord sets me free from this thing."*

While I admire his dedication and consecration, still, he can stay in that room, spend every available moment in prayer, and fast to the extent that, proverbially speaking, they can pull him through a keyhole, and he still won't have victory within his life.

THE TRUTH

Jesus said, *"And you shall know the Truth, and the Truth shall make you free"* (Jn. 8:32). In fact, this Word, as given by our Lord, is the secret of all Abundant Life in Christ. The *"Truth"* is *"Jesus Christ and Him Crucified,"* which alone is the answer to the problems of man. But, the sadness is, most Believers simply don't know the Truth.

When Christians do spiritual things, such as we've just mentioned regarding prayer, they somehow think that this will bring about victory. It won't! Read carefully what Paul said:

"For Christ sent me not to baptize, but to preach the Gospel: not with wisdom of words, lest the Cross of Christ should be made of none effect" (I Cor. 1:17).

Was Paul denigrating Water Baptism? Of course not! Was he meaning it wasn't important? Of course not! He was merely saying that Believers were not to put their faith and confidence in the ordinance of Water Baptism, as important as it is, and as Scriptural as it is in its own right. You could say the same thing about the Lord's Supper, etc.

Millions of Christians, as sincere as they know how to be, are placing their faith in their church membership, their association with a certain religious denomination, in a particular preacher, a specific Christian discipline, or the money they give to the Work of God, etc. While some or all of these things are good in their own right, nothing that we've named, and a whole lot we haven't named, will bring one victory over sin. Again we state, it is our Faith in Christ and the Cross exclusively which gives the Holy Spirit latitude to work within our hearts and lives and, thereby, to give us Victory. Let us say it again:

Placing one's faith in anything, irrespective as to what it might be and how good it might be in its own right, other than the Cross of Christ, is constituted by the Lord as *"walking after the flesh."* Such a direction will bring defeat every time. In fact, there is no victory in that direction. Now, let's look at *"walking after the Spirit."*

WALKING AFTER THE SPIRIT

Most Christians think that doing spiritual things constitutes walking after the Spirit. While those things may be very good, that is not walking after the Spirit.

Some time back I picked up a booklet containing a Message written by one of the greatest men of God I ever knew. I will leave him nameless at this time simply because of what I'm about to say.

His Message was on the subject of *"walking after the Spirit."* He made the mistake of so many Christians. This is what he said, and what most Christians erroneously believe.

He went into some detail, but, actually, he was saying, *"the doing of spiritual things"* constituted walking after the Spirit. It doesn't!

I addressed a small group of Christians sometime back, incidentally, people who were close to God, and who loved the Lord very much.

I asked, *"What do you think 'walking after the Spirit' actually means?"*

One said, *"It means being faithful to church!"* Another said, *"It pertains to us supporting with our finances the Work of God!"* Another said, *"It refers to witnessing to souls about the Lord!"*

Quite a few answers were in this vein. All the things they named were very good, but actually, all the things they named were merely Christian disciplines, in other words, that which every good Christian ought to do and, in fact, will do.

Not a single one who I was addressing knew the answer to the question, and yet, knowing these people as I did, I knew every one of them loved the Lord very much. Please understand that it doesn't matter how much one loves the Lord, how consecrated to the Lord that one might be, how sincere that one might be, or how great his prayer life might be. If that person doesn't understand what *"walking after the Spirit"* actually means, he will find the sin nature ruling him in some way. It is inevitable!

THE SCRIPTURAL MEANING

"Walking after the Spirit," refers to the fact that we do what the Spirit of God does. And, what is that?

It is the Cross of Christ which gives the Holy Spirit the legal means to do all that He does for us. It was at the Cross that Jesus paid the price, which means that He atoned for all sin, past, present, and future, at least, for all who will believe (Jn. 3:16). With all sin removed, meaning that the sin debt is lifted from the head and heart of every single Believer, this gives the Holy Spirit latitude to work within our lives. As we have repeatedly stated, the Holy Spirit works entirely within the parameters of the Finished Work of Christ. He will not work outside of those parameters. Now, as I've also said several times, He doesn't demand much of us, but He does demand one thing and that is:

We as Believers must understand that everything we receive from God comes to us from Jesus Christ as our Source and by the Cross as the Means by which all of this is made possible, all superintended by the Holy Spirit. Understanding that, we must place our Faith constantly in Christ and the Cross and not allow it to be moved elsewhere. Placing our Faith in the Cross of Christ and keeping it in the Cross of Christ gives the Holy Spirit the freedom, the liberty, and the latitude, one might say, to carry out His Mission in our lives, which is to rid us of all sin, and among other things, to give us Victory in every capacity over the world, the flesh, and the Devil. That is *"walking after the Spirit."*

This is so important, placing our Faith exclusively in Christ and the Cross, that it is referred to as *"the Law."* Paul said:

THE LAW OF THE SPIRIT OF LIFE IN CHRIST JESUS

"**For the Law** *(that which we are about to give is a Law of God, devised by the Godhead in eternity past [I Pet. 1:18-20]; this Law, in fact, is 'God's Prescribed Order of Victory')* **of the Spirit** *(Holy Spirit, i.e., 'the way the Spirit works')* **of Life** *(all life comes from Christ, but through the Holy Spirit [Jn. 16:13-14])* **in Christ Jesus** *(any time Paul uses this term or one of its derivatives, he is, without fail, referring to what Christ did at the Cross, which makes this 'life' possible)* **has made me free** *(given me total Victory)* **from the Law of Sin and Death** *(these are the two most powerful Laws in the Universe; the 'Law of the Spirit of Life in Christ Jesus' alone is stronger than the 'Law of Sin and Death'; this means that if the Believer attempts to live for God by any manner other than Faith in Christ and the Cross, he is doomed to failure)*" **(Rom. 8:2).**

THE NATURAL THING

It is natural for Believers to gravitate toward the flesh. We are human beings, and we are accustomed to doing this, as would be obvious. So, in trying to live for God, it's very easy to continue in that vein because it comes naturally. The supernatural way is the Holy Spirit. We have to train ourselves to function *"after the Spirit,"* instead of our normal way of functioning, *"after the flesh."* It is the Work of the Holy Spirit to bring us to the place that walking after Him becomes the natural thing to do. This will not come quickly or easily simply due to the fact that oftentimes when we think we are walking after the Spirit, we are actually walking after the flesh. But, as we humble ourselves before the Lord, allowing Him to have His Perfect Way within our lives, gradually, His Way will become our way.

"I am Thine, O Lord,
"I have heard Your Voice,
"And it told Your Love to me;
"But I long to rise in the arms of Faith,
"And be closer drawn to Thee."

"Consecrate me now,
"To Your Service, Lord,
"By the Power of Grace Divine;
"Let my soul look up with a steadfast hope,
"And my will be lost in Thine."

"Oh, the pure delight,
"Of a single hour,
"That before Your Throne I spend,
"When I kneel in prayer, and with You, my God,
"I commune as friend with friend."

"There are depths of love,
"That I cannot know,
"Till I cross the narrow sea,
"There are heights of joy that I may not reach,
"Till I rest in peace with Thee."

CHAPTER NINE

Spiritual Adultery

SPIRITUAL ADULTERY

Most modern Christians have never even heard the term *"spiritual adultery,"* much less understand what it is. And yet, most of the modern church, and we speak of those who truly love the Lord, who truly desire to do His Will, and who truly hunger and thirst after Righteousness are, in fact, and sadly so, living in a state of *"spiritual adultery."*

To be brief, spiritual adultery constitutes the Believer looking to other things, whatever they might be, and no matter how correct they may be in their own right, thereby, placing his faith in something other than the Cross of Christ. Such constitutes spiritual adultery, which means that such a Believer, even though doing so ignorantly, is being unfaithful to Christ. We as Believers are to look exclusively to Christ for all things, and we are, as well, to understand that everything He gives us, and I mean everything, is done so by the Means of the Cross, in other words, the price He there paid. Consequently, the Cross of Christ must ever be the Object of our Faith, and the Cross of Christ alone! Now, most Believers would read that statement and automatically exclaim that they are looking solely to Christ. However, the Truth is that most modern Believers have absolutely no knowledge whatsoever as to the part the Cross of Christ plays in all of this. They do not understand that everything we receive from the Lord comes from Christ as the Source and the Cross as the Means. Most Christians understand the Cross of Christ relative to Salvation, or at least they have a modicum of knowledge in this respect, but they know absolutely nothing about the Cross of Christ relative to Sanctification, i.e., how we live for God, how we conduct ourselves, or how we order our behavior. In fact, there is a great segment of the modern church in the charismatic realm which actually repudiates the Cross of Christ, referring to it as *"past miseries"* and *"the greatest defeat in human history."* I speak of the so-called Word of Faith people. Consequently, they will not even sing songs about the Blood, about the Cross, about Calvary, or about the price that Jesus paid, claiming that such is defeatism. They claim that the Cross of Christ was just another incident with the real work of Redemption being carried out, of all places, in Hell.

THE JESUS DIED SPIRITUALLY DOCTRINE

Truthfully, most of the people who subscribe to the Word of Faith doctrine and attend churches of that stripe have little or no knowledge at all of the *"Jesus died spiritually doctrine."* They have embraced that doctrine for other reasons.

In brief, this doctrine claims that Jesus became a sinner on the Cross, with some even stating that He actually became demon possessed, and when He died, He then went to Hell, and we speak of the burning side of the Pit where all unredeemed go at death. They claim that Satan, along with many, many demon spirits, beat up on Christ for three days and nights, claiming victory over the Son of God. At the end of the three days and nights, God the Father, looking down from Heaven, declared that Jesus had suffered enough, and then the Son of God, they claim, was Born-Again just like any sinner is Born-Again. They derive that belief from the Passage which states:

"For whom He *(God)* did foreknow *(God's foreknowledge)*, He also did predestinate *to be* conformed to the Image of His Son *(it is never the person that is predestined, but rather, the Plan)*, that He *(Jesus)* might be the Firstborn among many Brethren" (Rom. 8:29).

This Scripture doesn't mean that Jesus was Born-Again as a sinner as these people teach, but rather, that He is the Father of the Salvation Plan, having paid the price on the Cross, which made it all possible.

The Greek word for *"firstborn"* is *"prototokos,"* and means *"foremost in order or importance."* As Paul uses the word, it is referring to Jesus as the Father of the Salvation Plan and being so by what He did at the Cross. Actually, the word *"first-born"* can be used literally, which refers to the first child born in the family, or figuratively, as Paul is using it here. In fact, every time it refers to Christ it is in that manner. When Paul made the statement, *"Who is the Image of the invisible God, the Firstborn of every creature,"* he wasn't meaning that Jesus was a created being, but rather, that He is the Creator of all things (Col. 1:15; Jn. 1:1-3).

As well, when He spoke of Jesus as *"the Head of the Body, the Church: Who is the beginning, the Firstborn from the dead,"* he is meaning that Jesus is, in fact, the Resurrection and the Life (Col. 1:18). In other words, our Lord is the Father of all Creation, the great Salvation Plan which was carried out at Calvary, and of the Resurrection.

The Greek scholars tell us that there is no suitable English equivalent of the Greek word *"prototokos."* The word *"first-born"* is the nearest they can come to properly explaining it, which falls short, they say. At any rate, Jesus did not become a sinner on the Cross, but rather, a sin-offering (Isa. 53:10); neither upon His Death did He go to the burning side of Hell and neither was He Born-Again. You won't find any of that in the Bible, and the reason is that it does not exist.

WHAT HAPPENED FROM THE CROSS TO THE THRONE?!

When Jesus died on the Cross, His Soul and Spirit went down into the nether world, with the Bible recording that He did two specific things.

1. It seems that He went to the underworld prison and there made an announcement to fallen Angels, who were locked up there and are still there presently. The Scripture says:

"**By which also He went** *(between the time of His Death and Resurrection)* **and preached** *(announced something)* **unto the spirits in prison** *(does not refer to humans,* *but rather to fallen Angels; humans in the Bible are never referred to in this particular manner; these were probably the fallen Angels who tried to corrupt the human race by cohabiting with women [II Pet. 2:4; Jude, Vss. 6-7]; these fallen Angels, as stated, are still locked up in this underworld prison);"*

DISOBEDIENT ANGELS

"**Which sometime** *(in times past)* **were disobedient** *(this was shortly before the Flood)*, **when once the long-suffering of God waited in the days of Noah** *(refers to this eruption of fallen Angels with women taking place at the time of Noah; this was probably a hundred or so years before the Flood)*, **while the Ark was a preparing** *(these fallen Angels were committing this particular sin while the Ark was being made ready, ever how long it took; the Scripture doesn't say!)*, **wherein few, that is, eight souls were saved by water.** *(This doesn't refer to being Saved from sin. They were saved from drowning in the Flood by being in the Ark)*" **(I Pet. 3:19-20).**

Jude had something to say about this as well.

ANGELS WHICH KEPT NOT THEIR FIRST ESTATE

"**And the Angels which kept not their first estate, but left their own habitation** *(these particular Angels did not maintain their original position in which they were created, but transgressed those limits to invade territory foreign to them, namely the human race; they left Heaven and came to Earth, seeking to cohabit with women, which they did [Gen. 6:4])*, **He** *(the Lord)* **has reserved in everlasting chains under darkness unto the Judgment of the Great Day** *(these Angels are now imprisoned [II Pet. 2:4], and will be judged at the Great White Throne Judgment,* *then placed in the 'Lake of Fire' where they will remain forever and forever [Rev. 20:10])."*

STRANGE FLESH

"**Even as Sodom and Gomorrah, and the cities about them in like manner** *(the Greek Text introduces a comparison showing a likeness between the Angels of Verse 6 and the cities of Sodom and Gomorrah; but the likeness between them lies deeper than the fact that both were guilty of committing sin; it extends to the fact that both were guilty of the same identical sin)*, **giving themselves over to fornication, and going after strange flesh** *(the Angels cohabited with women; the sin of Sodom and Gomorrah, and the cites around them, was homosexuality [Rom. 1:27])*, **are set forth for an example, suffering the vengeance of eternal fire** *(those who engage in the sin of homosexuality and refuse to repent will suffer the vengeance of the Lake of Fire)*" **(Jude, Vss. 6-7).**

As to exactly what Jesus announced to these fallen Angels, we aren't told.

The Greek word used by Peter concerning Jesus preaching to the spirits in prison is *"kerusso,"* and means, *"to make an announcement, to proclaim an announcement."* The usual word for *"preached"* is *"euaggelizo,"* and means, *"to announce good news,"* etc. However, Jesus didn't announce good news to these fallen Angels, at least, good news as it concerned them. It was most definitely good news as it regarded mankind, but not the Angels. He probably announced to them that the Cross was now a fact, and that their master, Satan, was totally defeated. That meant that they now had no hope of ever getting out of this place.

PARADISE

2. The second thing the Bible says that Jesus did while in

the underworld and before His Resurrection was to deliver all the souls that were in Paradise.

Before the Cross, every Believer who died was taken to Paradise, which was in the heart of the Earth, actually very near to the burning side of Hell. The two places were separated by a gulf (Lk. 16:26). Due to the fact that the blood of bulls and goats could not take away sins (Heb. 10:4), this meant that the sin debt remained, even over the heads, so to speak, of the godliest. As a result, when they died, they could not be taken to Heaven, but were rather taken down into Paradise where they were actually captives of Satan. He could not harm them, but still, they were under his domain, after a fashion. Jesus gave us an account of this in the Sixteenth Chapter of Luke.

When Jesus atoned for all sin at the Cross, Satan had no more claim on any of those individuals who were in Paradise, for the sin debt was totally and completely eradicated. Now, they could be taken to Heaven. So, Paul wrote concerning this:

HE LED CAPTIVITY CAPTIVE

"Wherefore He said *(Ps. 68:18)*, When He ascended up on high *(the Ascension)*, He led captivity captive *(liberated the souls in Paradise; before the Cross, despite being Believers, they were still held captive by Satan because the blood of bulls and goats could not take away the sin debt; but when Jesus died on the Cross, the sin debt was paid, and now He makes all of these His Captives)*, and gave Gifts unto men. *(These 'Gifts' include all the Attributes of Christ, all made possible by the Cross.)*"

THE LOWER PARTS OF THE EARTH

"(Now that He ascended *(mission completed)*, what is it but that He also descended first into the lower parts of the earth? *(Immediately before His Ascension to Glory, which would be done in total triumph, He first went down into Paradise to deliver all the believing souls in that region, which He did!)*

"He Who descended is the same also Who ascended *(this is a portrayal of Jesus as Deliverer and Mediator)* up far above all Heavens *(presents His present location, never again having to descend into the nether world),* that He might fill all things.) *(He has always been the Creator, but now He is also the Saviour)*" (Eph. 4:8-10).

Those are the only two things the Bible relates to us that Jesus did during the three days and nights He was in the heart of the Earth after His Death on Calvary.

1. He made an announcement to the fallen Angels locked away in the underworld prison.

2. He delivered all of the souls out of Paradise, which included every Believer who ever lived before the Cross, and took them with Him to Heaven.

There is no mention, as stated, of Jesus going to the burning side of Hell, as some claim. After going through the litany of Jesus becoming a sinner on the Cross and then going down to the burning side of Hell, where He was tortured and tormented for three days and nights, and then Born-Again as any sinner is Born-Again, and then raised from the dead, one particular preacher stated, *"You won't find this in the Bible, it has to be given to you by revelation,"* or words to that effect.

NOT IN THE BIBLE!

Now, I want you to think about that statement for a moment concerning this so-called great truth not being found in the Bible.

They are saying that the great Plan of God, the Plan of Redemption, that predicted by the Prophets of old and elaborated on by the Apostles of the New Testament, is not found in the Bible! Can you figure anything in the world that's more stupid than that statement?

The weird story of Jesus dying spiritually on the Cross and going to the burning side of Hell is not found in the Bible because it never happened. The idea of something so wonderful, so beautiful, so powerful, so dramatic, actually the fulfillment of all the Prophecies, and yet God did not put it in the Bible? How foolish can we be?!

No, the great Plan of Redemption is portrayed in the Word of God in no uncertain terms. In fact, in the four Gospels a blow-by-blow account is given of everything that took place. In the Epistles, the Apostle Paul, and all others who wrote, referred to this great event over and over again, but they never once mentioned this wild story of Jesus dying as a sinner on the Cross. They didn't mention it because it did not happen.

THE ATONEMENT

The Cross of Christ constitutes the Atonement, which is the very heart of the Gospel. Please allow me to say the following:

If a person has a hangnail, that's one thing. While it might evidence some discomfort, it's not going to kill him; but, when a person has a problem with his heart, that can kill him.

The Atonement, what Jesus did at the Cross, is the very heart of the Gospel. To tamper with the Atonement is to tamper with one's Salvation.

What am I saying?

I am saying that those who believe this pernicious doctrine of Jesus dying spiritually on the Cross, meaning that He became a sinner on the Cross and went to the burning side of Hell, and then was Born-Again in Hell like any sinner is Born-Again, is in danger of losing his soul.

The Atonement, as stated, is the heart of the Gospel, which means that there is nothing in the world more important than this Message. God help us to understand it correctly as given to us in the Word of God. And, as clearly as it is given, there is no excuse for us not understanding what it says.

Paul said:

ONE MEDIATOR

"For *there is* one God *(manifested in three Persons
— God the Father, God the Son, and God the Holy Spirit)*,
and one Mediator between God and men, the Man
Christ Jesus *(He can only be an adequate Mediator Who
has sympathy with and an understanding of both parties,
and is understandable by and clear to both; in other
words, Jesus is both God and Man, i.e., 'Very God and
Very Man')*;

"Who gave Himself a ransom for all *(refers to the
fact that our Lord's Death was a spontaneous and voluntary Sacrifice on His Part; the word 'ransom' refers to the
price He paid, owed by man to God, which was His Precious Blood [I Pet. 1:18-20])*, to be testified in due time.
*(This refers to the planning of this great Work, which took
place 'before the foundation of the world' [I Pet. 1:18-20],
unto the 'due time' of its manifestation, which refers to
when Christ was Crucified)*" **(I Tim. 2:5-6).**

SPIRITUAL ADULTERY

Paul deals with the subject of spiritual adultery in the first
four Verses of the Seventh Chapter of Romans. He said:

"Know ye not, Brethren *(Paul is speaking to Believers)*, (for I speak to them who know the Law,) *(he is
speaking of the Law of Moses, but it could refer to any type
of religious Law)* how that the Law has dominion over a
man as long as he lives? *(The Law has dominion as long
as he tries to live by Law. Regrettably, not understanding
the Cross regarding Sanctification, virtually the entirety of
the church is presently trying to live for God by means of
the Law. Let the Believer understand that there are only
two places he can be, Grace or Law. If he doesn't understand the Cross as it refers to Sanctification, which is the*

only means of victory, he will automatically be under Law, which guarantees failure.)"

THE EXAMPLE GIVEN

"For the woman which has an husband is bound by the Law to *her* husband so long as he lives *(presents Paul using the analogy of the marriage bond)*; but if the husband be dead, she is loosed from the Law of *her* husband *(meaning that she is free to marry again).*

"So then if, while *her* husband lives, she be married to another man, she shall be called an adulteress *(in effect, the woman now has two husbands, at least in the Eyes of God; following this analogy, the Holy Spirit through Paul will give us a great truth; many Christians are living a life of spiritual adultery; they are married to Christ, but they are, in effect, serving another husband, 'the Law'; it is quite an analogy!)*: but if her husband be dead *(the Law is dead by virtue of Christ having fulfilled the Law in every respect)*, she is free from that Law *(if the husband dies, the woman is free to marry and serve another; the Law of Moses, being satisfied in Christ, is now dead to the Believer and the Believer is free to serve Christ without the Law having any part or parcel in his life or living)*; so that she is no adulteress, though she be married to another man *(presents the Believer as now married to Christ, and no longer under obligation to the Law).*"

EVERY BELIEVER IS MARRIED TO CHRIST

"Wherefore, my Brethren, you also are become dead to the Law *(the Law is not dead per se, but we are dead to the Law because we are dead to its effects; this means that we are not to try to live for God by means of 'Law,' whether the Law of Moses, or religious Laws made up by other men or of ourselves; we are to be dead to all religious*

Law) **by the body of Christ** *(this refers to the Crucifixion of Christ, which satisfied the demands of the broken Law we could not satisfy; but Christ did it for us; having fulfilled the Mosaic Law in every respect, the Christian is not obligated to Law in any fashion, only to Christ and what He did at the Cross)*; **that you should be married to another** *(speaking of Christ)*, **even to Him Who is raised from the dead** *(we are raised with Him in Newness of Life, and we should ever understand that Christ has met, does meet, and shall meet our every need; we look to Him exclusively, referring to what He did for us at the Cross)*, **that we should bring forth fruit unto God** *(proper fruit can only be brought forth by the Believer constantly looking to the Cross; in fact, Christ must never be separated from the Work of the Cross; to do so is to produce 'another Jesus' [II Cor. 11:4])*" **(Rom. 7:1-4).**

HOW BAD IS THE SIN OF SPIRITUAL ADULTERY?

To answer the question, *"How bad is the sin of spiritual adultery?"* we will ask another question!

How bad is the sin of physical adultery?

I think all of us should know and understand the terrible strain that literal adultery would place on a marriage. In fact, most marriages do not survive such. Thankfully, the Lord does not function as a human being but rather as the Lord of Glory. He said a long time ago:

"God is not a man, that He should lie; neither the Son of man that He should repent: has He said, and shall He not do it? or has He spoken, and shall He not make it good?" (Num. 23:19). The patience and longsuffering of the Lord are totally unlike anything that is peculiar to humans. The truth is this:

Every single Believer who has ever lived, at one time or the other, has committed the sin of *"spiritual adultery,"* which means that we have trusted things other than Christ and the Cross. Sadly, that is the truth; however, the great problem is that most Christians never graduate from this particular difficulty, continuing to live in a state of spiritual adultery. They do so because they do not understand the Cross of Christ as it regards Sanctification, or else, they register unbelief in connection with their lack of understanding.

HOW DOES THE SIN OF SPIRITUAL ADULTERY AFFECT THE HOLY SPIRIT?

I want to say that the sin of spiritual adultery affects the Holy Spirit exactly as it would a husband or wife in the natural who has been sinned against in this fashion; however, the truth is, it affects Him to a much greater degree. Loving us as He does, He knows what this sin will do to us as Believers. In fact, there is a very peculiar Scripture that deals with this very question. It says:

THE HOLY SPIRIT IS ENVIOUS OF ANY CONTROL THE FALLEN NATURE MIGHT HAVE OVER THE BELIEVER

"**Do you think that the Scripture says in vain** *(James was quoting several Scriptures [Gen. 15:6; 49:10; Ex. 17:6; Ps. 78:16; Ezek. 47:9; Joel 2:28-29])*, **The Spirit Who dwells in us lusts to envy?** *(This refers to the Holy Spirit, which means that the word 'Spirit' should have been capitalized.*

"*The word 'lusteth' here means 'to earnestly or passionately desire.' Of what is He envious, and what does He passionately desire?*

"*The Holy Spirit is envious of any control the fallen nature might have over the Believer, and is passionately desirous that He control all our thoughts, words, and deeds. He is desirous of having the Believer depend upon Him for His Ministry to Him, so that He might discharge His responsibility to the One Who sent Him, namely God the Father)*" **(James 4:5).**

ONE OF THE NAMES OF GOD IS *"JEALOUS"*

Moses wrote:

"For you shall worship no other god: for the LORD,
Whose Name is Jealous, is a jealous God *(in this sense, the
jealousy of God is of the essence of His Moral Character, a
major cause for worship and confidence on the part of His
People, and a ground for fear on the part of His enemies;
the Lord will not share His People with Satan; as well,
the jealousy evidenced by the Lord is in no way selfish, as
it is with mankind [Deut. 4:24; 5:9; 6:15; Josh. 24:19])"*
(Ex. 34:14).

As a man would not want his wife consorting with other
men, as should be overly obvious, likewise, the Lord doesn't
want us consorting with that which He knows is unfaithfulness
to Him and will, thereby, cause us tremendous problems. The
Holy Spirit is extremely limited as to what He can do in our
hearts and lives for our good and our betterment when we are
living in a state of spiritual adultery. I think it would be obvious as to the harm that such brings about. Yet, and as stated,
most of the church, simply because of not understanding the
Cross of Christ as it refers to Sanctification, is, in fact, living
in a state of spiritual adultery. Such hinders their Spiritual
Growth, if not stopping it altogether, and to be sure, makes life
a lot less than it ought to be and, in fact, can be.

ASKING FORGIVENESS FOR THE GOOD AND THE BAD

Christians need to repent not only of the bad things they
have done, whatever that might be, but also, of the good things.
Now, that may seem strange, but I say that because of the
following:

All of the so-called good things that we do oftentimes tend
to make us believe that these things contribute something

toward our Salvation, or at least, toward our Sanctification.

They don't!

To be frank, more than likely, this is the biggest sin of most Christians. We think our good deeds, our good things, all which are done in the Name of the Lord, affords us something with God. It's hard for us to realize and admit that they don't. That's why Paul said:

"For if Righteousness come by the Law, then Christ is dead in vain!" (Gal. 2:21).

There is absolutely nothing good that a Believer can do to make himself holy, to make himself righteous. While we aren't demeaning the good things per se, we are demeaning the attitude which thinks that such earns something from God. It doesn't, and they don't!

Every iota of Righteousness and Holiness possessed by a Believer is a Gift from God, all made possible by Christ and what He did for us at the Cross. Upon simple Faith, not merit, not works, but simple Faith, all of these things are awarded to us. But, as we have repeatedly stated, they are made available to us altogether by what Jesus did for us at the Cross. In other words, it is the Cross that made it possible. The song says:

"O the love that drew Salvation's Plan,
"O the Grace that brought it down to man,
"O the mighty gulf our God did span,
"At Calvary."

The following has been quoted in an earlier part of this Volume; however, it is so important that I would ask your permission to quote it again.

THE CRUCIFIED LIFE

Man, even believing man, somewhat balks at this position given here by the Holy Spirit through Paul concerning the Crucified Life (Gal. 2:20). Man likes to have some credit and some position. He likes that which he can see and handle. He refuses to be treated as vile and incapable of good, and is angered that he and his religious efforts should be condemned to annihilation.

Oh yes! He will willingly practice efforts to annihilate himself; for that ministers to his own importance. But to accept the absolute judgment of death upon his nature, his religious energies, and his moral virtues, and to be commanded to be silent, and, as a dead sinner, to trust the life-giving Saviour, finding in Him all that is needful for Righteousness and worship, is distasteful and repelling, hence, the offense of the Cross. But, this is the Doctrine of Galatians 2:20.

Once again, let me approach the subject.

Man loves to think that his good deeds merit him something with God. He loves to think that these things contribute somewhat to his Righteousness and Holiness. He likes to think, *"God likes me because I do thus and so!"* He is loath to admit what the Lord actually says about these things. The Prophet Isaiah tells us:

"But we are all as an unclean thing, and all our righteousnesses are as filthy rags; and we all do fade as a leaf; and our iniquities, like the wind, have taken us away" (Isa. 64:6).

While the doing of good things is not to be condemned, it's our attitude of self-righteousness which oftentimes stems from these things that must be condemned. In effect, that's what self-righteousness is.

SELF-RIGHTEOUSNESS

Self-righteousness is that we think we are righteous because we do certain good things or don't do certain bad things. Now, while those things most definitely do have an effect, as ought to be obvious, still, we must ever understand that we cannot work, earn, or merit our way into Righteousness. It cannot be done. God cannot accept anything of that nature.

The Righteousness which He has, He will freely give to

us without price, and without price of any nature, if we will only place our Faith in Christ and what Christ did for us at the Cross. That being the case, God will impute to us a perfect, pure, spotless Righteousness, made possible by Christ and what He did at the Cross. We must ever understand the Source of all of these things, which is Christ, and the Means by which they are made available to us, which is always the Cross. Anything else constitutes spiritual adultery!

At the expense of being overly repetitious, please allow me one more time to say the following:

• We must ever understand and realize that the Lord Jesus Christ is the Source of all things that we receive from God (Jn. 14:6).

• We must ever realize that the Cross of Christ must ever be the Object of our Faith, and that alone (Gal. 6:14; Col. 2:14-15).

• We must know that the Holy Spirit, without Whom we can have nothing, works entirely within the framework of the Finished Work of Christ. In other words, He superintends all things (Rom. 8:1-2, 11).

"In shady green pastures, so rich and so sweet,
"God leads His dear Children along;
"Where the water's cool flow bathes the weary one's feet,
"God leads His dear Children along."

"Sometimes on the mount where the sun shines so bright,
"God leads His dear Children along;
"Sometimes in the valley in the darkest night,
"God leads His dear Children along."

"Though sorrows befall us, and Satan oppose,
"God leads His dear Children along;
"Through Grace we can conquer, defeat all our foes,
"God leads His dear Children along."

"Away from the mire, and away from the clay,

"God leads His dear Children along;
"Away up in Glory, eternity's day,
"God leads His dear Children along."

"Some through the waters, some through the flood,
"Some through the fire, but all through the Blood;
"Some through great sorrows, but God gives a song;
"In the night season and all the day long."

CHAPTER TEN

The Good Fight Of Faith

THE GOOD FIGHT OF FAITH

If the Lord helps me to properly explain this great subject of *"fighting the good fight of Faith,"* it could be one of the most important Chapters in this Volume. In fact, even as we shall see, *"Faith"* is the key that unlocks every door as it pertains to the Lord, and Faith alone! In fact, that's where the battle rages; as always, it is between *"Faith"* and *"works."* If the Believer has a problem, this is generally where the problem begins. Paul said:

FIGHT THE GOOD FIGHT OF FAITH

"But you, O man of God, flee these things *(the Holy Spirit is unequivocally clear in His Command; we can follow the Lord, or we can follow other things; we can't follow both!)*; and follow after Righteousness, Godliness, Faith, Love, Patience, Meekness. *(In a sense, this is Fruit of the Spirit, or at least that which the Spirit Alone can bring about in our lives, which He does by the Cross ever being the Object of our Faith.)*

"Fight the good fight of Faith *(in essence, the only fight we are called upon to engage; every attack by Satan against the Believer, irrespective of its form, is to destroy or seriously weaken our Faith; he wants to push our Faith from the Cross to other things)*, lay hold on Eternal Life *(we do such by understanding that all Life comes from Christ, and the Means is the Cross)*, whereunto you are also Called *(Called to follow Christ)*, and have professed a good profession before many witnesses. *(This does not refer to a particular occasion, but to the entirety of his life for Christ.)*"

A CHARGE

"I give you charge in the sight of God *(in essence,*

the mantle is soon to be passed to this young Preacher), **who quickens** *(makes alive)* **all things** *(presents Christ here as the Preserver, rather than the Creator)*, **and** *before* **Christ Jesus** *('I charge you before Christ')*, **who before Pontius Pilate witnessed a good confession** *(the confession of Christ was the model confession for all martyrs, insofar as it was a bold confession of the Truth, even with the sentence of death before His Eyes)***;"**

THE COMMANDMENTS

"That you keep *this* **Commandment without spot, unrebukeable** *(the Gospel of Christ and Him Crucified must not be compromised in any fashion)*, **until the appearing of our Lord Jesus Christ** *(the statement refers to both the Rapture and the Second Coming)*" **(I Tim. 6:11-14).**

THE INGREDIENT OF FAITH

The whole of God's vast Creation stems from the ingredient of Faith. Paul said:

"Through Faith we understand that the worlds were framed by the Word of God *(refers to Creation, along with everything that goes with Creation)*, **so that things which are seen were not made of things which do appear.** *(God began with nothing, thereby, speaking into existence the things needed to create the universe)*" **(Heb. 11:3).**

As such, all the inhabitants of Planet Earth, and it has been that way from the beginning, operate, whether they realize it or not, from the position of faith.

That's the reason that capitalism, that is, if it's halfway honest, is the engine that drives prosperity. It is the reward at the end of the proverbial rainbow, all built upon faith.

In fact, every human being in the world has faith and

operates accordingly. Capitalism, if operated honestly, creates an incentive, which, within itself, is faith. In fact, such is Biblical, and it is what has made this nation great. Of course, capitalism, as any other attribute or philosophy, can be weakened or even destroyed by dishonesty.

Scientists claim that they will not accept anything on the basis of faith, when all the time, they are functioning from this element. They labor in the laboratory for untold amounts of time, investing their mind and their ability in the realm of development. It is faith. Even the atheist, who claims he doesn't believe in God, evidences faith constantly. In fact, he has faith in his lack of faith. But, none of this is Faith that God will recognize, which we will deal with to a greater degree momentarily.

This is the reason that socialism and communism will not work. It tries to function without faith, and such is impossible.

• Communism is when the government owns everything, all the houses, all the businesses, all the land, all the factories, etc. The entirety of the population who has the misfortune to be in such a climate works exclusively for the state. In such a climate, there is no incentive to do anything well simply because there will be no reward for doing well in that philosophy. So, it is a failed system and on all accounts.

• Socialism, someone has said, contains nine points of the ten of communism. At any rate, under this philosophy, the people own their homes, the land, the factories, the businesses, etc.; however, the government tells the businesses what they can manufacture, what they can charge for it, etc. It, too, is an unworkable solution because it contains no faith.

• Capitalism is when the people own everything, and the free market decides what is manufactured and what should be charged.

In capitalism, however, the government must exercise certain regulations. The love of money is so strong in people that they will do things to the hurt of society if not properly regulated; however, the government must be careful that it does not over-regulate, even as it must be careful that it does regulate enough.

So, understanding that God operates solely from the premise of Faith, it would do us well to garner all understanding that we can muster as it regards this all-important subject.

WHAT IS FAITH?

The Biblical definition is:

"Now Faith is the substance *(the title deed)* **of things hoped for** *(a declaration of the action of Faith)***, the evidence of things not seen.** *(Faith is not based upon the senses, which yield uncertainty, but rather on the Word of God)*" **(Heb. 11:1).**

I think one could say without fear of Scriptural contradiction that the subject of Faith, and its link to Salvation, is the very first Revelation of such magnitude to be given to man. In fact, it was given to Abraham. It is referred to as *"Justification by Faith."* Concerning this, the Scripture says:

JUSTIFICATION BY FAITH

"And he *(Abraham)* **believed in the LORD** *(exercised Faith, believing what the Lord told him)***; and He** *(the Lord)* **counted it to him** *(Abraham)* **for Righteousness.** *(This is one of the single most important Scriptures in the entirety of the Word of God. In this simple term, 'Abraham believed the LORD,' we find the meaning of Justification by Faith. Abraham was Saved by Grace through Faith, not by his good works. There is no other way of Salvation anywhere in the Bible. God demands Righteousness; however, it is the Righteousness afforded strictly by Christ and Christ Alone. Anything else is self-righteousness, and totally unacceptable to God. Directly the sinner believes God's*

Testimony about His Beloved Son, he is not only declared righteous, but he is made a son and an heir)" **(Gen. 15:6).**

As it regards *"Justification by Faith,"* this means that a thrice-Holy God can justify and, in fact, will justify even the worst of sinners, which means to declare such a one *"not guilty,"* upon such a person evidencing simple Faith in Christ and what Christ has done for us at the Cross. In fact, Justification can come by no other means.

THE MEANING OF JUSTIFICATION

One is made to wonder as to how a thrice-Holy God can maintain His integrity and at the same time declare an obviously guilty sinner *"not guilty."* How can He do that?

He does it on the basis of the Lord Jesus Christ and what Christ did at the Cross. That's the reason Faith is required, which means to simply believe in Christ. It means to believe that He is the Son of God, and that He paid the price for us at the Cross of Calvary. In other words, Jesus did for us what we could not do for ourselves. He lived a life perfectly, never failing even one time, not in word, thought, or deed. Again, He did that solely for us as our Representative Man. Also, He addressed the broken Law, of which all of us were guilty, by going to the Cross and giving Himself in Sacrifice, thereby, satisfying the debt we owed but could not pay. In other words, He paid it for us. Thereby, having Faith in Him and what He did for us simply means that we believe in Him and what He did. It's not something difficult; it's not something hard. It's just simply a matter of believing.

THE REAL MEANING OF JUSTIFICATION

Upon simple Faith expressed in Christ and what He did for us at the Cross, such a person is instantly justified by God and, thereby, given a spotless, pure, perfect Righteousness, all made possible by Christ and His Sacrificial Atoning Death at

Calvary's Cross. Justification means:

- One is declared *"not guilty."*
- One is declared innocent of all charges.
- One is looked at by God as though he has never sinned, not even one time.
- The absolute Perfection of Jesus Christ is granted to such a person.

Please understand that God cannot accept anything less than perfection. Understanding that there is no perfection in the human race, such Perfection must come from His Son and our Saviour, the Lord Jesus Christ. So, when the Lord looks at us, and I speak of those who have accepted Christ, He really doesn't see us, but rather, sees His Son, as stated, our Saviour.

ARE THINGS RECEIVED FROM GOD ACCORDING TO THE DEGREE OF OUR FAITH?

No! Things are not received from God according to the degree of our Faith.

While most definitely Faith is required in all of our actions with God, and while there definitely is such a thing as *"weak Faith"* and, as well, *"great Faith,"* still, a little forethought will debunk the idea that the degree of Faith decides what we receive or don't receive.

If that were the case, then one could use his Faith to get anything he wanted from the Lord, irrespective if it were the Lord's Will or not. We know that's not true. God will never allow His Word to be used against Himself.

What do we mean by that?

If an increase of Faith guaranteed anything we wanted, we would soon be telling God what He should do. We all know that the Lord will never surrender His Sovereignty. The Disciples thought this same thing, that the greater their Faith, the greater the reward, etc. They said to the Lord:

"**Increase our Faith** *(this is the request of many; however,* *the answer the Lord will give is extremely interesting).*

"**And the Lord said, If you had faith as a grain of mustard seed** *(a very small seed, telling us, in effect, that it's not really the amount of faith, but rather the correct Object of Faith; the correct Object is the Cross [I Cor. 1:18]),* **you might say unto this sycamine tree, Be thou plucked up by the root, and be thou planted in the sea; and it should obey you** *(the removal of trees and mountains were proverbial figures of speech among the Jews at that time, expressing the overcoming of great difficulties)*" **(Lk. 17:5-6).**

The Lord was telling His Disciples and us, as well, that it's not the quantity of Faith that one has, but rather, the quality of Faith that one has. Quality has to do with the correct Object which, at all times, must be the Cross of Christ.

HOW DOES ONE ACQUIRE FAITH?

Concerning this question the Scripture says:

"**So then Faith** *comes* **by hearing** *(it is the publication of the Gospel, which produces Faith in it),* **and hearing by the Word of God** *(Faith does not come simply by hearing just anything, but rather by hearing God's Word, and believing that Word)*" **(Rom. 10:17).**

Every answer as it pertains to God and His Ways, which includes Faith, is found in the Word of God. In fact, it is impossible for a person to have proper faith outside of the Word of God. That's the reason the Scripture also says:

"**If we believe not** *(believe what He did at the Cross),* *yet* **He abides Faithful** *(despite the unbelief of many, He will be Faithful to Redeem all who come to Him in Faith):* **He cannot deny Himself.** *(Heaven will never change the*

Plan of Redemption and Victory, which is the Cross.)

"**Of these things put *them* in remembrance** *(has special reference to the issues of life and death set out in the previous three Verses)*, **charging *them* before the Lord that they strive not about words to no profit** *(if the Cross is abandoned, 'Christ shall profit you nothing' [Gal. 5:2])*, ***but* to the subverting of the hearers** *(refers to overthrowing their Faith).*"

STUDY TO SHOW YOURSELF APPROVED

"**Study to show yourself approved unto God** *(refers to a workman who has been put to the test and, meeting these specifications, has won the approval of the one who has subjected him to the test)*, **a workman who needs not to be ashamed** *(Faith placed exclusively in the Cross will never bring shame; faith placed elsewhere will, without fail, bring shame)*, **rightly dividing the Word of Truth.** *(If one doesn't properly understand the Cross, one cannot rightly divide the Word of Truth.)*"

SHUN PROFANE AND VAIN BABBLINGS

"**But shun profane *and* vain babblings** *(this means no false doctrine leaves its victims as they were found, but rather worse, much worse!)*: **for they will increase unto more ungodliness.** *(If the preacher is teaching anything other than the Cross of Christ, it is construed by the Holy Spirit as no more than 'vain babblings,' and is guaranteed to increase ungodliness more and more. In fact, it cannot be any other way!)*" **(II Tim. 2:13-16).**

THE RIGHT KIND OF STUDY BIBLE

If you are to truly have the Word of God, you must have a translation, such as the King James, which is a word-for-word translation. This means that the scholars, when it was translated from the Hebrew (Old Testament) and the Greek (New Testament), did their very best to bring the exact meaning that was given in the original Text over into the translation. Those who have the thought for thought translations, to be frank, have no Bible at all.

All of our quotes in this Volume come from THE EXPOSITOR'S STUDY BIBLE. It is, we think, the very finest Study Bible, to help one more perfectly understand the Word of God, in the world today. If you don't have a copy, I would strongly advise you to get a copy. If you do, you know what I'm talking about, and you should make every effort to place a copy into the hands of your friends and loved ones. It would be the greatest favor you ever did for them. Anything that will help one understand the Word of God to a greater degree is worth its weight, proverbially speaking, in pure gold.

The Bible is the Word of God and, in fact, the only Word of God in the world. Because it is the Word of God, it must be studied, and studied constantly. In fact, every Believer should read the Bible completely through at least once every year. As you begin to study its contents, you will find that it is inexhaustible. In other words, no matter how much we may learn its contents, there is still much more to be learned.

A PERSONAL EXAMPLE

Some years ago, the Lord gave me some special instructions regarding His Word that proved to be very valuable to my heart and life. It was very simple, yet, very meaningful.

At that particular time, the Ministry, it seemed, was suffering every attack that Satan could muster our way. The problems seemed to be without end, with no way to be solved.

Every morning I would go out in front of the house where we have a circular drive and walk on that drive and pray. I had done that for years, and that particular morning was no exception.

THE HEAVENS SEEMED TO BE BRASS

I tried to pray, but, all to no avail! I couldn't keep my mind on what I was saying, with my thoughts constantly going to one problem after the other, wondering how in the world they could be solved. I finally gave up and went back in the house. Also, as my custom always was, after prayer, I would study the Word for a period of time. Actually, most of the time, I spent time in the Word before going to prayer. However, that morning, for some particular reason, I went to prayer first. I suppose, if I remember correctly, the problems were so overwhelming that I felt I had to talk to the Lord about them; however, as stated, I couldn't pray.

In my study of the Word of God, I have always read the Bible straight through. In other words, I begin with Genesis and go all the way through to Revelation. I would read the Bible completely through several times a year. Actually, I have read it completely through over fifty times.

I sat down on the couch and opened my Bible to the place I had finished the day before. In my study the day before, I had finished the Book of Ecclesiastes. I would now begin with the *"Song of Solomon."*

To be frank, as my eyes fell on the first page of this great Book, my first thoughts were, *"I wish my study was somewhere else in the Word. I would much rather be in I Samuel to study about David, or the Psalms, or the Gospels, or the Book of Acts,"* etc. In my state of mind, I felt that would be much more encouraging.

Nevertheless, as I began to read, I quickly came to the Third Verse. It said:

"Because of the savour of Your good ointments Your Name is as ointment poured forth, therefore do the virgins love you" (Song of Sol. 1:3).

YOUR NAME IS AS OINTMENT POURED FORTH

As I read that short phrase, *"Your Name is as ointment*

poured forth," all of a sudden, the Spirit of God settled upon me. Whatever it was that Solomon meant when he wrote these words, I now knew that it actually referred to the Lord Jesus Christ.

I sat there for a few moments with tears rolling down my face and the Presence of God all over me. I learned that morning that:

• Every statement in the Word of God holds a great meaning for us. If we don't see it, it's just because of a lack of understanding. To be sure, that great meaning is there, and it is for us personally.

• I learned that His Name is a medicine for us and is equal to any task.

That morning, the Lord poured His Love like ointment over me, with it covering me, proverbially speaking, from head to toe.

Whenever I arose to go to the office that morning, I was a different person than I was when I began that morning. Yes, the problems were still there. Not a one had gone away; however, with the Presence of the Lord having filled my heart, I knew that He was telling me that whatever those problems were, He was equal to the task. Not only did He do that for me, proclaim His Power to help, to Save, and to deliver, but, as well, it was like He poured medicine, a soothing balm, all over my mind and my spirit. I learned, as stated, *"Your Name is as ointment poured forth."*

If one wants to use such a term, this is the Lord's psychiatry. This is His therapy, and what a therapy it is. The little chorus says:

"His Name is as Ointment poured forth,
"Jesus, Jesus, Jesus, Jesus,
"His Name is as Ointment poured forth,
"His Name is as Ointment poured forth."

The more that one knows the Word, studies the Word, and understands the Word, the more that Faith will be developed in one's life.

THE CORRECT OBJECT OF FAITH

The only Faith that God will actually recognize is Faith in Christ and what He did for us at the Cross. That and that alone is true Faith simply because the meaning of the Cross is, in effect, the meaning of the New Covenant. It is that to which all the Prophets of old pointed, and it is that to which all the Apostles point as well. The Cross of Christ must be the Object of our Faith.

In the last two Chapters of the Book of Revelation, the Holy Spirit opens up to us the perfect world that is to come, which will be a world without end. In fact, God will literally change His Headquarters from Planet Heaven, so to speak, to Planet Earth. That great city referred to as the New Jerusalem will be 1,500 miles wide, 1,500 miles long, and then, believe it or not, 1,500 miles high (Rev. 21:16).

In other words, if you put the southeast corner of this city in Dallas, Texas, the southwest corner in Los Angeles, California, with the northwest corner in Vancouver, British Colombia, Canada, and the northeast corner in Minneapolis, Minnesota, that would be the footprint of this city. And then, when you consider, as stated, that it is 1,500 miles high, that completely goes beyond our powers of comprehension.

But, the point of this is, the last two Chapters of Revelation picture, as stated, the Perfect Age to come. It will be an Age without sin, without Satan, without demon spirits, and without transgression of any nature. As a result, this perfect world to come will be absolutely beyond our comprehension. Yet, in these final two Chapters, the Holy Spirit through John the Beloved, as he wrote the Text, had him to use the word *"Lamb"* some seven times as it refers to our Lord (Rev. 21:9, 14, 22-23, 27; 22:1, 3).

Why did the Holy Spirit choose to use the appellative *"Lamb"*?

The title *"Lamb,"* as it refers to Christ, speaks of the Cross and what He there did. As well, the number *"seven"* speaks of completion, totality, universality, and perfection. It is God's number.

Considering that there is no more sin, no more Satan, no more iniquity, and no more transgression, why would the Holy Spirit use the name *"Lamb"* seven times?

I'm sure that the Holy Spirit had reasons beyond our capabilities of understanding; however, I personally feel that the real reason the word or name *"Lamb"* is used at that time, and done so seven times, is to let us know, and forever, that all of this grandeur, all of this glory, and God with us, are all made possible by what Jesus did for us at the Cross. This must never be forgotten! It is the Cross! The Cross! The Cross!

THE CROSS OF CHRIST ALONE
STOPS THE WRATH OF GOD

Paul said:

"**For the Wrath of God** *(God's Personal Emotion with regard to sin)* **is revealed from Heaven** *(this anger originates with God)* **against all ungodliness and unrighteousness of men** *(God must unalterably be opposed to sin)*, **who hold the truth in unrighteousness** *(who refuse to recognize Who God is, and What God is)*" **(Rom. 1:18).**

WHY IS GOD SO OPPOSED TO SIN?

Sin is more than a mere act. In all its forms, it carries with it the seed of death. That's the reason the Scripture says:

"**For the wages of sin** *is* **death** *(speaks of spiritual death, which is separation from God)*; **but the Gift of God** *is* **Eternal Life through Jesus Christ our Lord** *(as stated, all of this, without exception, comes to us by the Means of what Christ did at the Cross, which demands that the*

Cross ever be the Object of our Faith, thus giving the Holy Spirit latitude to work within our lives and bring forth His Fruit)" **(Rom. 6:23).**

This not only means physical death, but it speaks of death in all its forms. Sin, by the means of death, is the cause of all pain, all suffering, all war, all evil, and all of man's inhumanity to man. It's all because of sin, which is characterized by death. At this very moment, millions of marriages are dying. At this moment, millions of human beings are dying before their time, and all because of sin. At this moment, sickness ravages billions of human bodies, and all because of sin. It places the mark of death on everything it touches. And, it doesn't matter how strong, how rich, or how powerful the thing may be; when sin begins to take its toll, death is always the result.

Understanding that, we know, as stated, why God has to be, must be, unalterably opposed to sin in any and every form. It is the blight of Planet Earth, the blight of His most choice Creation, man, and, in fact, the blight of the Universe. He cannot condone it in any fashion, cannot tolerate it in any fashion, and the only thing that stands between Him pouring out His Wrath upon the whole of the human race is the Cross of Christ. If, in fact, that is true, and it most definitely is, then we should start to realize just how significant is that which Jesus did in the giving of Himself as a Sacrifice on the Cross of Calvary. We must remember that the Crucifixion of Christ is an event which took place in a period of time that is past, but has continuing results, in fact, results which will never be discontinued. That's why Paul referred to it as *"The Everlasting Covenant"* **(Heb. 13:20).**

Understanding this, it should become overly obvious to us as to the reason the Cross of Christ must ever be the Object of our Faith.

ANOTHER JESUS

If the Cross of Christ is somehow divorced from our Lord,

meaning that the Cross of Christ is little looked at as the Means of all that we receive from the Lord, such a direction could be constituted as *"another Jesus,"* fostered by *"another spirit,"* which presents *"another gospel,"* which is, as Paul also said, no Gospel at all (Gal. 1:6-7).

Concerning this very thing, and we continue to speak of *"another Jesus,"* Paul said:

GODLY JEALOUSY

"Would to God you could bear with me a little in *my* folly: and indeed bear with me. *(In effect, the Apostle is saying, 'Indulge me.')*

"For I am jealous over you with Godly jealousy *(refers to the 'jealousy of God' [Ex. 20:5; 34:14; Nah. 1:2])*: for I have espoused you to one husband *(not jealous of the Corinthians' affection for himself, but of their affection for Christ)*, that I may present *you as* a chaste virgin to Christ. *(They must not commit spiritual adultery, which refers to trusting in things other than Christ and the Cross.)*"

THE SIMPLICITY OF CHRIST

"But I fear, lest by any means, as the serpent beguiled Eve through his subtilty *(the strategy of Satan)*, so your minds should be corrupted from the simplicity that is in Christ. *(The Gospel of Christ is simple, but men complicate it by adding to the Message.)*"

ANOTHER JESUS, ANOTHER SPIRIT, ANOTHER GOSPEL

"For if he who comes preaching another Jesus *(a Jesus who is not of the Cross)*, whom we have not preached *(Paul's Message was 'Jesus Christ and Him Crucified';*

anything else is 'another Jesus'), **or** *if* **you receive another spirit** *(which is produced by preaching another Jesus),* **which you have not received** *(that's not what you received when we preached the True Gospel to you),* **or another gospel, which you have not accepted** *(anything other than 'Jesus Christ and Him Crucified' is 'another gospel'),* **you might well bear with** *him. (The Apostle is telling the Corinthians that they have, in fact, sinned because they tolerated these false apostles who had come in, bringing 'another gospel' which was something other than Christ and the Cross)"* **(II Cor. 11:1-4).**

Unfortunately, *"another Jesus"* is basically what the modern church is now presenting to the world. It's Jesus the example, Jesus the Miracle Worker, Jesus the motivator, Jesus the financier, Jesus the doctor, Jesus the therapist, Jesus the psychologist, etc. While, in a sense, Christ may most definitely be all of these things and much, much more, the Jesus the world needs, and desperately, is Jesus the Saviour, which He is and can be only by the Means of the Cross. So, if our message is *"another Jesus,"* that which man desperately needs, he cannot receive.

A GOOD FIGHT

While it is a fight, and of that there is no doubt, still, it is a good fight because it's the right fight. It's the *"good fight of Faith."*

As we have already stated, the individual is sorely mistaken if he thinks that upon understanding the Message of the Cross, and understanding it correctly, this will end all opposition by Satan. Nothing could be further from the truth.

Every attack by Satan, and irrespective as to what form it takes, whether physical, financial, domestical, or spiritual, is for but one purpose, and that is to destroy our Faith, or else, seriously weaken it. Satan wants you to quit, in other words, to throw over the Message of the Cross, and if he can't do that, he wants the Message weakened, and he does that by adding certain things, whatever they might be, to the Cross.

THE WEAPONS OF OUR WARFARE

We must never forget this conflict in which we are engaged is *"war."* And, I mean all out war until Satan has no hold at all in our life or living.

Those who are truly doing Satan harm, and to be sure, those who have their Faith exclusively in Christ and the Cross most definitely are doing Satan harm, are the ones he is going to contest with every fiber of his power. I related to our people at FAMILY WORSHIP CENTER one Sunday morning a few weeks ago that if they embrace the Message of the Cross, thereby, aligning themselves with this Church, they can expect, to be blunt, all Hell to break loose. I realize that's not very good public relations, but it is the truth. I went on to tell them that they would face opposition like they've never faced it before, with even their own families possibly turning against them.

But, then I went on to tell them, and I'm telling you, as well, while you will suffer opposition from the Evil One, and severely so, the truth is, you are going to cause him tremendous damage by seeing souls Saved, lives changed, Believers baptized with the Holy Spirit, sick bodies healed, and people delivered from the bondages of darkness, all by the Power of God. So, inasmuch as you are now a tremendous threat to Satan, expect the worst, but, as well, expect Victory, and a Victory like you have never known before.

Concerning this warfare, Paul said:

THIS IS WAR

"For though we walk in the flesh *(refers to the fact that we do not yet have Glorified Bodies)*, we do not war after the flesh *(after our own ability, but rather by the*

Power of the Spirit):
"(For the weapons of our warfare *are* not carnal *[carnal weapons consist of those which are man-devised]*, but mighty through God *[the Cross of Christ (I Cor. 1:18)]* to the pulling down of strongholds;)"

THE OBEDIENCE OF CHRIST

"Casting down imaginations *(philosophic strongholds; every effort man makes outside of the Cross of Christ)*, and every high thing that exalts itself against the Knowledge of God *(all the pride of the human heart)*, and bringing into captivity every thought to the obedience of Christ *(can be done only by the Believer looking exclusively to the Cross, where all Victory is found; the Holy Spirit will then perform the task, whatever it might be)*" **(II Cor. 10:3-5).**

"Send forth the Gospel! Let it run,
"Southward, northward, east and west;
"Tell all the Earth Christ died and lives,
"Who gives pardon, life, and rest."

"Send forth Your Gospel, Mighty Lord!
"Out of this chaos bring to birth,
"Your Own Creation's promised hope;
"The better days of Heaven on Earth."

"Send forth Your Gospel, Gracious Lord!
"Thine was the Blood for sinners shed;
"Your Voice still pleads in human hearts;
"To You Your other Sheep be led."

"Send forth Your Gospel, Holy Lord!
"Kindle in us love's sacred flame;
"Love giving all, and grudging naught,

"For Jesus' Sake in Jesus' Name."

"Send forth the Gospel! Tell it out!
"Go, Brothers, at the Master's Call;
"Prepare His Way, Who comes to reign,
"The King of kings, and Lord of all."

CHAPTER ELEVEN

Various Laws

VARIOUS LAWS

In the last few Verses of Romans 7, the Holy Spirit through Paul listed some three Laws. In the second Verse of Chapter 8, He listed another Law, making a total of four.

These are all Laws devised by the Godhead in eternity past and, to be sure, these *"Laws"* will function exactly as they were designed. They are:

1. The Law of God: (Rom. 7:22, 25).
2. The Law of the Mind: (Rom. 7:23).
3. The Law of Sin and Death: (Rom. 7:23, 25; 8:2).
4. The Law of the Spirit of Life in Christ Jesus: (Rom. 8:2).

Let's look at these Laws one by one.

THE LAW OF GOD

The Law of God is the Ten Commandments, the moral part of the Law of Moses. While Jesus fulfilled all Law in His Life and Living, and especially in His Death and Resurrection, the moral Law, as should be obvious, is still incumbent upon all Believers and, in fact, every human being in the world, Believers or not. Moral Law cannot change. It is objective, meaning that what it was three thousand years ago, it is the same presently.

HOW SHOULD CHRISTIANS ADDRESS THEMSELVES TO THE MORAL LAW OF GOD?

We should have an understanding, and if we are truly Born-Again, most definitely will have an understanding, that the Ten Commandments, the moral Law of God, is to be kept. Keeping it is not the question; how it is done is the great question.

Considering that the notes in THE EXPOSITOR'S STUDY BIBLE shed some light on these particular Laws, even though it's quite voluminous, I think it would be proper for us to copy it directly from THE EXPOSITOR'S STUDY BIBLE. These Laws are:

ONE
"YOU SHALL HAVE NO OTHER GODS BEFORE ME"

"You shall have no other gods before Me *(the manner in which this First Commandment is given indicates that each individual of the nation is addressed severally, and is required personally to obey the Law, a mere general national obedience being insufficient; this Commandment requires the worship of one God Alone, Jehovah; it implies, in point of fact, that there is no other God)."*

TWO
"YOU SHALL NOT MAKE UNTO YOURSELF ANY GRAVEN IMAGE"

"You shall not make unto yourself any graven image, or any likeness of anything that is in heaven above, or that is in the Earth beneath, or that is in the water under the Earth.

"You shall not bow down yourself to them, nor serve them: for I the LORD your God am a jealous God, visiting the iniquity of the fathers upon the children unto the third and fourth generation of them who hate Me;

"And showing mercy unto thousands of them who love Me, and keep My Commandments. *(The prohibition intended here does not forbid the arts of sculpture, painting, photography, etc., or even to condemn the use of them, but to disallow the worship of God under material forms. Those who ignore this Commandment are guilty of the sin of idolatry. Also, many have tried to derive from Verse 5 that which they refer to as the 'family curse'; however, let it be known and understood, every curse was addressed at the Cross of Calvary [Gal. 3:13-14]. As well, Jesus has perfectly kept all the Commandments, and all who trust Him, and what He did for us at the Cross, are participants of God's Gracious Mercy.)"*

THREE
"YOU SHALL NOT TAKE THE NAME OF THE LORD YOUR GOD IN VAIN"

"You shall not take the Name of the Lord your God in vain; for the LORD will not hold him guiltless who takes His Name in vain *(taking the Name of the Lord in vain pertains to all blasphemy, all swearing, all perjury and, in fact, all irreverent use of God's Name in ordinary life)."*

FOUR
"REMEMBER THE SABBATH DAY, TO KEEP IT HOLY"

"Remember the Sabbath Day, to keep it holy.

"Six days you shall labor, and do all your work:

"But the seventh day is the Sabbath of the LORD your God: in it you shall not do any work, you, nor your son, nor your daughter, your manservant, nor your maidservant, nor your cattle, nor your stranger that is within your gates:

"For in six days the LORD made Heaven and Earth, the sea, and all that in them is, and rested the seventh day: wherefore the LORD blessed the Sabbath Day, and hallowed it. *(The seventh day was not so much to be a day of worship, as we think of such now, but rather a day of 'rest.' Even the very beasts, pressed into man's service since the Fall, shall rest. All were to observe this day. Everything pertaining to the Law of Moses, in some way, spoke of Christ. The 'Sabbath' was no exception. It was meant to portray the fact that there is 'rest' in Christ and, in fact, that there is rest 'only in Christ' [Mat. 11:28-30]. So, when a person presently accepts Christ, they are, in effect, keeping the Sabbath, which speaks of the 'rest' that we have in Christ — rest from self-effort to attain unto Righteousness. Even though there was no written command by the Holy Spirit to do so, gradually we find Believers, during the time of the Early Church, as recorded in the Book of Acts, making Sunday, the first day of the week, the day of our Lord's Resurrection, their day of worship, etc., which is different than the Sabbath of old, because Christ has fulfilled in totality the old Jewish Sabbath.)*"

FIVE
"HONOR YOUR FATHER AND YOUR MOTHER"

"Honor your father and your mother: that your days may be long upon the land which the LORD your God gives you *(honoring the father and the mother sets the stage for the honoring of God; the first five Commandments have to do with man's obligation toward God, while the last five have to do with his obligation toward his fellowman)***."**

SIX
"YOU SHALL NOT KILL"

"You shall not kill *(should have been translated, 'Thou shalt do no murder'; God, in His Holy Word, commands magistrates to put evil men to death [Rom. 13:4]; that is not murder; to 'kill' and to 'commit murder' are two different verbs in the Hebrew Text)***."**

SEVEN
"YOU SHALL NOT COMMIT ADULTERY"

"You shall not commit adultery *(regarding this sin, both man and woman are placed in the same category; our duty toward our neighbor is to respect the bond on which the family is based, and that conjugal honor which to the true man is dearer than life; marriage, according to the original institution, makes the husband and wife 'one flesh' [Gen. 2:24]; and to break in upon this sacramental union was at once a crime and a profanity; it is a sin against man* *and against God)."*

EIGHT
"YOU SHALL NOT STEAL"

"You shall not steal *(as it regards our neighbor, we are to respect his property; we simply don't take that which doesn't belong to us)."*

NINE
"YOU SHALL NOT BEAR FALSE WITNESS AGAINST YOUR NEIGHBOUR"

"You shall not bear false witness against your neighbour *(false witness is of two kinds, public and private; we may either seek to damage our neighbor by giving false evidence against him in a court of justice, or simply culminate him to others in our social intercourse with them)."*

TEN
"YOU SHALL NOT COVET"

"You shall not covet your neighbour's house, you shall not covet your neighbour's wife, nor his manservant, nor his maidservant, nor his ox, nor his ass, nor anything that is your neighbour's *(covetousness addresses what causes the evil deed; this Commandment teaches men that there is One Who sees the heart; to Whose Eyes 'all things are naked and open'; and Who cares far less for the outward act than the inward thought or motive from which the act proceeds)"* **(Ex. 20:3-17).**

NOW THE QUESTION: HOW DO MODERN CHRISTIANS KEEP THE COMMANDMENTS?

We, as Believers, are to place our Faith exclusively in Christ

and the Cross, which then gives the Holy Spirit latitude to work within our lives, and then the Commandments will be kept without us even thinking about them. If we set out to try to live for God by the means of Commandments, i.e., *"trying to keep Commandments,"* we will fail every time. Jesus has already kept every Commandment for us. He did it as our Representative Man, and He did so in thought, word, and deed. As stated, He did it all for us. Please know and understand that we have broken the Commandments, which are incumbent upon every human being, and the sentence for such is death, which means separation from God forever and forever, and the destination is the Lake of Fire. But at the Cross, Christ paid the price for our Redemption, satisfied the claims of heavenly Justice, which had demands on all of us, and did so by the giving of Himself as a Perfect Sacrifice. As such, upon simple Faith in Him and what He did at the Cross, the slate is wiped clean, and we can then say that we are no longer wanted by the Law. However, this freedom from the curse of the Law cannot come except by one way, and that is by simple Faith in Christ and His Atoning Work at the Cross of Calvary. Concerning this, Paul wrote:

CHRIST IS THE HEAD

"**And you are complete in Him** *(the satisfaction of every spiritual want is found in Christ, made possible by the Cross)*, **which is the Head of all principality and power** *(His Headship extends not only over the Church, which voluntarily serves Him, but over all forces that are opposed to Him as well [Phil. 2:10-11])*.

"**In Whom also you are circumcised with the Circumcision made without hands** *(that which is brought about by the Cross [Rom. 6:3-5])*, **in putting off the body of the sins of the flesh by the Circumcision of Christ** *(refers to the old carnal nature that is defeated by the Believer placing his Faith totally in the Cross, which gives the Holy Spirit latitude to work)*:"

BURIED WITH HIM

"**Buried with Him in Baptism** *(does not refer to Water Baptism, but rather to the Believer baptized into the Death of Christ, which refers to the Crucifixion and Christ as our Substitute [Rom. 6:3-4]),*"

RISEN WITH HIM

"**Wherein also you are risen with *Him* through the Faith of the operation of God, Who has raised Him from the dead.** *(This does not refer to our future physical Resurrection, but to that Spiritual Resurrection from a sinful state into Divine Life. We died with Him, we are buried with Him, and we rose with Him [Rom. 6:3-5], and herein lies the secret to all Spiritual Victory.)*"

FORGIVEN ALL TRESPASSES

"**And you, being dead in your sins and the uncircumcision of your flesh** *(speaks of spiritual Death [i.e., 'separation from God'], which sin does!)*, **has He quickened together with Him** *(refers to being made spiritually alive, which is done through being 'Born-Again')*, **having forgiven you all trespasses** *(the Cross made it possible for all manner of sins to be forgiven and taken away)*;"

REMOVED THE PENALTY OF THE LAW

"**Blotting out the handwriting of Ordinances that was against us** *(pertains to the Law of Moses, which was God's Standard of Righteousness that man could not reach)*, **which was contrary to us** *(Law is against us, simply because we are unable to keep its precepts, no matter how hard we try)*, **and took it out of the way** *(refers to the penalty of the Law being removed)*, **nailing it to His Cross** *(the Law with its decrees was abolished in Christ's Death, as if Crucified with Him);"*

THE GREAT TRIUMPH

"*And* having spoiled principalities and powers *(Satan and all of his henchmen were defeated at the Cross by Christ atoning for all sin; sin was the legal right Satan had to hold man in captivity; with all sin atoned, he has no more legal right to hold anyone in bondage)*, He *(Christ)* made a show of them openly *(what Jesus did at the Cross was in the face of the whole Universe)*, triumphing over them in it. *(The triumph is complete and it was all done for us, meaning we can walk in power and perpetual Victory due to the Cross.)*"

NO MORE LAW

"Let no man therefore judge you in meat, or in drink, or in respect of an holyday, or of the new moon, or of the Sabbath *Days (the moment we add any rule or regulation to the Finished Work of Christ, we have just abrogated the Grace of God)*:

"Which are a shadow of things to come; *(the Law, with all of its observances, was only meant to point to the One Who was to come, Namely Christ)*; but the Body *(Church)* is of Christ *(refers to 'substance and reality,' as opposed to shadow)*" (Col. 2:10-17).

Paul had much to say regarding Christians embracing law, and I speak of religious law of any kind. Please note the following:

CHRIST SHALL PROFIT YOU NOTHING

"Stand fast therefore in the liberty wherewith Christ

has made us free *(we were made free, and refers to freedom to live a Holy life by evidencing Faith in Christ and the Cross)*, and be not entangled again with the yoke of bondage. *(To abandon the Cross and go under law of any kind guarantees bondage once again to the sin nature.)*

"Behold *('mark my words!')*, I Paul say unto you *(presents the Apostle's authority regarding the Message he brings)*, that if you be circumcised, Christ shall profit you nothing. *(If the Believer goes back into law, and law of any kind, what Christ did at the Cross on our behalf will profit us nothing. One cannot have it two ways.)*"

A DEBTOR TO THE LAW

"For I testify again to every man who is circumcised *(some of the Galatian Gentiles were being pressured by false teachers to embrace the Law of Moses, which meant they would have to forsake Christ and the Cross, for it's not possible to wed the two; as well, it's not possible to wed any law to Grace)*, that he is a debtor to do the whole Law *(which, of course, is impossible; and besides, the Law contained no Salvation)*."

FALLEN FROM GRACE?

"Christ is become of no effect unto you *(this is a chilling statement, and refers to anyone who makes anything other than Christ and the Cross the Object of his Faith)*, whosoever of you are justified by the Law *(seek to be Justified by the Law)*; you are fallen from Grace *(fallen from the position of Grace, which means the Believer is trusting in something other than the Cross; it actually means, 'to apostatize')*."

THROUGH THE HOLY SPIRIT

"For we through the Spirit *(the Holy Spirit works*

exclusively within the parameters of the Sacrifice of Christ; consequently, He demands that we place our Faith exclusively in the Cross of Christ) **wait for the Hope of Righteousness** *(which cannot come about until the Resurrection)* **by Faith** *(refers to Faith in Christ and what He did for us at the Cross).*

"For in Jesus Christ neither Circumcision avails anything, nor uncircumcision *(has no spiritual bearing on anything)*; **but Faith which works by Love.** *(The evidence of true Faith is the fact of the Love which emanates from such Faith)*" **(Gal. 5:1-6).**

EVERY CHRISTIAN IN THE WORLD IS UNDER GRACE OR LAW

There is no other place to be; it is either one or the other. Paul also said:

"For sin shall not have dominion over you *(the sin nature will not have dominion over us if we as Believers continue to exercise Faith in the Cross of Christ; otherwise, the sin nature most definitely will have dominion over the Believer)*: **for you are not under the Law** *(means that if we try to live this life by any type of law, no matter how good that law might be in its own right, we will conclude by the sin nature having dominion over us)*, **but under Grace** *(the Grace of God flows to the Believer on an unending basis only as long as the Believer exercises Faith in Christ and what He did at the Cross; Grace is merely the Goodness of God exercised by and through the Holy Spirit, and given to undeserving Saints)*" **(Rom. 6:14).**

Any and every Believer who does not have his Faith exclusively in Christ and the Cross, which constitutes living under Grace, is going to be under Law, whether he understands that or not. Such a position guarantees failure, in other words, guarantees that the Commandments will not be kept. They can be kept by understanding that Jesus has already kept them on our behalf, and our Faith in Him and His Work on Calvary gives the Holy Spirit the wherewithal to work within our lives, Who, in essence, keeps the Commandments for us. In other words we keep them without even thinking about them because it's all in Christ.

THE LAW OF THE MIND

What did the Holy Spirit mean when He spoke through Paul regarding *"the Law of the Mind?"*

When anyone comes to Christ, the Holy Spirit through the great Apostle said:

"... *he is* a new creature *(a new creation)*: old things are passed away *(what we were before Salvation)*; behold, all things are become new. *(The old is no longer useable, with everything given to us now by Christ as 'new.')*

"And all things *are* of God *(all these new things)*, Who has reconciled us to Himself by Jesus Christ *(which He was able to do as a result of the Cross)*, and has given to us the Ministry of Reconciliation *(pertains to announcing to men the nature and conditions of this Plan of being reconciled, which is summed up in the 'preaching of the Cross' [I Cor. 1:21, 23])*" **(II Cor. 5:17-18).**

Then the great Apostle said:

A LIVING SACRIFICE

"I beseech you therefore, Brethren *(I beg of you please)*, by the Mercies of God *(all is given to the Believer, not because of merit on the Believer's part, but strictly because of the 'Mercy of God')*, that you present your bodies a Living Sacrifice *(the word 'Sacrifice' speaks of the Sacrifice of Christ, and means that we cannot do this which the Holy Spirit demands unless our Faith is placed strictly in Christ and the Cross, which then gives the Holy Spirit latitude to carry out this great work within our lives)*, **holy** *(that which the Holy Spirit Alone can do)*, **acceptable unto God** *(actually means that a holy physical body, i.e., 'temple,' is all that He will accept)*, **which is your reasonable service.** *(Reasonable if we look to Christ and the Cross; otherwise impossible!)*."

THE RENEWING OF YOUR MIND

"**And be not conformed to this world** *(the ways of the world)*: **but be you transformed by the renewing of your mind** *(we must start thinking Spiritually, which refers to the fact that everything is furnished to us through the Cross, and is obtained by Faith and not works)*, **that you may prove what** *is* **that good** *(is put to the test and finds that the thing tested meets the specifications laid down)*, **and acceptable, and perfect, Will of God** *(presents that which the Holy Spirit is attempting to bring about within our lives, and can only be obtained by ever making the Cross the Object of our Faith)*" **(Rom. 12:1-2).**

CHANGE

When a person comes to Christ, everything changes. That's what we've tried to establish by giving the Scriptures just quoted. The things we once hated (the Ways of the Lord), we now love. The things we once loved (sin), we now hate! Now the Divine Nature rules us, or, at least, it is supposed to. The *"Law of the Mind"* upon conversion wants to please God, wants to obey the Lord, wants to do what is required of him, etc. However, as noble as this is, the *"Law of the Mind,"* although renewed, is no match for *"the Law of Sin and Death."* Regrettably, most modern Believers are trying to live for God merely by the *"Law of the Mind."* In other words, they want to do right, they desire to do right, they are struggling to do right, but they find themselves unable to do so. In other words, those who try to live for the Lord by the means of the *"Law of the Mind"* are trying to do so by the means of willpower. While willpower is important, it within itself is not enough to do what needs to be done. This is what frustrated the Apostle Paul.

He found that he wanted to live for God and wanted to do things right, but found that he couldn't, no matter how hard he tried. Let us say it again:

While the Law of the Mind is very much essential to the Child of God and, of course, will become a part of our nature once we accept Christ, still, if we try to live for God by the means of the *"Law of the Mind"* alone, which most modern Believers are attempting to do, we will fail, as fail we must!

That's why the great Apostle said in Romans 7:25 that with his mind he desired to live for God, be what God wanted him to be, and to obey the Lord in every respect, but found that his *"flesh"* wanted something else, with the *"Law of Sin and Death"* overriding the *"Law of the Mind."* That is what is happening millions of times each day all over the world with Christians. As we've already discussed in this Volume, millions are struggling, trying to live for God, and despite all they can do, are failing, and they don't understand why they are failing (Rom. 7:15).

"THE LAW OF SIN AND DEATH"

This Law devised by the Godhead in eternity past is the second most powerful Law in the Universe, the most powerful being *"the Law of the Spirit of Life in Christ Jesus."* This *"Law of Sin and Death"* has soaked the earth with blood, filled it with graves, brought about enough sorrow and heartache for ten eternities, and is so powerful that it can only be defeated in one way, and that is, as stated, by *"the Law of the Spirit of Life in Christ Jesus."* But, most Believers, to whom we have already addressed ourselves, are trying to live for God, trying to overcome this *"Law of Sin and Death,"* by the *"Law of the Mind,"* and they find every time that they are unable to do so.

When the person comes to Christ, as Paul found out, the *"Law of Sin and Death"* is not quarantined. It roams free! If the Believer doesn't understand how to overcome this Law — the *"Law of Sin and Death"* — he will find this Law overcoming him every single time, which makes for less than a satisfactory life in Christ. Yet, by not understanding the Cross of Christ as it refers to our life and living, our Sanctification, most Believers are controlled by the Law of Sin and Death exactly as Paul was before the Lord gave him the meaning of the New Covenant, which he has given to us.

"THE LAW OF SIN AND DEATH" AND HUMANISTIC PSYCHOLOGY

Trying to overcome the world of spiritual darkness, i.e., the *"Law of Sin and Death,"* by means of humanistic psychology is about the same as trying to stop a Louisiana hurricane with a palm branch, but that's where the modern church finds itself. It has embraced humanistic psychology in totality. And, please allow the following to be stated:

Either one, humanistic psychology or the Way of the Lord, which is the Cross of Christ, cancels out the other. In other words, one cannot have both. Jesus said:

"No man can serve two masters: for either he will hate the one, and love the other; or else he will hold to the one, and despise the other. You cannot serve God and mammon *(this is flat out, stated as, an impossibility; it is total devotion to God, or ultimately it will be total devotion to the world; the word, 'mammon' is derived from the Babylonian 'Mimma,' which means 'anything at all')"* (Mat. 6:24).

This Passage not only covers humanistic psychology but

every other way devised by man in order for us to live the life
we ought to live. It is God's Way, which is the Cross of Christ,
or it is no way. What is God's Way?

"THE LAW OF THE SPIRIT OF LIFE IN CHRIST JESUS"

Even though we have already given the following Scripture and comments in this Volume, still, due to the extreme
significance of this particular subject, please bear with the
repetition.

Paul now gives us the answer to *"the Law of Sin and Death."*
It is *"the Law of the Spirit of Life in Christ Jesus."* He said:

"For the Law *(that which we are about to give is a
Law of God, devised by the Godhead in eternity past
[I Pet. 1:18-20]; this Law, in fact, is 'God's Prescribed
Order of Victory')* **of the Spirit** *(Holy Spirit, i.e., 'the way
the Spirit works')* **of Life** *(all life comes from Christ, but
through the Holy Spirit [Jn. 16:13-14])* **in Christ Jesus**
*(anytime Paul uses this term or one of its derivatives, he
is, without fail, referring to what Christ did at the Cross,
which makes this 'life' possible)* **has made me free** *(given
me total Victory)* **from the Law of Sin and Death** *(these
are the two most powerful Laws in the Universe; the 'Law
of the Spirit of Life in Christ Jesus' alone is stronger than
the 'Law of Sin and Death'; this means that if the Believer
attempts to live for God by any manner other than Faith in
Christ and the Cross, he is doomed to failure)"* **(Rom. 8:2).**

IN CHRIST JESUS

As we said in the notes above, any time and every time that
Paul uses the term *"in Christ Jesus,"* or one of its derivatives
such as, *"in Him,"* or *"in Whom,"* or *"in Christ,"* etc., without
fail, he is speaking of what Christ did at the Cross on behalf of
lost humanity. The key with Paul was the Cross, and the key

with us had better be the Cross.

THE THEOLOGY OF THE CROSS

The Cross of Christ is the central theme of the Gospel. If one removes the Cross, Christianity is nothing more than a vapid, empty philosophy. While everything Christ did was of utmost significance, as should be obvious, still, everything revolves around the Cross.

Some have tried to make the Resurrection the center of all doing; however, Paul shot that down immediately. He said, *"For Christ sent me not to baptize, but to preach the Gospel: not with wisdom of words, lest the Cross of Christ should be made of none effect"* (I Cor. 1:17). He did not say, *"Lest the Resurrection of Christ should be made of none effect."*

He also said, *"For the preaching of the Cross is to them who perish foolishness; but unto us who are Saved it is the Power of God"* (I Cor. 1:18). He did not say, *"For the preaching of the Resurrection. . . ."*

He said, *"But we preach Christ Crucified . . ."* (I Cor. 1:23). He did not say, *"But we preach Christ Resurrected. . . ."*

He said, *"For I determined not to know anything among you, save Jesus Christ, and Him Crucified"* (I Cor. 2:2). He did not say, *"For I determined not to know anything among you, save Jesus Christ, and Him Resurrected."*

Now, most definitely, he did preach the Resurrection, as is overly obvious from I Corinthians, Chapter 15; however, as it regarded Atonement, Redemption, Justification, and Sanctification, in other words, the ingredients of the Gospel, he placed the Cross of Christ, while never demeaning the other attributes of Christ, as the very Foundation of the great Plan of God. If we do less, we sin!

DEFINING THE THEOLOGY OF THE CROSS

The Cross of Christ is the well, so to speak, which produces all things that pertain to Redemption. But, possibly in abbreviated form, the following will help define the theology of the Cross.

• The Cross brings home the full seriousness of sin.
• The Cross declares the powerlessness of fallen humanity to achieve Salvation.
• The Cross exposes human delusions of self-righteousness.

THE SERIOUSNESS OF SIN

Perhaps it can be explained best in this manner:

To fully understand the seriousness of sin, how bad that sin is, how awful that sin is, that it kills everything that it touches, and how that God is unalterably opposed to sin, even as God must be unalterably opposed to sin, we can only partially understand its consequences by understanding, at least as best we can, the price that was paid in order to save man from sin. That price was God giving His Only Son as a Sacrifice for sin on the Cross of Calvary. In order for this to be done, God would have to become man, which is referred to as the Incarnation. He did so for many purposes and reasons, but the greatest reason of all, by far the greatest reason, was to go to the Cross. Concerning that, the great Prophet Isaiah said:

"For the Lord GOD will help Me; therefore shall I not be confounded: therefore have I set My face like a flint, and I know that I shall not be ashamed. *(Lk. 9:31, 51, fulfilled this Verse. The 'help' that His Father gave Him was that He might finish the task of redeeming mankind. The idea of redeeming someone who responds only with hate cannot be comprehended by the mortal mind, especially when one considers what that Redemption costs!*

"The phrase, 'I set My face like a flint,' refers to the resolve of accomplishing a certain thing despite all the scorn and hatred. That certain thing was the Cross)" (Isa. 50:7).

While I realize that the Fifty-Third Chapter of Isaiah is quite lengthy, at least as it regards the complementary notes in THE EXPOSITOR'S STUDY BIBLE, still, I feel that in order to properly explain this tremendous subject, the single most important subject on the face of the Earth, the following from THE EXPOSITOR'S STUDY BIBLE would be helpful.

THE EYE OF FAITH

"**Who has believed our report? and to whom is the Arm of the LORD revealed?** *('Our report,' refers to this very Prophecy, as well as the other Messianic Prophecies delivered by Isaiah. To Israel was 'the Arm of the LORD revealed.' And to Israel is ascribed the 'unbelief,' which destroyed them.*

"The Revelation of 'the Arm of the LORD' requires the eye of Faith to see it. Unbelief can always assign the most plainly providential arrangements to happy accident. It takes Faith to believe the report that is revealed.)"

NO BEAUTY THAT WE SHOULD DESIRE HIM

"**For He shall grow up before Him as a tender plant, and as a root out of a dry ground: He has no form nor comeliness; and when we shall see Him, there is no beauty that we should desire Him.** *(To God's Eye, Israel, and the entirety of the Earth for that matter, was a 'dry ground,' but that Eye rested with delight upon one tender plant which had a living root. It was Jesus!*

"The Hebrew verbs in these Verses [through Verse 7] are to be regarded as 'perfects of prophetic certitude.' This means that in the mind of God all has been finished before the foundation of the world and done so in the Divine Counsels [I Pet. 1:18-20].

"The words, 'before Him,' mean 'before Jehovah' — under the fostering care of Jehovah. God the Father had

*His Eye fixed upon the Son with a watchfulness and ten-
derness and love.*

*"This 'sapling' from the house of David shall become
the 'root' out of which His Church will grow. The Messiah
will be a fresh sprout from the stump of a tree that had been
felled, i.e., from the destroyed Davidic Monarchy.*

*"The words, 'He has no form nor comeliness,' refer to
the fact that He had none during His Sufferings, but now
He has it more than anyone else except the Father and
the Holy Spirit [Eph. 1:20-23; Phil. 2:9-11; Col. 1:15-18;
I Pet. 3:22].*

*"The words, 'There is no beauty that we should desire
Him,' refer to His Sufferings, which include His peasant
upbringing and, as a consequence, His poverty, as well as
His lack of association with the aristocracy!)"*

REJECTED OF MEN

**"He is despised and rejected of men; a man of sor-
rows, and acquainted with grief: and we hid as it were
our faces from Him; He was despised, and we esteemed
Him not.** *(Him being 'rejected of men' means 'One from
Whom men held themselves aloof.' Why? He was pure
Holiness and they were pure corruption.*

*" 'A man of sorrows,' refers to Jesus taking all the sor-
rows of humanity upon Himself.*

*" 'Acquainted with grief,' actually refers to diseases
and sicknesses, for that's what the word 'grief' in the
Hebrew means.*

*" 'And we hid as it were our faces from Him,' describes
the treatment of the Servant by His fellowmen. Again,
Why? He was not the type of Messiah they wanted!*

*" 'He was despised, and we esteemed Him not,' refers
to the fact that the religious leadership of Israel esteemed
Him not at all. He came to deliver men from sin, but that
wasn't the type of deliverance they desired!)"*

SMITTEN OF GOD, AND AFFLICTED

"**Surely He has borne our griefs, and carried our sorrows: yet we did esteem Him stricken, smitten of God, and afflicted.** *(Twelve times within the space of nine Verses the Prophet asserts, with the most emphatic reiteration, that all the Servant's sufferings were vicarious; i.e., borne for man to save him from the consequences of his sins, to enable him to escape punishment. In other words, Jesus did this all for us.*

" 'Yet we did esteem Him stricken, smitten of God, and afflicted,' proclaims the fact that because He died on a Cross, Israel assumed that He died under the curse of God, because Moses had said, 'For he who is hanged is accursed of God' [Deut. 21:23].

"What they did not understand was that He was not accursed, neither in Himself was cursed, but, in fact, was 'made a curse for us.'

"Israel assumed He was 'smitten of God,' and, in a sense, He was. He suffered in our stead, actually as our Substitute, which means that the blow that should have come to us instead went to Him. But yet, it was not for His sins, because He had none, but instead was for our sins. He was 'afflicted' for us. As stated, He was our Substitute.)"

WOUNDED FOR OUR TRANSGRESSIONS

"**But He was wounded for our transgressions, He was bruised for our iniquities: the chastisement of our peace was upon Him; and with His stripes we are healed.** *('He was wounded for our transgressions,' pertains to the manner in which He died, which was the price He paid for the Redemption of humanity.*

" 'He was bruised for our iniquities,' means that what He suffered was not at all for Himself, but all for us. It was

for our iniquities. Look at the Cross, and then say, 'My sin did this.'

" 'The chastisement of our peace was upon Him,' means that if peace between God and man was to be restored, all which Adam lost, then Jesus would have to bring it about. Here is the simple Doctrine of the Gospel — the Death of Christ. All other founders of religions base their claims upon their life and their teaching — their death was a calamity, and without significance. But the Death of Christ was His Glory, and forms the imperishable foundation of the one and only Salvation. His purpose in coming was to die.

" 'And with His stripes we are healed,' definitely pertains to physical healing, but is far greater in meaning than that. Its greater meaning refers to being healed of the terrible malady of sin.)"

ALL WERE LAID ON HIM

"**All we like sheep have gone astray; we have turned every one to his own way; and the LORD has laid on Him the iniquity of us all.** (Sheep without a shepherd get lost easily. Man as sheep has wandered from the right path; he has become so hopelessly lost that it is impossible for him, within his own means, to come back to the right path. Therefore, the Lord had to come from Heaven down to this wilderness called Earth and, thereby, seek and save man, who is lost.

" 'We have turned every one to his own way,' refers to the fact that the whole world, collectively and individually, has sinned and come short of the Glory of God. This 'erroneous way' has led to death, suffering, sorrow, heartache, loneliness, despair, and pain. This is the reason that everything that man touches dies! Whereas everything that God touches lives! So man desperately needs God's Touch, i.e., 'the Atonement of Calvary.'

*" 'And the LORD has laid on Him the iniquity of us all,'
refers to the total price He paid for our total Salvation.
The penalty for every sin for all of humanity and for all
time was laid on Christ. God the Father, as the primary
disposer of all things, lays upon the Son the burden which
the Son voluntarily accepts. He comes into the world to
do the Father's Will, and the Father's Will is to secure the
Salvation of man, at least for those who will believe.)"*

AS A LAMB TO THE SLAUGHTER

**"He was oppressed, and He was afflicted, yet He
opened not His Mouth: He is brought as a lamb to the
slaughter, and as a sheep before her shearers is dumb,
so He opens not His Mouth.** *(The first phrase refers to
all that was done to Him in His humiliation, suffering, and
agony. He could so easily have vindicated Himself from
every charge; therefore, He self-abased Himself.*

*"It seemed like an admission of guilt and, in fact, was,
but not His guilt, but the guilt of those who were accusing
Him, as well as the entirety of the world.*

*"Of all the Levitical Offerings [five total], the 'lamb'
was the animal most used; hence, John the Baptist would
say, 'Behold the Lamb of God, which takes away the sin of
the world' [Jn. 1:29].)"*

FOR THE TRANSGRESSION OF MY PEOPLE

**"He was taken from prison and from judgment:
and who shall declare His generation? for He was cut
off out of the land of the living: for the transgression of
My People was He stricken.** *('He was taken from prison
and from judgment,' refers to a violence which cloaked
itself under the formalities of a legal process.*

*" 'And who shall declare His generation,' refers to the
fact of Him being 'cut off' [Dan. 9:26], which means that*

He would have no posterity.

" 'For the transgression of My People was He stricken,' can be summed up in what He suffered, and all on our behalf. This must never be forgotten: Every single thing He suffered was not at all for Himself, or for Heaven in any capacity, but all for sinners.)"

HIS GRAVE

"And He made His grave with the wicked, and with the rich in His death; because He had done no violence, neither was any deceit in His mouth. *('And He made His grave with the wicked,' means that he was appointed such by the religious hierarchy of Israel, but Joseph of Arimathea, a rich man, asked that Jesus be buried in his personal tomb instead, and so He was.*

" 'Because He had done no violence, neither was any deceit in His mouth,' proclaims the sinlessness of Christ, and forms the main argument in the Epistle to the Hebrews for the superiority of the New Covenant over the Old [Heb. 7:26-28; 9:14].

"As no other man was ever without sin, it follows that the Servant of this present Chapter is, and can be no other than, Christ.)"

IT PLEASED THE LORD TO BRUISE HIM

"Yet it pleased the LORD to bruise Him; He has put Him to grief: when You shall make His soul an offering for sin, He shall see His seed, He shall prolong His days, and the pleasure of the LORD shall prosper in His hand. *('Yet it pleased the LORD to bruise Him,' refers to the sufferings of Christ, which proceeded from the 'determinate counsel and foreknowledge of God' [Acts 2:23], and which, being permitted by Him, were in some way His doing. It 'pleased Him' moreover that they should be* *undergone, for the Father saw with satisfaction the Son's self-sacrifice, and He witnessed with joy man's Redemption and Deliverance effected thereby.*

"'He has put Him to grief,' actually says 'He has put Him to sicknesses' or 'He has made Him sick.' This spoke of the time He was on the Cross bearing our sins and 'sicknesses' [Mat. 8:16-17; I Pet. 2:24]. And yet, while all sin and sickness were atoned at the Cross, the total effects of such will not be completely dissipated until the coming Resurrection [Rom. 8:23].

"'When You shall make His soul an offering for sin,' is powerful indeed! The word 'offering' in the Hebrew is 'Asham,' and means 'a Trespass Offering,' an 'offering for sin.'

"Offerings for sin, or 'guilt offerings,' were distinct from 'sin offerings.' The object of the former was 'satisfaction'; of the latter, 'expiation.' The Servant of Jehovah was, however, to be both. He was both the 'Sin Offering' and the 'Guilt Offering.'

"This completely destroys the idea that Jesus died spiritually on the Cross, meaning that He became a sinner on the Cross, and died and went to Hell as all sinners, and was Born-Again in Hell after three days and nights of suffering, etc. None of that is in the Word of God. While Jesus definitely was a 'Sin Offering,' He was not a sinner, and did not become a sinner on the Cross. To have done so would have destroyed His Perfection of Sacrifice, which was demanded by God. In other words, the Sacrifice had to be perfect, and He was Perfect in every respect.

"'He shall see His seed,' refers to all His 'true followers,' which include all who have ever been Born-Again.

"'He shall prolong His days,' refers to His Resurrection.

"'And the pleasure of the LORD shall prosper in His Hand,' refers to the great Victory that He would win at Calvary, which will ultimately restore everything that

Adam lost.)"

JUSTIFICATION

"He shall see of the travail of His Soul, and shall be satisfied: by His knowledge shall My righteous Servant justify many; for He shall bear their iniquities. *(The 'travail of His Soul' pertains to His Sacrifice for sin, which has resulted in the Restoration of man, at least for those who will believe.*

"'And shall be satisfied,' refers to the fact that even though the price was high, actually beyond comprehension, still, it was worth the Redemption it accomplished.

"What Jesus did at the Cross made it possible for man to be fully and totally 'justified' in the Eyes of God, which comes about by man exhibiting Faith in Christ and what Christ did at the Cross.)"

HE POURED OUT HIS SOUL UNTO DEATH

"Therefore will I divide Him a portion with the great, and He shall divide the spoil with the strong; because He has poured out His Soul unto death: and He was numbered with the transgressors; and He bore the sin of many, and made intercession for the transgressors. *(To be appointed with the great and to divide the spoil with the strong is figurative language expressive of full Victory. It means here that Christ, by His Death, delivers from Satan mankind who was held captive.*

"'Because He has poured out His Soul unto death,' means that Christ not only died for man, but, as it were, 'poured out His Soul' with His Own Hand to the last drop. The expression emphasizes the duration and the voluntariness of the Messiah's sufferings. In other words, He laid down His Own Life and no man took it from Him [Jn. 10:18]."

NUMBERED WITH THE TRANSGRESSORS

"*'And He was numbered with the transgressors,' refers to the actions of the Jews toward Him. He was crucified between two thieves. He was condemned as a 'blasphemer' [Mat. 26:65], crucified with malefactors [Lk. 23:32], called 'that deceiver' [Mat. 27:63], and regarded generally by the Jews as accursed [Deut. 21:23].*

"*'And He bore the sin of many, and made Intercession for the transgressors,' is, in the Hebrew, an act, though begun in the past, not yet completed. The 'Intercession for transgressors' was begun on the Cross with the compassionate words, 'Father, forgive them; for they know not what they do' [Lk. 23:34]. This Intercession for Believers has continued ever since and will ever continue [Rom. 8:34; Heb. 7:25]; such Intercession is made possible by what Christ did at the Cross)*" **(Isa., Chpt. 53).**

THE INABILITY OF MAN TO SAVE HIMSELF

After seeing the seriousness of sin, we now come to the inability of man to redeem himself. The Cross of Christ proclaims the fact as to what it took to redeem man, which is beyond the pale of human ability.

In Adam all died. Paul said:

"**For as in Adam all die** *(spiritual death, separation from God)*, **even so in Christ shall all be made alive.** *(In the first man, all died. In the Second Man, all shall be made alive, at least, all who will believe [Jn. 3:16])*" **(I Cor. 15:22).**

The manner and way that Adam was created was totally different than the creation of the Angels. Evidence is that when the Angels were created, they were all created at the same time and created fully mature. In other words, there is no such thing as a baby Angel. When man was created, however, only a pair was created, Adam and Eve, but given the power of pro-creation, which means to bring offspring into the world. So, in Adam's loins, so to speak, was every human being who would ever be born up to this point and will be until the Perfect Age to come. So, whatever happened to Adam would happen to the entirety of the human race; therefore, when he by transgression fell, fell from a position of total God-consciousness down to the far, far lower level of total self-consciousness, meaning to be ruled by the sin nature, all who would be born thereafter would be born under the curse of sin, referring to original sin. So, polluted man could in no way redeem himself.

Poor Eve did not understand this, thinking when Cain was born that he was the promised one. She even said, *"I have gotten a man from the LORD"* (Gen. 4:1). The name or title *"LORD"* means *"Covenant God."* Every evidence is that the Lord had explained to the First Family the means by which sin could be forgiven and a modicum of fellowship be had with God. It would be by the means of the slain lamb, which would serve as a substitute until the coming of the Lord Jesus Christ. At any rate, Eve thought that Cain was the one. As stated, she did not know or understand that sinful, fallen man could not bring anything into the world that God could honor. She found to her dismay that her firstborn was to be a murderer. In fact, it would take some four thousand years before the Redeemer would come into the world. The truth is, man does not know how lost he really is, and Believers do not know how Saved they really are.

Not respecting Jehovah, man ever since has been trying to fashion another god, the work of his own hands, which would allow him to bring his own salvation into focus. Irrespective, man cannot save himself in any capacity. In fact, when it comes to things spiritual, if the Holy Spirit doesn't give birth to the idea and bring about its conception, it cannot be accepted by the Lord. It is hard for believing man to understand that, but it is the truth.

Salvation is simple and easy. One has only to believe in

Christ and accept what He did for us at the Cross, and such a one will be Saved. In fact, Paul said:

"That if you shall confess with your mouth the Lord Jesus *(confess that Jesus is the Lord of Glory, and the Saviour of men, and that He died on the Cross that we might be Saved)*, and shall believe in your heart that God has raised Him from the dead *(pertains to the Bodily Resurrection of Christ, as is obvious)*, you shall be Saved *(it is that simple!)*.

"For with the heart man believes unto Righteousness *(presents the word 'believing' in a mode of 'thinking,' not of feeling; the 'believing' has to do with believing Christ, and that His Sacrifice of Himself atoned for all sin)*; and with the mouth confession is made unto Salvation *(when Faith comes forth from its silence to announce itself and proclaim the Glory and the Grace of the Lord, its voice 'is confession')*."

THE WORD OF GOD

"For the Scripture says *(combining parts of Isa. 28:16 with 49:23)*, Whosoever believes on Him *(proclaims the fact that Salvation is reachable by all)* shall not be ashamed *(in essence says, 'shall not be put to shame,' but rather will receive what is promised)*.

"For there is no difference between the Jew and the Greek *(should read, 'between the Jew and the Gentile'; all must come the same way, which is by and through Christ and what He did at the Cross on our behalf)*: for the same Lord over all is rich unto all who call upon Him *(the riches of Grace will be given to all who truly call upon the Lord)*.

"For whosoever *(anyone, anywhere)* shall call upon the Name of the Lord shall be Saved *(speaks of the sinner coming to Christ, but can refer to any Believer and with whatever need; the Cross is the means by which all of this is done)"* **(Rom. 10:9-13).**

THE CROSS EXPOSES SELF-RIGHTEOUSNESS

The theology of the Cross insists upon the Cross being given priority over all other events in the history of Salvation.

We must understand that the Cross is not a Chapter in the history of the Resurrection in which the Resurrection excels the Cross in importance. Rather, the Resurrection gives meaning to the Cross, with the Cross being the real center of gravity, so to speak. One might also say that the Resurrection is a Chapter in a book on the Theology of the Cross. Before Paul, the Cross of Jesus formed the question which answered the Message of the Resurrection. The Apostle decisively reversed this way of looking at things. In his controversy with the enthusiasts it was precisely the interpretation of the Resurrection which turned out to be a problem, a problem which can only be answered in the light of the Cross. That's why Paul said:

"For if we have been planted together *(with Christ)* **in the likeness of His Death** *(Paul proclaims the Cross as the instrument through which all Blessings come; consequently, the Cross must ever be the Object of our Faith, which gives the Holy Spirit latitude to work within our lives),* **we shall be also** *in the likeness* **of** *His* **Resurrection** *(we can have the 'likeness of His Resurrection,' i.e., 'live this Resurrection Life,' only as long as we understand the 'likeness of His Death,' which refers to the Cross as the Means by which all of this is done)"* **(Rom. 6:5).**

This tells us that Paul's emphasis on the Cross appears intended to stress that the Cross cannot be bypassed on the way to Resurrection. Before sharing in the Resurrection Life and all its fullness, Believers must first pass through the shadow of the Cross, which continues to fall across the entire range of

Christian experience.

And yet, wherever the Church takes the Cross of Christ seriously, it can expect to encounter hostility.

HOSTILITY TO THE CROSS

The Cross of Christ exposes error, and above all, exposes self-righteousness. That does not sit well with most people.

The church now, as in the time of Paul, is constantly coming up with one fad after the other which is supposed to enable the Believer to live as he or she should live. Outside of the Cross of Christ, let it be understood, there is no other way. Faith in anything other than the Cross of Christ produces self-righteousness, which is an invention of man.

Religious man does not mind at all hardships placed upon him by others because he thinks that the doing of such, i.e., the doing of religion, will affect in himself righteousness and holiness, in other words, that the Lord will be pleased with him. The Cross slams these things up beside the head, so to speak. It doesn't sit well and invites hostility.

Religious man doesn't enjoy being told that his schemes and stratagems of righteousness and holiness are of no spiritual worth whatsoever. In fact, instead of drawing one closer to the Lord, they push one further away. There is only one thing that pleases God, and that is for the Believer to express his Faith in Christ and what Christ has done for us at the Cross, and to do so totally and completely.

Religion is devised by man and caters to man's self-importance. So, he will undergo basically any type of hardship, in effect, saying, *"Look what I have done!"*

As an example, a particular preacher announces that fasting so many days will give one victory over sin. Now, while fasting is definitely Scriptural, that is, if done in the right spirit and for the right reason, it will not give anyone victory over sin. The Cross of Christ alone, which refers to Faith in the Finished Work of Christ, will give Victory. To be told that, however, does not sit well with the proponents of such, just as the Judaizers in the time of Paul being told that circumcision was to no avail. They didn't enjoy hearing that, so they fought against the great Apostle. It is the same presently! That's the reason that the Cross of Christ is an offense. Paul plainly said:

"And I, Brethren, if I yet preach Circumcision, why do I yet suffer persecution? then is the offense of the Cross ceased" (Gal. 5:11). As stated, the Cross of Christ exposes self-righteousness, which religious man does not enjoy at all and normally, in fact, opposes greatly.

ONE'S VIEW OF THE CROSS IS ONE'S VIEW OF GOD

Now, I want the reader to study that heading very closely. It simply means that if one has a correct view of the Cross, then one has a correct view of God. If one has an incorrect view of the Cross, then one of necessity has an incorrect view of God. In other words, the only way that one can properly understand God is to understand Christ and what Christ did at the Cross.

If the Cross of Christ is ignored, then one finds man being placed at the center of circumference with God being relegated to the outskirts, if given any recognition at all.

Misinterpreting the Cross brings about a misinterpretation of God. For instance, the Word of Faith people, which is no faith whatsoever, at least that God will recognize, claim that the Cross of Christ is none other than *"past miseries,"* and *"the greatest defeat in human history."* As such, they relegate the Cross to insignificance, actually stating that if the Preacher preaches the Cross, he is preaching death. That is strange when one considers that Paul said, *"For the preaching of the Cross is to them who perish foolishness, but to we who are Saved it is the Power of God"* (I Cor. 1:18).

In that genre, God is relegated to none other than an errand boy who is to cater to man's wishes. I would hope that the folly of that thinking is obvious!

Let us say it again, if one does not properly understand the Cross, one cannot properly understand God. When Paul used the term, which he did again and again, *"in Christ Jesus,"* probably those three words describe Biblical Christianity as nothing else.

"I dare not be defeated,
"With Calvary in view,
"Where Jesus conquered Satan,
"When all His Foes He slew.
"Come, Lord, and give the Vision,
"To nerve me for the fight,
"Make me an overcomer,
"Clothed with Your Spirit's Might."

"I dare not be defeated,
"Since Christ, my conquering King,
"Has called me to the battle,
"Which He did surely win.
"Come, Lord, and give me courage,
"Your conquering Spirit give,
"Make me an overcomer,
"In power within me live."

"I dare not be defeated,
"When Jesus leads me on,
"To press through hellish regions,
"To share with Him His Throne;
"Come, Lord, and give Your Soldier,
"The power to wield the sword,
"Make me an overcomer,
"Through Your inerrant Word."

"I dare not be defeated,
"Just as the set of sun,
"When Jesus waits to whisper,

"'Well done, beloved, well done!'
"Come, Lord, bend from the Glory,
"On me Your Spirit cast,
"Make me an overcomer,
"A victor to the last."

CHAPTER TWELVE

Victory

VICTORY

All Victory is found in Christ, and all is made possible solely by the Cross.

Jesus is God, and as such, He could have done and can do anything. The Scripture plainly says, *"For with God nothing shall be impossible"* (Lk. 1:37). In other words, God could have found another way to redeem man other than the Cross; however, He chose the Cross because, evidently, that was the best way.

It must always be understood that while God has the Knowledge and the Power to do anything, He will never use that Knowledge and that Power against His Nature and against His Character. His Nature and Character demand certain things, and that He will do.

For instance, His Nature and His Character demanded that sin not be stricken from the books by a mere word, which He had the Knowledge and the Power to do, but rather, that it be addressed in totality and the price paid in full. That price was the Incarnation, God becoming Man, and doing so for the purpose of going to the Cross. Paul said:

"**Blotting out the handwriting of Ordinances that was against us** *(pertains to the Law of Moses, which was God's Standard of Righteousness that man could not reach)*, **which was contrary to us** *(Law is against us, simply because we are unable to keep its precepts, no matter how hard we try)*, **and took it out of the way** *(refers to the penalty of the Law being removed)*, **nailing it to His Cross** *(the Law with its decrees was abolished in Christ's Death, as if Crucified with Him)*;"

THE DEFEAT OF ALL EVIL FORCES

"*And* **having spoiled principalities and powers** *(Satan and all of his henchmen were defeated at the Cross* *by Christ atoning for all sin; sin was the legal right Satan had to hold man in captivity; with all sin atoned, he has no more legal right to hold anyone in bondage)*, **He** *(Christ)* **made a show of them openly** *(what Jesus did at the Cross was in the face of the whole Universe)*, **triumphing over them in it.** *(The triumph is complete and it was all done for us, meaning we can walk in power and perpetual Victory due to the Cross)"* **(Col. 2:14-15).**

CONSIDERING THIS, HOW IS IT THAT SATAN CONTINUES TO HOLD UNTOLD MILLIONS IN BONDAGE?

That's a good question!

As we said in the notes, sin gives Satan the legal right to hold man captive. Yet, considering that Jesus atoned for all sin at the Cross, past, present, and future, at least for those who will believe, how can Satan hold man in bondage?

The key is in the *"believing,"* or the lack thereof. If you'll notice, we said, *"that Jesus atoned for all sin, past, present, and future, for those who will believe."* If man doesn't believe, the sin remains, and the bondage continues.

THE UNREDEEMED

Every unsaved person in this world can instantly be delivered from the powers of darkness, if they will only accept Christ, but most won't; therefore, they remain in bondage to Satan in one way or the other.

Now, that is understandable, but how do we explain Christians who are held captive by Satan?

CHRISTIANS HELD CAPTIVE BY SATAN

The problem with the unredeemed, which is a lack of believing, is the same problem with the Believer. As it regards the Believer, he is either ignorant of the provision made by our Lord that we walk in victory, in other words, that the sin nature not have dominion over us, or else, he simply doesn't believe that what Jesus did there solves the problem. Or, it could be a combination of both.

As we said in the last Chapter, the Cross of Christ exposes self-righteousness, and many do not like that. Any effort at living for God outside of God's Prescribed Order, which is Faith in Christ and what Christ did at the Cross, and that exclusively, always concludes in self-righteousness. That's the reason the church is full of self-righteousness, in fact, as it always has been. It is because of one placing one's faith in something other than Christ and the Cross.

A proper theology of the Cross treats the Cross as the center of all Christian thought in that from its center radiates every Christian thought. As an example, the Doctrines of Revelation and Salvation, so easily detached from one another, converge on the Cross. The Cross — more accurately, the Crucified Christ — thus acts as the Foundation of authentic Christian ways of thinking about God. Let us say it again. One's view of the Cross is one's view of God. If our thinking concerning the Cross is wrong, our thinking concerning God will be wrong as well! We must ever understand that the theology of the Cross insists upon the Cross being given priority over all other events in the history of Salvation.

REDEMPTION

The idea of *"Redemption"* has strong links with the world of a slave market or prison. The dominant theme is that of liberation from being *"under the power of sin"* (Rom. 3:9). Sin is here understood as a power or force, which exercises authority and dominion over sinful humanity. The Death of Christ makes it possible for this power to be broken, enabling humans to achieve the glorious liberty of the Children of God. The theology of the Cross reminds us that it is the Cross, the

Crucified Christ, that lies at the heart of the Christian Gospel. Actually, the word *"Cross,"* at least in Paul's thinking, is merely a synonym for the Gospel. In other words, the Cross of Christ is the Gospel.

THE THREE MEANINGS OF REDEMPTION

Actually, the very word *"Redemption"* speaks of being released from prison.

1. *"Garazo"*: the word in the Greek refers to one who is purchased as a slave from an auction.

2. *"Exgarazo"*: this word speaks of a person purchased off the auction block of slavery, never to be put up again for sale.

3. *"Lutroo"*: this Greek word means that such a price was paid, the Cross of Christ, that neither Angels nor anyone in the future will ever be able to say that the price was insufficient.

HOW TO BE AN OVERCOMER

In Chapters 2 and 3 in the Book of Revelation, Jesus preached seven short Messages to the seven Churches of Asia which, in fact, are meant to cover the entirety of the Church Age, which has lasted now nearly 2,000 years. At any rate, at the close of each Message He spoke to the overcomer.

Regarding the Church at Ephesus He said, *"To him who overcomes will I give to eat of the Tree of Life, which is in the midst of the Paradise of God"* (Rev. 2:7).

To the Church at Smyrna He said, *"He who overcomes shall not be hurt of the second death"* (Rev. 2:11).

To the Church at Pergamos He said, *"To him who overcomes will I give to eat of the hidden Manna, and will give him a white stone, and in the stone a new name written, which no man knows saving he who receives it"* (Rev. 2:17).

And then to the Church at Thyatira, *"And he who overcomes, and keeps My Works unto the end, to him will I give power over the nations"* (Rev. 2:26).

And to the Church at Sardis, *"He who overcomes, the same shall be clothed in white raiment; I will not blot out his name out of the Book of Life, but I will confess his name before My Father, and before His Angels"* (Rev. 3:5).

And to the Church at Philadelphia, *"Him who overcomes will I make a pillar in the Temple of My God, and he shall go no more out: and I will write upon him the Name of My God, and the Name of the city of My God, which is New Jerusalem, which comes down out of Heaven from My God: and I will write upon him My new Name"* (Rev. 3:12).

And finally, to the Church at Laodicea, *"To him who overcomes will I grant to sit with Me in My Throne, even as I also overcame, and am set down with My Father in His Throne"* (Rev. 3:21).

I think one should get the idea from all of these statements how important being an overcomer actually is. I'm also certain that many of you have read these statements over and over again somewhat with fear. You would look at your life and know that you didn't quite measure up to that which is demanded. And yet, you did not know how to fix it.

What I'm going to give you is what the Lord gave me, and I think that it will become much clearer.

YOU ARE AN OVERCOMER . . .

You are an overcomer, at least, if your Faith is exclusively in Christ and what Christ has done for you at the Cross (Rom. 6:3-5). If you keep looking at yourself that means you're not looking to Christ. That which you must do, that which you must be, for all of your efforts, you cannot bring it to pass. Only He can do so! Let me say it this way:

The moment you place your Faith exclusively in Christ, looking exclusively to Him and what He did for you at the Cross of Calvary, understanding that Jesus Christ is always the Source, and the Cross is the Means, at that very moment, you become *"an overcomer."*

The immediate reaction to that statement is, *"But Brother Swaggart, there are still some problems in my life that I need to have removed. How can I be an overcomer with those problems remaining?"*

As long as you look at yourself and your own personal problems, you'll never get to the place that you're trying to go. The only way it can be done, and I mean the only way, is by Faith in Christ, with you beginning to confess what you are in Christ, and because of what Jesus has done for you. Whenever we look at ourselves, the Holy Spirit becomes very limited as to what He can do. When we look solely to Christ, then the Holy Spirit can go to work and rid us of those difficulties in our lives that have been such a hindrance for all of these years.

I AM CRUCIFIED WITH CHRIST

The great Apostle, in dealing with this very subject said:

"**I am Crucified with Christ** *(as the Foundation of all Victory; Paul, here, takes us back to Rom. 6:3-5)*: **nevertheless I live** *(have new life)*; **yet not I** *(not by my own strength and ability)*, **but Christ lives in me** *(by virtue of me dying with Him on the Cross, and being raised with Him in Newness of Life)*: **and the life which I now live in the flesh** *(my daily walk before God)* **I live by the Faith of the Son of God** *(the Cross is ever the Object of my Faith)*, **Who loved me, and gave Himself for me** *(which is the only way that I could be Saved)*."

FRUSTRATING THE GRACE OF GOD

"**I do not frustrate the Grace of God** *(if we make anything other than the Cross of Christ the Object of our Faith, we frustrate the Grace of God, which means we stop its action, and the Holy Spirit will no longer help us)*: **for if Righteousness** *come* **by the Law** *(any type of religious* *law)*, **then Christ is dead in vain.** *(If I can successfully live for the Lord by any means other than Faith in Christ and the Cross, then the Death of Christ was a waste)"* **(Gal. 2:20-21).**

Any number of great statements is made in these two Verses. They are:

CRUCIFIED WITH CHRIST

How is a Believer crucified with Christ?
It is all by Faith. Let me explain!
When Jesus, the Son of the Living God, died on the Cross of Calvary, He did so as our Representative Man, actually, our Substitute. It would have done us no good to have been hung on a Cross. We were a very imperfect sacrifice, unacceptable to God. So, our Lord stood in for us.
When you as a Believer came to Christ, you exhibited Faith in Christ, at least, what little you then knew, and in the Mind of God, you were literally placed in Christ in His Death, Burial, and Resurrection. That's the way that you were Crucified with Christ. As stated, it was all and is all by Faith.

NEVERTHELESS I LIVE

The short phrase, *"nevertheless I live,"* refers to the Believer living an overcoming, Christlike life. In fact, a person doesn't really live until that person has accepted Christ. Everything else is a sham, a farce, a lie! The person who accepts Christ has just begun to live and has just begun to enjoy life, in fact, the *"more abundant life"* given to us by Christ (Jn. 10:10).

YET NOT I

Those three words, *"yet not I,"* are probably some of the most important words in the entirety of the New Covenant.

With those three words, the Apostle Paul is saying that what is needed, what he is supposed to be and supposed to do, he doesn't have the means to do it. It must be done by the Power of the Holy Spirit, Who Works exclusively within the parameters of the Finished Work of Christ.

We can go back to the overcoming spectacle just discussed! There is no way that you can make yourself into an overcomer, I don't care what you do. You will still come short no matter who you are. However, when you place your Faith exclusively in Christ and the Cross, you will then find the Holy Spirit beginning to work in your life, doing what you could never do. But, it's hard for religious man to say *"yet not I!"* You see, religion is doing, doing, doing. Christ is *"done, done, done!"*

Religious man loves the *"doing,"* because it somehow ministers to his self-importance, or at least, he thinks it does! People work very hard at religion.

A LETTER I RECEIVED

Among all of the hundreds of thousands of letters that we have received over a period of time, a goodly number stand out. The following is one of them. I do not quote the lady verbatim, only paraphrasing from memory.

She wrote and told me how that she had seen the telecast the previous Sunday morning and had given her heart to Christ. However, the following is the ironical thing about it.

She had been a member of a Baptist church almost all of her life. In fact, she went on to say that she knew Baptist Doctrine so well that she taught the new convert's class.

She stated how that she was involved in all of the activities of the church, so much so that she very seldom even had a night off for her family. But, watching the Telecast, she went on to say, the Lord began to convict her, and she suddenly came to the acute realization that she had never really been Born-Again. Religious, yes! Saved, no!

That morning she beautifully and wonderfully said *"yes"*

to Jesus Christ. She went on to say:

"Brother Swaggart, I now know what it is to be Saved. I've never experienced anything so wonderful in all of my life."

The purpose of this statement is that all of this dear lady's work, labor, and efforts, all trying to earn or gain something in the Lord, were to no avail. Now, more than likely, some of the things she was doing were very good and very needy, and we do not demean that. However, if we do these things, no matter how good they might be, thinking that they earn us something with the Lord, then we have just run aground, so to speak.

It's very hard for the individual to say, *"yet not I,"* meaning that whatever it is that I need, I cannot bring it about, that only being done so by the Power of the Holy Spirit, Who always operates within the boundaries of the Cross of Christ.

CHRIST LIVES IN ME

As we said in the notes, Christ lives in us by virtue of me dying with Him on the Cross and being raised with Him in Newness of Life. In fact, Christ lives within us by the Means of Faith on our part and through the Person, Agency, Work, and Office of the Holy Spirit (I Cor. 3:16).

The word *"lives"* means that Christ is very active in our hearts and lives and done so by and through what He did at the Cross. You see, the Cross is a work completed in times past, actually nearly 2,000 years ago, but has continuing results, and results which will never be discontinued.

I LIVE BY THE FAITH OF THE SON OF GOD

Once again, the word *"live"* has to do with life and living, an everyday affair, how we order our behavior.

The *"Faith of the Son of God,"* has to do with what our Lord did at Calvary's Cross. In fact, it can be referred to as *"the Faith."* If we are involved in *"the Faith,"* where every Christian ought to be, this and this alone is the road to Victory.

In fact, it is Victory!

WHO LOVED ME, AND GAVE HIMSELF FOR ME

Paul begins with the Cross with the first phrase of Verse 20 and now closes with the Cross in the last phrase. This *"Faith of the Son of God,"* made possible by what Christ did at the Cross, was carried out simply because the Lord loved us; therefore, He *"gave Himself for us."*

The type of love of which Paul mentions here is *"agape love,"* and refers to the *"God kind of love."* It's a love that a person cannot have until he first of all accepts Christ.

I DO NOT FRUSTRATE THE GRACE OF GOD

Whenever a Believer places his or her faith in anything except Christ and the Cross, this frustrates the Grace of God, which means that our actions impede this life-giving flow. The Grace of God is simply the *"Goodness of God"* extended to undeserving people. God has all kinds of good things for us, and He wants to give them to us, but He can only do such in one capacity, and that is according to our Faith, which refers to Faith in Christ and the Cross, and that exclusively.

The Grace of God is all made possible, and in its entirety, by the Cross of Christ. It was at the Cross that Jesus atoned for all sin, past, present, and future, at least for all who will believe (Jn. 3:16). In fact, the Lord has no more Grace today than He did some 3,000 years ago, but due to the fact that before the Cross animal blood was woefully insufficient to take away sins, the Lord was limited as to what He could do for humanity. Since the Cross, which lifted the sin debt, the Goodness of God, i.e., *"the Grace of God,"* can now flow to us in an uninterrupted manner. However, the sad fact is that virtually the entirety of the modern church, and we speak of those who truly love the Lord, are, in fact, frustrating the Grace of God, and because something other than the Cross of Christ is the object of their Faith.

RIGHTEOUSNESS AND THE LAW

Bluntly and plainly the Apostle tells us here, *"If Righteous-ness come by the Law, then Christ is dead in vain."* In other words, the Righteousness of God can only come to me by being given to me, for I certainly cannot earn it. It is given upon one premise, and one premise only, and that is by the person evidencing Faith in Christ and His Atoning Work. The idea is that if Righteousness could come by the means of Law, works, etc., then Jesus did not have to come down here and die on a Cross. In other words, if what we need from the Lord can be garnered in that fashion, and we mean by the flesh, by Law, by merit, etc., then the Death of Christ was a waste. But, the truth is, *"Righteousness cannot come by the Law."*

What did Paul mean by Righteousness coming by the Law?

He is speaking of the Law of Moses or any type of religious law made up by ourselves or others, in other words, anything other than the Cross of Christ. It doesn't really matter what else the other thing might be, how good it might be in its own way, or in its own right. If it's not the Cross of Christ that is the Object of our Faith, then it's faith that the Lord will not and, in fact, cannot recognize.

ONLY THE CROSS?

Somebody said, *"Brother Swaggart, you are concluding that everything comes to us from the Lord by Means of the Cross."*

You are exactly right. Now you are beginning to understand what we are saying. It is the Cross of Christ for Salvation, and it is the Cross of Christ for Sanctification.

Do you realize that the entirety of the Bible, with the exception of possibly one half of one percent, is given over to telling us how to live for God? Of course, what it does say about Salvation is to the point and exactly what needs to be said; however, the Word of God is a Book for Believers. Actually, those who are unsaved do not understand it and, therefore, little bother with it. As stated, the Word of God is for Believers.

One might say, I think, at least as it regards life and living, that everything centers up in the Sixth Chapter of Romans. But unfortunately, most Christians little understand that because they think that Paul is there speaking of Water Baptism. That being the case, they reason, they've already been baptized in water, so the balance of the Chapter holds little meaning for them. The truth is, Paul is not speaking there of Water Baptism, not at all! He is speaking of the Crucifixion of Christ and our being baptized into His Death, etc.

Some object to that, thinking that the word *"baptize,"* according to Strong's Dictionary, means to be dipped under water, etc. But, what they do not realize, Strong's Dictionary, at least the version I use, also states that the word *"baptize"* can be used literally or figuratively. Paul is using it figuratively in Romans 6:3-5.

In fact, John the Baptist also used it both literally and figuratively. He said, *"I indeed baptize you (literally) with water unto Repentance: but He Who comes after me is mightier than I, Whose Shoes I am not worthy to bear: He shall baptize you (figuratively) with the Holy Spirit and with fire"* (Mat. 3:11).

So, thinking that the word *"baptize"* in Romans 6 speaks of Water Baptism, most Christians completely miss what the great Apostle is saying, which is the greatest truth that the Believer can know.

In this Chapter he tells us as Believers how to have Victory over the sin nature. It is by virtue of the Cross of Christ and our Faith in that Finished Work.

Please note carefully the following little formula. I'm going to, first of all, give it the way it ought to be and then the way it is commonly used in the modern church, of which the latter speaks of failure.

FOCUS: The Lord Jesus Christ (Jn. 14:6).

OBJECT OF FAITH: The Cross of Christ (Rom. 6:3-5).
POWER SOURCE: The Holy Spirit (Rom. 8:1-2, 11).
RESULTS: Victory! (Rom. 6:14).

Now, let's use the same formula, but let's turn it around the way that it's mostly being used by the modern church.

Focus: works.

Object of Faith: our performance.

Power Source: self.

Results: defeat!

"Are you hungering for the fullness,
"Of the Blessing Christ does give?
"Longing now to learn the secret,
"Of the life He bids you live?
"In His Word your answer stands,
"Christ Who is our Life it says;
"Open now your heart, and trust Him,
"There to dwell, henceforth, by Faith."

"Christ, the Lord's Anointed, reigning,
"Over the life He died to win,
"Daily shall reveal more fully,
"His Great Power, without, within.
"What you never could accomplish,
"Shall His Spirit work through thee,
"While your soul this witness beareth,
"Tis not I, but Christ in me."

"In Him dwells all God's Fullness,
"In Him you are made complete;
"Rise, and claim your heavenly birthright,
"Kneeling at your Father's Feet.
"He will never disappoint thee,
"Praise Him that the gift is thine;
"Then go forth to live each moment,
"On sufficiency Divine."

"Lord, I come, and simply resting,
"On Your faithful, changeless Word,
"I believe the Blood does cleanse us,
"And that Christ is crowned Lord.
"Grant henceforth a ceaseless outflow,
"Of Your Life and Love through me;
"Reaching those who sit in darkness,
"Winning priceless souls to Thee."

CHAPTER THIRTEEN

How Satan Tries To Hinder

HOW SATAN TRIES TO HINDER

Once the Lord began to give me the Revelation of the Cross, at least as it regards Sanctification, immediately we began to preach it and teach it far and wide. To be sure, it is a grand Message, in fact, the grandest the world has ever known. It is the meaning, as we have previously stated, of the New Covenant. For the soul that has tried and failed, and tried and failed, this Message is like a breath of fresh air. It's like the sun that's rising after a long night of darkness. As stated, it is the liberating Message, the Message that sets the captive free. And to be sure, life is what it ought to be once the person in Christ learns what Jesus did for us at the Cross. Once we learn how the Holy Spirit Works within the parameters of the Finished Work of Christ and begin to apply it to our lives, Victory is ours. It is that which the Lord gave to the Apostle Paul (Gal. 1:12), and the great Apostle gave this great Truth to us. We read in the Seventh Chapter of Romans how the great Apostle struggled for years, not knowing how to live for God, trying and failing. The culmination of that effort was, and always is, *"O wretched man that I am! Who shall deliver me from the body of this death?"* (Rom. 7:24).

But then, the Lord opened up to Paul all to which the Prophets of old had pointed. It was and is the culmination of everything that God has given us.

Then I began hearing some saying, *"The Cross of Christ may work for others, but it doesn't work for me,"* or words to that effect.

WHY IS IT THAT THE CROSS DOESN'T WORK FOR ME?

One Baptist Preacher made the statement that some say, or words to this effect, *"The Cross of Christ may work for others, but it doesn't work for me."*

The Preacher went on to say, and rightly so, *"No, the Cross of Christ does not fail. It's me and you who fail."* He could not be more right!

If we think that hearing this Message and then applying it to our hearts and lives will stop all temptation and all efforts by the Devil, with all problems ended, then we have a wrong understanding of this great Message of Redemption. Let me say:

I don't care how much you know about the Cross of Christ, which is the answer to all life and living, and it doesn't matter how strong you may be in the Lord, and it doesn't matter how much knowledge you may have, Satan is never going to quit his attacks against you. If one thing doesn't work, he'll try another. You can expect that until the Trump sounds or the Lord calls you home.

VICTORY CAN BE YOURS

However, one thing is certain. If we follow the Lord as we should, which means to follow His Word, it may take some time, and there may be many failings along the way, but we can rest assured that the Holy Spirit is going to bring us into a position of life and living, which will truly be, as Peter said, *"Joy unspeakable and full of glory."*

When the Lord turned over the Promised Land to the Children of Israel, they had to learn that there was quite a distance between the Promise and the possession. In other words, the land was filled with Amalekites, Jebusites, Hittites, etc. Now, the Lord with His Almighty Power could easily have rid the Promised Land of every foe, but He didn't. He could stop Satan from attacking us ever, but He won't.

Why?

WHY THE LORD ALLOWS TEMPTATION AND TESTING

The Lord allows temptation and testing to teach us Faith and Trust in Him. As well, it is for reasons of discipline.

The Lord is making something of us. All of this is the dress rehearsal for eternity, so to speak. So, in the Lord, don't expect a life that is event free! Chapter 12 in Genesis is extremely important for it records the first steps of Abraham in the path of Faith. To be sure, there were Believers before him, but the Scripture speaks of him as the father of all Believers. The Lord said to him, *"Come with Me unto a land that I will show you."* He went out not knowing where he went, but Faith was rewarded for Verse 5 in this Twelfth Chapter of Genesis says, *"into the land of Canaan he came."* He actually found himself in the Promised Land.

Thus it is today. The Holy Spirit says, *"Believe on the Lord Jesus Christ and you shall be Saved."* The sinner believes, and he is Saved. Into, Scripturally speaking, *"the land of Canaan"* he comes. This is the first step in the life of Faith.

THE CANAANITE IS IN THE LAND

But, what an unexpected experience for Abraham! He finds the hateful, impure, and hostile Canaanite in God's Land. This was Faith's first trial; his heart would be tempted to question the fact that this was God's Land, for how could the Canaanite be in God's Land!

HOSTILITY TO CHRIST

So, in this present-day the young Believer expects after conversion to find nothing in his nature hostile to Christ, but is distressed and somewhat perplexed very soon to painfully learn that, alas, the Canaanite is in the land, and that he is now commencing a lifelong battle with that which the New Testament calls *"the Flesh."*

However, the Believer must also realize that if the Canaanite is in the land, so also is Jehovah. Directly upon Abraham reaching Sychem, the Lord appears to him and promises him a son, who was to be the progenitor of the Redeemer of all nations. To enjoy these conscious *"appearings"* of Jesus to the soul, the Believer must keep in the path of Faith and take the succeeding steps of obedience in that path.

GOD ALWAYS TESTS FAITH

Faith is always tested, and great Faith is always tested greatly.

Not enjoying having to say it, but having to say it we must, there will be failings along the way. It was with Abraham, and it will be with you and me.

When the famine came to Canaan, Abraham's Faith broke down in the presence of this trial. It was indeed a mystery that Abraham could not solve, why there should be the Canaanite in the land and, as well, a famine in God's Own chosen Land. His heart may have whispered to him that he was under a delusion; how could such things be found in a land that God had led him into? But, as stated, God always tests Faith, and as with Abraham, so with all young converts, and even with those that are not so young.

Soon after we have entered upon the path of Faith comes the test, that is, the famine. And, as well, this is something that will never end. It is something that we can grow to the place that we overcome, in other words, we pass the test, but even that does not come quickly or easily.

Abraham went down into Egypt, which was Satan's plan. Satan had schemed to get Abraham into Egypt, which was a lack of faith on the part of the great Patriarch, with Sarah being taken into Pharaoh's house in order that she might become the mother of a child by the Egyptian king, thus defeating the Messianic Promise made to Abraham.

To be sure, Abraham in Egypt presents a repulsive picture of contemptible and abject cowardice. To save himself, he denies his wife and places her in the home of another man to be his wife. Such is the deep depth to which the Christian readily falls directly after he leaves the path of Faith. God had said to Abraham on the day of his conversion, *"I will bless you and you shall be a blessing,"* but, in the land of Egypt, he was a curse. Because of Abraham and his failure before the Lord, Pharaoh and his family are plagued with great plagues, and this heathen prince hurries this Man of God out of his land as he would chase away a pestilence. How degrading! How embarrassing.

In the path of Faith the Christian is a blessing to the world, but in the path of self-will, a curse.

THE GRACE OF GOD

If Abraham went *"down"* into Egypt, Grace brings him *"up"* out of Egypt, and then, famine or no famine, led him to that mountaintop where his tent had been at the beginning, *"Unto the place of the Altar, i.e., 'the Cross,' which he had made there at the first."* And there, doubtless with tears and shame, he called, by sacrifice, on the Name of the Lord, that is, on the Saving Name of Jesus. His backslidings were forgiven, his soul was restored, and he resumed his true life as a pilgrim and a worshipper with his tent and his Altar, neither of which he had in Egypt.

Abraham was an example of that which happens to every single Believer in one way or the other. Abraham could have said, *"The Cross doesn't work,"* but instead, when he failed, he took that failure to the Lord and did so by the way of the Altar, i.e., the Cross. That is the only place for the Child of God, whether victorious or failing! And, there will be both in the life of every Believer.

I sense the Presence of the Lord even as I dictate these words, and I believe that you who read them sense the same!

Please remember, the Lord is not trying to wash us out, but rather, bring us over the top. While it may be three strikes and you are out as it regards baseball, the Lord has no limit on the number of times we can swing at that ball, so to speak. The Lord loves you, and He loves you supremely. While He most definitely is grieved at our failures, and sorely grieved, still, He promised that He would never leave us nor forsake us. He said what He meant and meant what He said! While the Cross needs no improvement, the truth is, you and I need an awful lot of improvement. It is so easy for us to think that we are *"walking after the Spirit,"* when all the while, we are *"walking after the flesh."* Our spiritual deficiencies aren't easily rectified. It takes time; it takes much trial and error but, as stated, if you won't quit on the Lord, the Lord will never quit on you.

THE WORD THE LORD GAVE UNTO ME

As stated, I was hearing some people say, *"The Cross may work for others, but it doesn't work for me,"* or *"Others may be strong enough to do this, but I'm not!"* In other words, the excuses came thick and fast.

It was a Saturday night, and I had retired for bed. If I remember correctly, I either had not gone to sleep, or else I had gone to sleep and had awakened. I don't exactly remember what time it was, possibly about 1:00 a.m., in the dead of night. All of a sudden, the Lord brought to me what Satan will do when the Believer begins to hear the Message of the Cross and begins to walk in a life of Victory that is absolutely unparalleled. The Lord took me to the Fifth Chapter of Exodus. To be sure, that is very appropriate, considering that it proclaims the beginning of the deliverance of the Children of Israel from Egyptian bondage. There could be no greater example. What I had was not a dream, but it very well could have been a Vision. It was that the Lord opened up this great Truth to me to help me see what was happening with Believers, and how that maybe I could help them. The Lord laid out to me three great particulars as it regards Satan's attacks against us. I will copy the Text and the notes directly from THE EXPOSITOR'S STUDY BIBLE.

LET MY PEOPLE GO

This was the first Command of the Lord to Pharaoh, *"Let My People go."* It came directly from the Throne of God through His Servant Moses and was delivered to Pharaoh. In effect, the Lord is saying the same thing to Satan about you,

"Let My Child go." It is the Word of the Lord given in the Word of God. Paul wrote and said:

"For sin shall not have dominion over you: for you are not under the Law, but under Grace" (Rom. 6:14). And yet, it seems that sin is most definitely, despite your Faith, continuing to have dominion over you. The idea is, the Lord has said, *"Let My People go,"* and if we keep believing, Satan will ultimately have to let go of his grip. But, as stated, it won't come easily, and it may not come quickly. Let's look at the Text:

> "And afterward Moses and Aaron went in, and told the Pharaoh (*according to many authorities, the Pharaoh at that time was 'Menephthap,' the son and successor of 'Rameses II'; history records that he was a weak individual, but, because of certain events, had an exalted opinion of himself; the close of Chapter 4 presents the people worshipping in believing joy; the close of Chapter 5 sets before the reader the same people filled with unbelieving bitterness; the glad tidings of Salvation is one thing; the struggle against the power that tries to keep the soul in bondage is quite another*), Thus says the LORD God of Israel, Let My People go, that they may hold a feast unto Me in the wilderness. (*If it is to be noticed, the Holy Spirit, in giving Moses direction regarding the Sacred Text, in no way recognizes the splendor of Egypt. The character of the Message that Moses was to deliver to Pharaoh was not calculated to compromise or pacify)*" (Ex. 5:1).

In other words, the Gospel of Jesus Christ is not a lesson in diplomacy, but rather, an ultimatum!

SALVATION IS ONE THING, BUT THE STRUGGLE AGAINST THE POWER THAT TRIES TO KEEP THE SOUL IN BONDAGE IS QUITE ANOTHER

Read the heading again very carefully, for this is what all

of this is about. This is the Christian life; this is the Christian struggle. Paul referred to it as *"warfare"* (II Cor. 10:4). This is a challenge, and a challenge it is that is incumbent upon every Believer. None are exempt. And to be sure, the more that one is used of God, the more that Satan is allowed his latitude and leeway to hinder. That's why Jesus said, *"For unto whomsoever much is given, of him shall be much required"* (Lk. 12:48).

That's why Peter said, *"Beloved, think it not strange concerning the fiery trial which is to try you, as though some strange thing happened unto you"* (I Pet. 4:12).

There is only one Way to overcome this struggle, to win this war, to come out victor, only one Way, and that is by and through the Cross of Jesus Christ. This is the Way, the Way of the Cross, that God has provided, and to be sure, He has provided no other, because no other is needed. If we try to bring about victory within our hearts and lives another way, a way other than the Cross, we will fail, irrespective as to the grand scheme of our planning. Once again, Paul nailed it shut when he said, *"If Righteousness come by the Law, then Christ is dead in vain"* (Gal. 2:21).

LAW

And, once again, allow me to approach the subject of Law.

Most Christians give it little thought because they know that the Law of Moses was fulfilled in Christ, so they automatically assume that they are not involved with law. Have you ever stopped to consider how much that Paul addressed Law, even though he was addressing Gentiles, who, in fact, knew very little, if anything, about the Law of Moses? The idea is this:

While it's not so much the Law of Moses that plagues modern Christians, that having been addressed totally in Christ, it is law nevertheless. What do we mean by that?

Anytime we concoct a scheme or make ready a particular plan, no matter how religious it may be, and no matter how many Scriptures we load upon it, if it's not the Cross of Christ, it is religious law — and it is that which God cannot honor, cannot bless! Let me give some examples:

Anything the preacher holds up as an answer to sin, other than our Faith in Christ and what He did for us at the Cross, is unacceptable.

I had two of the leading lights of the charismatic movement, gracious brothers, I might quickly add, who said to me that if there is sin in the life of a Believer, that means he has a demon that is responsible for that particular sin. In other words, if it's lust, he has a demon of lust; if it's alcohol, there is a demon of alcohol; if it's gambling, there is a demon of gambling; or, if it's unforgiveness, it's a demon of unforgiveness, etc. Hands are supposed to be laid on the individual, with that demon cast out, and then the problem, they say, will be solved.

No, it won't!

While demon spirits most definitely do get involved wherever there is sin, still, that doesn't mean that the Believer is demon possessed, etc. There is nothing in the Bible that lends credence to such thinking. To the contrary, Jesus said, *"You shall know the Truth, and the Truth shall make you free"* (Jn. 8:32). The Truth is the Cross. That's why Paul said:

"Christ sent me not to baptize, but to preach the Gospel: not with wisdom of words, lest the Cross of Christ should be made of none effect" (I Cor. 1:17).

That's why the great Apostle also said, *"But God forbid that I should glory, save in the Cross of our Lord Jesus Christ, by Whom the world is Crucified unto me, and I unto the world"* (Gal. 6:14).

In this Passage the Holy Spirit through Paul plainly tells us that it is by the Cross alone that we can have Victory over the world, the flesh, and the Devil, etc.

THE WORD OF GOD

Invariably, in reading about the great Prophets of the Old Testament and the Apostles of the New Testament, the writer will bring it out as to how these individuals were influenced by certain things, etc., and that's why, they will go on to say, that they wrote the things they did, etc.

Not so!

These men wrote the Word of God as they were moved upon by the Holy Spirit. Inspiration says that the Holy Spirit searched through their vocabulary to find each distinct word that He wanted for each sentence. That doesn't mean that they were in some type of trance as it regards automatic writing. Far from such! When they wrote the Word of God, they were just as lucid as you and me. The Holy Spirit used their knowledge, their education, their vocabulary, whatever it may have been, to put down in writing what He wanted said. That's the reason that Jesus said:

"Man shall not live by bread alone, but by every Word that proceeds out of the Mouth of God" (Mat. 4:4).

The sadness is that the church stumbles from one fad to the other, all with the idea in mind that this is the answer, whatever it might be. However, there is only one answer, and that is the Cross of Christ. It needs nothing subtracted from it or added to it, but rather, to take it at face value.

WHO IS THE LORD . . .?

"And Pharaoh said, Who is the LORD, that I should obey His Voice to let Israel go? I know not the LORD, neither will I let Israel go. *(Satan will not easily allow his captives to go free; and God permits the bitter experience of Satan's power in order to exercise and strengthen Faith. Mackintosh says: 'When we contemplate Israel amid the brick kilns of Egypt, we behold a graphic figure of the condition of every child of Adam's fallen race by nature. There they were, crushed beneath the enemy's galling yoke, and having no power to deliver themselves. The mere mention of the word "liberty" only caused the oppressor to bind his captives with a stronger fetter, and to lade them with a still*

*more grievous burden. Consequently, it was absolutely
necessary that deliverance should come from without.'
Nevertheless, Pharaoh will soon find out exactly 'Who is
the Lord!')"* **(Ex. 5:2).**

SEVEN TIMES

We find from Chapter 5 of Exodus through Chapter 10
that Moses and Aaron appeared some seven times before Pharaoh with the same Message each time from the Mouth of the
Lord, which Moses and Aaron were to deliver, *"Let My People
go!"* The point is this:

It didn't matter to Pharaoh, who, incidentally, was a type
of Satan, as to what the Lord had said. Even though the
Word came directly from God Almighty, still, Pharaoh did not
buckle, so to speak. In other words, he showed no indication
whatsoever of letting Israel go from their slavery.

Once again, the point is, just because the Word of God has
said that *"sin shall not have dominion over you,"* doesn't mean
that Satan is going to roll over and cease his activity. In fact,
as we shall see, he will do the very opposite. Some Christians
think that just because they've heard the Message and tried it
one time, whatever that means, and it doesn't seem to work,
that it must not be real. To be sure, the Message that Moses
and Aaron delivered to Pharaoh was most definitely real. It
was straight from the Mouth of God, but that made no difference to this heathen monarch.

What if Moses and Aaron had ceased going simply because
there did not seem to be any headway being made? They
didn't do that. They kept standing before Pharaoh and deliv-
ering the Message until the Lord said it was enough. As stated,
they appeared before him seven times.

VICTORY DOESN'T COME EASILY

I should say in the heading that victory doesn't come easily or quickly. For that reason, many give up and never reap that which the Lord has intended for them to reap. In other words, they fall short of what God has intended, and actually, that for which He has paid such a price. But, please understand, if the Believer doesn't quit, doesn't give up, ultimately and eventually, the Believer is going to experience everything promised in the Word of God. Let us say it again, *"While we may fail, the Cross does not fail."*

INCREASED PRESSURE

The Children of Israel will now find that instead of being set free, they had their workload doubled, in fact, to a killing pace. This is another tactic of Satan.

Whenever you, the Believer, hear the great Message of the Cross, and you sense in your spirit that it is Biblical, which it definitely is, and you embrace it, as you should, don't think that all of a sudden the temptation is going to stop, the pressure is going to stop, etc. In fact, it very well could be that Satan will increase and will intensify his efforts against you. The temptation could very well increase, and the oppression could increase. The powers of darkness will do everything they can to try to hinder you.

If the Evil One can increase the pressure to such an extent that you will give up, he will have won, and that's what he is trying to do. So, don't think it strange concerning increased opposition, increased oppression, or an increase of temptation. It very well could happen just that way, and more than likely will. The Scripture says:

AT THE MENTION OF SACRIFICE, PHARAOH INCREASED THE PRESSURE

"And Pharaoh said, Behold, the people of the land now are many *(the Israelites)*, and you make them rest from their burdens.

"And Pharaoh commanded the same day the taskmasters of the people, and their officers, saying,

"You shall no more give the people straw to make brick, as heretofore: let them go and gather straw for themselves. *(Oftentimes, the setting to carry out the Will of God will result in Satan's anger, with opposition being increased.)*

"And the tale *(number)* of the bricks, which they did make heretofore, you shall lay upon them; you shall not diminish ought thereof: for they be idle; therefore they cry, saying, Let us go and sacrifice to our God. *(At the mention of Sacrifice, Pharaoh increased the pressure and the workload, almost to a killing pace. When the Believer first begins to hear the Message of the Cross, he will find the opposition of Satan greatly increasing. This will be confusing at first, but the Believer should take heart. The enemy does this because he knows the Believer has now found the source of Victory; therefore, he seeks to move the Believer's Faith from the Cross to other things, by discouragement, etc.).*

"Let there more work be laid upon the men, that they may labor therein; and let them not regard vain words. *(Pharaoh regarded the offering of 'Sacrifices' as 'vain words.' Regrettably, much of the modern church does the same, as it regards the Cross)*" **(Ex. 5:5-9).**

OPPOSITION FROM THE CHILDREN OF ISRAEL

This was Satan's next tactic, and probably, in some ways, was more difficult for Moses and Aaron than anything else. The Scripture says:

"And the officers of the Children of Israel did see that they were in evil case, after it was said, You shall not minish *(reduce)* ought from your bricks of your daily task.

"And they met Moses and Aaron, who stood in the

way, as they came forth from Pharaoh:

"And they said unto them, The LORD look upon you, and judge; because you have made our savour to be abhorred in the eyes of Pharaoh, and in the eyes of his servants, to put a sword in their hand to kill us" (Ex. 5:19-21).

Concerning this, the notes from THE EXPOSITOR'S STUDY BIBLE say:

"Moses was, no doubt, prepared for the rebuff which he had himself received from Pharaoh, for the Lord had plainly said that He would harden the king's heart. But, so far as the inspired record informs us, nothing has been told him that he would meet with discouragement and opposition from his own brethren. A real testing was this for God's servant, for it is far more trying to be criticized by our own Brethren, by those whom we are anxious to help, than it is to be persecuted by the world."

OPPOSITION FROM OUR OWN

Let it be understood, when the Cross of Christ begins to be preached, one can expect opposition, and most of the time, it will come from those who claim to be God's People. Oftentimes when Believers accept the Message of the Cross, their own families turn against them. Many times they are told to leave their church and friends.

Why?

The major problem is self-righteousness! As we've already said in this Volume, the Cross of Christ heavily impacts self-righteousness. It exposes it and shows it for what it really is. This does not sit well with most people, especially religious people. They like to think that all of these things they're doing, whatever these things might be, are contributing toward their righteousness, etc. Even though the individual who has embraced the Cross doesn't say anything, the very Message of the Cross itself says it all. It shows them for what they are, and without a word being said. As stated, they don't too very much like that! As we've also stated, most of the time this hurts more than anything else.

We have seen people have to leave churches and their friends, churches which they have attended for many, many years. Were they doing something wrong in the church? No! When they started talking about the Cross, as stated, it showed up the self-righteousness of all concerned, whoever and whatever that might be.

CAIN AND ABEL

It must be remembered, the account of the very first sacrifice, which portrays the Cross, which account was given in the Fourth Chapter of Genesis, concluded by Cain murdering his brother. The Lord rejected his sacrifice, which was the fruit of his own hands, and the sacrifice being rejected means that Cain was rejected as well. That didn't sit well with him at all! Never mind that his brother Abel had absolutely nothing to do with any of that; that's who suffered the brunt of Cain's rejection. In answer, he murdered his brother. Such opposition in one form or the other has been par for the course from then until now. Man loves his ways and is very angry when those ways are not accepted. So, all who accept the Way of the Lord must expect opposition, sometimes from our closest friends and even our closest loved ones.

SIN SHALL NOT HAVE DOMINION OVER YOU

But, if the Believer will persevere and not allow the efforts of the enemy to cause us to quit, Victory is guaranteed.

Paul said:

"For sin shall not have dominion over you *(the sin*

nature will not have dominion over us if we as Believers continue to exercise Faith in the Cross of Christ; otherwise, the sin nature most definitely will have dominion over the Believer): **for you are not under the Law** *(means that if we try to live this life by any type of religious Law, no matter how good that Law might be in its own right, we will conclude by the sin nature having dominion over us)*, **but under Grace** *(the Grace of God flows to the Believer on an unending basis only as long as the Believer exercises Faith in Christ and what He did at the Cross; Grace is merely the Goodness of God exercised by and through the Holy Spirit, and given to undeserving Saints)*" **(Rom. 6:14).**

The Lord's Way is a way of guaranteed Victory, and it is truly as Simon Peter said, *"joy unspeakable and full of glory."* We must not allow anything to deter us from this for which the Lord has paid such a price.

"Go worship at Emmanuel's Feet,
"See, in His Name what wonders meet;
"Earth is too narrow to express,
"His Worth, His Glory and His Grace.
"The whole Creation can afford,
"But some faint shadow of my Lord:
"Nature, to make His Beauties known,
"Must mingle colors not her own."

"Is He a Fountain? There I'll bathe,
"And heal the plague of sin and death,
"These waters all my soul renew,
"And cleanse my spotted garments too,
"Is He a Sun? His Beams are Grace,
"His Chorus is Joy and Righteousness.
"Is He a Tree? The world receives,
"Salvation from His Healing Leaves."

"Is He a Rose? Not Sharon yields,
"Such fragrancy in all her fields.
"Or if the Lily He assume,
"The valleys bless the rich perfume;
"Is He a Star? He breaks the night,
"And spreads for all the dawning light.
"I know His Glories from afar,
"I know the Bright, the Morning Star."

"Is He the Way? He Leads to God,
"The Path is drawn in line of Blood!
"There would I walk with hope and zeal,
"Till I arrive at Zion's Hill.
"Is He a Door? I'll enter in,
"Behold the pastures large and green,
"A Paradise Divinely fair,
"And all the Saints have freedom there."

"Is He a Rock? How firm He proves!
"The Rock of Ages never moves:
"Yet the sweet streams that from Him flow,
"Attend us all the desert through.
"Nor Earth, nor seas, nor sun, nor stars,
"Nor Heaven His full Resemblance bears,
"His Beauties we could never trace,
"Till we behold Him face-to-face."

BIBLIOGRAPHY

CHAPTER 6
Wuest, K. S. (1997, c 1984), *Wuest's Word Studies from the Greek New Testament: For the English reader (Jud 17).* Grand Rapids, Eerdmans.

Jimmy Swaggart
Books

$29.95 Each or $80 for all 4 (SA1007)

Plus Regular Postage, Shipping, and Handling

Brother Swaggart, Here Is My Question . . .

Here are samples of some of the questions:
- Who Is Satan, And Where Do Demon Spirits Come From?
- What Is Blaspheming The Holy Spirit?
- What Is The Difference Between The Great White Throne Judgment And The Judgment Seat Of Christ?
- What Should Be The Christian's Position In Respect To Alcohol?
- Are Homosexuals Born That Way? (426 pages)

09-097

Brother Swaggart, Here Is My Question About The Cross

The following are some of the subjects addressed:
- How Do I Apply The Cross To My Life Daily?
- How Does Satan Respond To The Message Of The Cross?
- Why Is The Cross Of Christ So Important As It Regards The Holy Spirit?
- How Do You Know That Romans 6:3-4 Speaks Of The Crucifixion, Instead Of Water Baptism?
- Why Is It That The Cross Doesn't Work For Me?
- How Does Christ Intercede For The Saints? (452 pages)

09-103

Brother Swaggart, How Can I Understand The Bible?

The following are some of the subjects addressed:
- The Doctrine Of The Bible
- The Doctrine Of Grace
- The Doctrine Of *"Justification By Faith"*
- The Doctrine Of Our Lord Jesus Christ
- The Doctrine Of Satan
- The Doctrine Of Sin
- The Doctrine Of The Baptism With The Holy Spirit (528 pages)

09-100

Brother Swaggart, Here Is My Question About Bible Prophecy

The Word of God alone gives us the account of the most astounding happenings for the future that Planet Earth will ever see. They are soon to come to pass. They are:
- The Rapture of the Church.
- The Rise of the Antichrist.
- The Great Tribulation.
- The Battle of Armageddon.
- The Second Coming of the Lord.
- The 1,000 Year Kingdom Age.
- The Perfect Age to come, which will last forever. (300 pages)

09-106

It's easy to order! Just call 1-800-288-8350, Baton Rouge residents call (225) 768-7000, or log on the internet at www.jsm.org, or mail in your order to:

JIMMY SWAGGART MINISTRIES
P.O. Box 262550 • Baton Rouge, LA 70826-2550